WOMEN, SOCIAL EXCLUSION AND INCLUSION

WOMEN, SOCIAL EXCLUSION AND INCLUSION

Sangeeta Krishna

KALPAZ

ISBN : 978-93-5128-072-9
Price: ` 900

First Published, 2015

Published by

Kalpaz Publications
C-30, Satyawati Nagar,
Delhi-110052
Ph. : 9212142040
E-mail: kalpaz@hotmail.com

Laser Typesetting: Sanya Computers, Delhi

Printed at: G. Print Process, Delhi
Printed at: G. Print Process, Delhi

Cataloging in Publication Data--DK
Courtesy: D.K. Agencies (P) Ltd. <docinfo@dkagencies.com>

Sangeeta Krishna, author.
Women, social exclusion and inclusion / Sangeeta Krishna.
pages cm
Includes bibliographical references (pages) and index.
ISBN 9789351280729

1. Dalit women--India--Social conditions. 2. Marginality, Social--India. 3. Social integration--India. I. Title.

DDC 305.420954 23

Dedicated

to

My affectionate and loving Parents

Contents

Contents

Preface

The hallmark of past twenty-five years has been a steady progress in achieving socio-economic development, providing wider support for democratic values and strengthening collaborative relationships among government, social institutions and civil society worldwide. However, at the same time inequality and social exclusion not only continues but are increasing menacingly in parts of the world both within and outside countries. Many societies are facing depressing social conditions such as widening social disparities and marginalisation of certain groups and/or communities. In Indian context the legacies of discrimination, marginalisation and denial are still enmeshed in its social composition on the basis of religion, sexual orientation, caste, descent, gender, age, disability, HIV status, migrant status or where one lives. To prevent the further increase of social tensions among their members it is vital that societies be equipped with strategies, and tools for addressing existing challenges in a more proactive, constructive and holistic way, so that they may become better prepared for new challenges and more resilient in confronting them and better able to adjust to emerging imbalances on peaceful, equitable and sustained basis.

The necessity of timely interventions has been felt more than ever in the current years. To make the Indian society truly egalitarian, the institution of higher learning need to address the issue of social exclusion and inclusion. The primary space where "Exclusion" can be studied understood and first transcended, are the universities which, can and must act as a symbol of hope for society. And once, that transpires, the Social Exclusion Studies would emerge as an academic discipline, a social exclusion perspective would become a space that the mainstream can seek to occupy and social exclusion would be recognised as another approach for the understanding of the world around us. The founding of the Centre was a reflection of the felt need for intervention in the education system in general and higher education in particular. The recently established UGC Centre for Study of Social Exclusion and Inclusive Policy in Babasaheb Bhimrao Ambedkar University engaged in exploring the conceptual/theoretical contours of social exclusion, historical and contemporary facets of social exclusion/ discrimination, nature of exclusion of deprived sections of the Indian society and their contributions to society, the theme of inclusive policies, etc., through its inter-disciplinary efforts. The Centre has four pronged activities—teaching research, action and extension activities. It is trying to highlight the importance of inclusive and emancipatory development perspective in the pursuit of knowledge as well as in defining policy and planning. The Centre inspired me to read more and more on the issue, carry some research have a better understanding of the theme. This academic exercise in the form of book has been the outcome of my some understanding of the issue and association with this Centre.

This book which has tried to bring out the concept of social exclusion and inclusion from a gender perspective is only a modest beginning in this direction.

Sangeeta Krishna

Acknowledgements

To start on a common note, there is a journey underlying every book. I do not intend to recount ups and downs of this particular journey, but would like come up with acknowledging the invaluable contribution of several individuals without whom this journey could not have been completed.

When I completed the project on Social Exclusion, Inclusion from gender perspective, I had never imagined that I would be able to develop this into a book. However after two years of reading, understanding and working on this I could muster some courage to translate my understanding into a book. As mentioned this book has been developed out of a project sponsored by my institution Babasaheb Bhimrao Ambedkar University. Therefore my first gratitude goes to it. My institution provided me space to look deeper into the issues of social exclusion. The establishment of the Centre for the Study of Social Exclusion and Inclusive Policy is one such platform, which gave me an opportunity to work on this important issue of social exclusion. This is very significant because the Central government is committed to working on the issues of excluded communities and providing some understanding based on facts and figures to the researchers and policy-makers to use the database for the equitable policy formulations. I express my gratitude to my former Vice Chancellor Prof. B. Hanumaiah for his unflinching support to the Centre and for granting financial assistance to undertake this project.

I am highly grateful for the wide-ranging and thought-provoking discussions with my former Co-ordinators, Prof. N.M.P. Verma and Prof. Kameshwar Choudhary. They have jointly and separately offered insightful comments, criticisms, challenges. My thanks also for their insistence that I use my expertise and long experience in the field of gender studies by working on the issue through a gendered lens. They have always stood by me at the time of crisis.

A number of friends have extended different kinds of support throughout the progress of this project. I am grateful to their insight, enthusiasm and friendship. Their ideas and views have encouraged me to think through the challenges. The shortcomings, however remain my own.

My special thanks to Ms. Madhu Patel, Data Entry Operator for boosting my morale and assisting me a lot in the compilation of this study.

I would like to express my intellectual debt of gratitude to numerous scholars whose researches and words have enriched the stream of literature in social exclusion and have been referred to through out this work.

For this project I have used several libraries at New Delhi, Lucknow, and Varanasi. I would like to extend my warm thanks to the librarians, who had helped me in providing books and relevant materials at the Nehru Memorial Library (Teen Murti), Centre for Women's Development Studies, New Delhi, Central Library and Centre for Women's Studies and Development, Banaras, Hindu University, Varanasi, Women's Studies Centre, Lucknow University and my own University Library.

Last but not the least, I must also thank to my entire family for nurturing my desire for self-expression from the very start. Their sacrifices have enabled to explore the boundless possibilities of my life. No words are adequate to describe the intensity of their love, pride and support. Besides, the pleasant thought about my little angels Puku, Gungun and Partha, was a constant source of positive energy for me. Their love created an effervescent atmosphere for me while shaping the project into a reality.

The study is a modest effort to bring the issues and debates concerning social exclusion and inclusive initiatives at various levels and strata among the policy-makers, academia and researchers. The study has been done from a gender perspective. The contemporary society has been witnessing the crisis and resilience in different aspects and forms. This has helped the academia and researchers to discuss about the excluded, segregated and marginalised communities like women and dalits. The notion about social exclusion varies from one society to another depending upon the changing context with time and space. Thus, there is need to reconceptualise and recontextualise this pertinent issue.

Introduction

"I am conscious of the fact that if women are conscientised the untouchable community will progress. I believe that women should organise and this will play a major role in bringing an end to social evils... the progress of the Dalit community should be measured in terms of the progress made by its womenfolk."

Dr. B. R. Ambedkar, Speech to the Dalit Mahila Federation in 1942

In the last couple of years, there has been a spurt of growing interest in and awareness about questions of social exclusion and inclusion. While the nature of exclusion in India has centred around the caste system, other disadvantaged groups such as tribals, women and the poor have also suffered from similar disabilities. This opens up a number of possibilities for future investigations. In the present work, I have focussed on exploration of the gendered nature of social exclusion. If we look at women today their lives are located at the intersection of caste, class and patriarchy/ies. In many areas they face exclusion, discrimination and remain in the margins. To understand (Dalit) women exclusion, marginalisation and discrimination, it is necessary to delineate both, internal and external (structural/institutional) factors that affects their lives.

The politics of exclusion and inclusion, censure and celebration of dalits show that they wish to be a part of the so called mainstream academic discourse and the development indicators and yet, cannot be. How it has become a part of the process is a matter of serious discussion and analysis. Now, the question is whether something has been done for the inclusion of these excluded groups at the level of pedagogy and praxis over these years? If so, in actual how far these efforts have been instrumental in translating the search for inclusivity and egalitarian society into a reality?

Social Exclusion: Concept and its Application

Let us begin with the term Social Exclusion. What does it mean and imply? How this term came into policy debates at the international and national level. The concept of Social Exclusion is of relatively recent origin and was first used in France in the 1970s.

The French Policy Context

In the French policy milieu, "exclusion sociale" had been used as a term to refer to a very selected category of people, who were excluded from the provision of social insurance in France. A French social policy analyst, Rene Lenoir, who published *Les Exclus: UN Francais sur dixin* 1974, identified ten categories or groups who came under the "uninsured" umbrella. They were the physically and mentally handicapped, "suicidal", aged invalids, abused children, substance abusers, delinquents, single parents (notably sole mothers), multi-problem household (where more than one of the factors existed at any one time), "marginals", "asocial" and "social misfits".

The European Union Context

The concept was later adopted by the European Union in the late 1980's as a key concept in social policy and in many instances replaced the concept of poverty. Most specifically the idea of poverty took a paradigm shift in Euro-centric discussion and it got replaced by the so-called term social exclusion (de Haan 1998). To understand "Social Exclusion", this requires an understanding of the policy mandate of the European Union. Over the 20 years of the Poverty Programmes (the policy initiatives that were the key carriers of the "social exclusion" discourse into member states) a significant "discursive shift" (where "discursive" refers to the ways in which poverty and exclusion were talked about and written about) occurred. (Peace, 2001)

The discursive shift in European Union social policy entailed a shift from a focus on "Poverty" to a focus "Social Exclusion" and attracted a great deal of (English-language) commentary, especially since the mid-1990s. Simultaneously the concept encouraged a shift away from the idea of extreme marginalisation.

It has been found that people generally see social exclusion as being very similar to the concept of poverty. So, many a times, people say this is a linguistic shift from poverty to exclusion and regarded social exclusion concept as nothing but the old wine in a new bottle. Thus, there is a need to go deeper into the features and debates, going around the concept.

'Exclusion' or 'Poverty'?

The primary use of the idea of exclusion, as stated above, relates to poverty, because much of the concern with 'solidarity' relates to the availability of systems of support to meet needs. Poverty is not seen simply as a matter of lacking resources; it implies that people who are not protected by solidarity, and so are not fully a part of society. The kind of concept of poverty favoured by Peter Townsend (1979), is very similar to the idea of social exclusion:

Individuals, families and groups in the population can be said to be in poverty when they lack the resources to obtain the types of diet, participate in the activities and have the living conditions and amenities which are customary in the societies to which they belong.

Townsend's stress on non-participation is directly compatible with the idea of 'exclusion' indeed. Townsend actually used the idea of exclusion in the classic work on poverty, though without assigning any special importance to it. The mechanisms through which people participate in the society, develop in terms of the pattern of social networks to which they belong. People who are unable to participate are seen as being on the margins of society, or excluded from it. But the same principles apply to many people who are not 'poor'. (Spicker, 2007)

One of the most popular arguments in favour of the social exclusion concept is that it takes into account more dimensions of people's lives than the poverty concept. (Ashland and Flotten, 2000)

Gradually, the concept came to be termed differently by different scholars like Amartya Sen, who came out with the idea of deprivation of opportunities. Sen pointed out how particularly in Asia, social exclusion results in deprivation and limits individual opportunities. Being excluded from social relations can lead to other relational deprivations such as lack of education, employment, and exclusion from markets resulting in economic impoverishment, which limits opportunities (in terms of economic exclusion) (Sen, 2000). Thus, Social Exclusion has various dimensions, for example social, political, economic, educational, and interactive and so on. Thus, the social exclusion debate goes beyond the debate of poverty.

Social Exclusion: Its Meaning and Definition

The core meaning of the idea was that some people were left out and that they were not part of the solidarity social networks that applied to others. The idea was immensely influential in France, and after a short time it was expressed in several of ways. Exclusion might be taken in a negative sense, contrasting those who are within the bounds of social networks unfavourably with those who are outside them. A French government circular in 1976, referred to exclusion as another way of understanding what in Britain might have been called the 'problem family'.

Families generally described as 'problem families' or 'anti-social', or more objectively, families which are 'marginal', 'excluded' or in the 'fourth world', who appear temporarily unable to resolve the problems they are confronted with.

This points to a second understanding of the idea of exclusion. At first it meant people, who were not protected. This became extended to people who were not part with the idea of 'marginality'. 'Deviants and marginals are not forgiven for their refusal to share in the "values of the system". In Britain, the idea of exclusion has been compounded with ideas relating to the 'underclass'. Tony Blair describes 'exclusion' as:

> "A short hand label for what can happen when individuals or areas suffer from a combination of linked problems such as unemployment, poor skills, low incomes, poor housing, high crime environments, bad health and family breakdowns."

The third meaning of exclusion, which follows from this, has been in referring to people who are socially rejected. In France, the term has been applied, for example, to people who are unemployed, young offenders, or people with AIDs. We are still talking about people who are not part of society, but they are not left out, or standing outside. They are pushed out.

When the European Union took up the idea of exclusion, then, there were already a variety of competing understandings of what the term might mean. It covered people who were left out, people who refused to take part in society, and people who were rejected making the idea of 'exclusion' more wider. And on this basis we can say that social exclusion affects individuals, groups of people and geographical areas. Social exclusion can be seen, not just in terms of income, but also in matters such as health, education, access to services, and housing and debt. Phenomena which result from social exclusion therefore include:

- the resurgence of homelessness,
- urban crises,
- rising long-term unemployment,
- persistent high levels of poverty.

The kinds of issues mentioned like racial issues or urban crises, point generally to the structure of social relationships as the focus for concern.

Exclusion is different mainly in the prescriptions it offers for policy. If the main issue is that people are excluded from society, then they need to be included. When provision was made for social assistance in France in the 1980s, it took a different form from the kind of welfare benefits offered in other countries. The revenue minimum d'insertion (RMI) offered a minimum income, but it also made provisions for 'insertion', or social inclusion. The RMI was introduced as:

> "One of the elements of a general provision in the struggle against poverty, directed toward the suppression of every kind of exclusion, in particular in the fields of education, employment, training, health and housing."

Schemes modelled on the French RMI have been introduced in Portugal, Northern Spain and in Italy.

Now coming to the definitional aspect, in it simplest sense, social exclusion can be defined as "the process through which individual or groups are wholly or partially excluded from full participation in the society in which they live".

The term 'social exclusion' is ambiguous and contested. Definitions range from little more than the re-naming of poverty (Burchardt *et al.,* 1999) to more broad-based concepts based on a lack of or inability to participate in society. Rodgers (1995) himself 'dissects' the concept into patterns which include, 'exclusion from goods and services', 'labour market exclusion',

'exclusion of land' and 'exclusion from security'. He criticises the notion for being 'at heart a normative, heavily-laden notion, evoking negative responses' (*Ibid*) as well as highlighting its 'incongruent' dimensions.

However, in recent years, debates have also been influenced by academic trends in post-structuralist theory which has increasingly focussed on the 'other', a term relevant to social exclusion. A new politics of 'difference' has emerged with the creation of political and social movements concerned with gender, race and ethnicity, sexual orientation and disability. There is recognition of the immense difficulties in managing fragmentation and these multiple identities.

A useful starting point for the conceptualisation of 'social exclusion' is to consider the different ways in which 'disadvantage' operates to circumscribe the opportunities and life chances of individuals and groups in a given society. Economic theories have focussed primarily on resource-based paradigms of disadvantage, generally taking the individual, or the individual household, as their unit of analysis. This, for instance, was the approach which influenced earlier conceptualisations of poverty within development studies which equated it with income or expenditure shortfalls. Even now, when poverty has come to be increasingly recognised to be a multi-dimensional phenomenon, encompassing income, assets, education, health, dignity and voice, it nevertheless continues to be *causally* understood in economic terms. The poor within this paradigm are believed to have little or no voice in determining resource allocations and institutional arrangements within a society because they are poor; they are rarely seen to be poor because *they have little or no voice* in determining resource allocations and social arrangements.

Thus, social exclusion is a universal phenomenon which has existed over time and space and recently, it has become central to policies and debates all over the world. The notion of Social Exclusion is a way of conceptualising society including (and with a focus on) the processes of deprivation that are integral part of that society. Definitions of social exclusion vary due to different political and intellectual traditions.

De Haan provides a range of definitions of social exclusion

that reflects the general literature. According to De Haan Social Exclusion:

> "Is defined as the opposite of social integration or social participation, which reflects the perceived importance of being part of the activities customary in that society; Is a multi-dimensional concept. It refers to exclusion in the economic social and political sphere. It goes beyond the analysis of recourse allocation mechanisms, and includes power relations, agency, culture and social identity; and can refer to a state or situation, but often refers to processes, to the mechanisms by which people are excluded."

The focus is on both the individual and the institutions that enable and constrain human interaction, and makes explicit the interplay between its material and non-material.

Thus, exclusion takes place at each level of society. Group formation is a fundamental characteristic of human society and this is accompanied by exclusion of others. The concept takes us beyond mere descriptions of deprivation and focusses attention on social relations and the processes and institutions that underlie and are part and parcel of deprivation (De Haan, 2001).

Hillary Silver has argued that the meaning of social exclusion depends on the nature of society or the dominant model of society from which social exclusion occurs and it varies in meanings according to national and ideological contexts. (Silver, 1994)

Even though Hillary Silver has tried to locate her paradigm of social exclusion on the nature of society, nevertheless such differentiated conceptions of nature of society would entail what exclusion and inclusion would really mean. This paradigm of nature of society calls for different conceptions of what constitutes exclusion and inclusion, thus making it even more difficult to devise a suitable means for promoting inclusion. In the same light, Jackson (1999) argues that dualistic opposition between exclusion and inclusion tends to emphasise exclusion as the opposite of integration, which limits exploration of contradictions in the multiplicity of exclusions or paradoxes of simultaneous exclusion and inclusion.

Reacting to the various meanings of social exclusion which are embedded in current political debate, Levitas (1998) develops a model which identifies three different approaches. The three different approaches have very different views of the causal relations between poverty and exclusion, and different implications for key indicators.

The first of these approaches is a redistributive discourse (RED) which derives from critical social policy, and which sees social exclusion as a consequence of poverty. As Peter Townsend (1979) argued that poverty should not be understood in terms of subsistence, but in terms of people's ability to participate in the customary life of society. He says, 'Individuals, families and groups can be said to be in poverty when... their resources are so seriously below those commanded by the average individual or family that they are, in effect, excluded from ordinary living patterns, customs and activities'. Although 'resources' here does not simply refer to cash incomes, and importantly includes access to collectively-provided services—a central element in the RED approach has been that since social exclusion results from poverty, raising benefit levels to reduce poverty is crucial to reducing exclusion.

Much of current policy, however, is implicitly or explicitly rooted in a different model of exclusion, in which the key element is labour-force attachment. This is supported by a discourse about Social Integration Discourse (SID) in which paid work is represented as the primary or sole legitimate means of integrating individuals of working age into society. The excluded are those who are 'workless', or, in the case of young people, at risk of becoming so. Unlike RED, SID leaves little room for the reward of unpaid work through the benefit system, and glosses over the ways in which paid work may fail to prevent exclusion (for example by being poorly paid), or even cause it where long and a social hours block other forms of social participation. While the lead indicator of social exclusion for RED is low income, for SID it is unemployment or 'economic inactivity'—a concept which intrinsically denies the value of unpaid, non-market work.

The third approach is a Moral Underclass Discourse (MUD), which emphasises moral and cultural causes of poverty and which is centrally concerned with the moral hazard of 'dependency', and thus with workless households rather than individual labour market attachment. MUD tends to replay recurrent themes about 'dangerous classes' (Morris, 1994; Murray 1990 and 1999) to focus on consequences of social exclusion for social order, and on particular groups, such as unemployed and potentially criminal young men, and lone parents, especially young never-married mothers. (Levitas, 2003)

Placing the groups in a single category may do little to aid the understanding of the specific difficulties than any one of them face or to help resolve these. A case in point has been illustrated by Jackson (1999), where she argues that early liberal western feminisms produced a universalising theory of marginality which tended to view the marginality of women 'as parallel in its form to marginalise the colonised, non-white or the poor. (Tsing, 1993 cited in Jackson 1999) which failed to take into account the divisions between women and the fact that gender marks social relations across and within groups. This position shifts the focus on the gendered construction of identities rather than on a bounded category of exclusion-based on gender.

She further argues that binary and polarised formulation of exclusion and inclusion is problematic for at least two reasons. First, it suggests a unitary notion of power in which the included are powerful and excluded are powerless rather than the one in which power is dispersed, contingent and unstable. Second dualist discourses can themselves be structures of control which deserves to be questioned and decentred. (Jackson, 1999)

Cursory reviews of the concept social exclusion clearly indicate different conceptions of what constitute social exclusion and inclusion. The concept and definitions vary both in academia and in development policies. For instance, some analysts see social exclusion as a cause of poverty and others suggest that it is both an expression and a determinant of poverty and most would probably agree that poverty is a form of social exclusion (De Haan, 1998 cited in Jackson, 1999). Although originally defined in terms of rupture of social bonds and applied to social disintegration rather than poverty *per se*, social exclusion has developed in a range of paradigmatic styles in different political and intellectual contexts. (Silver, 1995 cited in Jackson, 1999)

Social exclusion has been defined by the Department of International Development (DFID) as "a process by which certain groups are systematically disadvantaged because they are discriminated against on the basis of their ethnicity, race, religion, sexual orientation, caste, descent, gender, age, disability, HIV status, migrant status or where they live. Discrimination occurs in public institutions, such as the legal system or education and health services, as well as social institutions like the household" (DFID, 2005).

Whilst the concept arose in response to dissatisfaction with approaches to poverty that focussed on income alone, the term remains contested and there is no agreed definition. Most commonly, social exclusion is seen to apply to groups, involving the exclusion of individuals due to their membership of particular groups that suffer discrimination, i.e., according to racial, ethnic, gender, geographic or age characteristics. There are various understandings of social exclusion which emphasise different aspects: the groups at risk of being excluded, what people are excluded from, e.g., employment, education, citizenship, respect; the problems associated with the impact of social exclusion, e.g., low income, poor housing, the processes driving exclusion, and the agents and actors involved.

There is an agreement however, that social exclusion is multi-dimensional. One particularly useful feature of the concept of social exclusion is its focus on process and relations. It complements the concept of inequality, which focusses more on disparities between different categories of people.

In development practice the term 'exclusion' has become popular with non-economic social scientists. This popularity is due to its focus on societal institutions, actors, relationships and processes, of which measured disparity in income or lack of access to social services may be both an indicator and an outcome.

While the precise definition varies, there is broad agreement that social exclusion consists of 'exclusion from social, political and economic institutions resulting from a complex and dynamic set of processes and relationships that prevent individuals or groups from accessing resources, participating in society and asserting their rights' (Beall and Piron, 2004).

Social exclusion attempts to make sense out of multiple deprivations and inequities experienced by people and areas, and the reinforcing effects of reduced participation, consumption, mobility, access, integration, influence and recognition. Theorising Social Exclusion first reviews and reflects upon the existing thinking, literature and research into social exclusion and social connectedness, outlining an integrated theory of social exclusion across dimensions of social action and along pathways of social processes.

The disadvantages faced by the excluded tend to be inter-related people belonging to minorities or social drop-outs may have a greater risk of being unemployed or be employed in precarious jobs and hence be low paid, less-educated, recipients of social assistance, possess little political power and fewer social contacts.

Silver's 'monopoly paradigm' about social exclusion emphasises hierarchical power relations in the constitution of a social order. Group monopolies are seen as responsible for exclusion. Powerful groups restrict the access of outsiders through social closure. Inequality is thought to overlap with such group distinctions, but it is mitigated by social democratic citizenship and participation in the community.

People can and usually are excluded in some area (or dimensions) and included in others. Jackson in her critique of the notion of Social Exclusion emphasises that women are not categorically excluded but integrated in particular way through reproductive labour for example. (Jackson, 1998) In her view, in the social exclusion discourse the assumption that marginality is the problem remains pervasive. Also, marginality may produce the conditions for women to protest and to be included in collective organisations. However, social exclusion debate does not focus on bounded groups but stresses social relations and processes through which people are being deprived taking the debate beyond mere descriptions of people's situations.

Dimensions of Social Exclusion

Social Exclusion has several dimensions. It exists in various spheres and in many forms. Race and caste have however dominated the discourse on social exclusion. In its simplest understanding, social exclusion is lack of access to resources and consequent inability to utilise them. It is further accentuated by denial of opportunities which enhance access to resources and their utilisation. It can, therefore, be experienced by anyone who is in a position which is vulnerable to such aimpeding conditions. Thus, besides caste and race, religion, age, gender, social position and occupational hierarchy—are all potentially volatile to social exclusion. Now let us see a few dimensions of exclusionary processes.

- Political exclusion can include the denial of citizenship rights such as political participation and the right to organise, and also of personal security, the rule of law, freedom of expression and equality of opportunity. Bhalla and Lapeyre (1997) argue that political exclusion also involves the notion that the state, which grants basic rights and civil liberties, is not a neutral agency but a vehicle of a society's dominant classes, and may thus discriminate between social groups.

- Economic exclusion includes lack of access to labour markets, credit and other forms of 'capital assets'.
- Social exclusion may take the form of discrimination along a number of dimensions, for example gender, ethnicity, age—which effectively reduces the opportunity for such groups to gain access to social services and limits their participation in the labour market.
- Cultural exclusion relates to the extent to which diverse values, norms and ways of living are accepted and respected. At one extreme, diversity is accepted in all its richness and at the other there can be situations of stigma and discrimination.

Moving ahead Amartya Sen (Sen, 2000) too draws attention to its various dimensions. Distinction is drawn between the situation where some people are kept out (or at least left out), and where some people are being included (may even be forcibly included)—at greatly unfavourable terms; and describes these two situations as 'unfavourable exclusion' and 'unfavourable inclusion'. 'Unfavourable inclusion', with unequal treatment may have the same adverse effects as 'unfavourable exclusion'.

Sen also differentiates between 'active and passive exclusion'—defined 'active exclusion' as the deliberate exclusion of people from opportunities through government policies or other means. 'Passive exclusion' works through the social processe in which there are no deliberate attempts to exclude, but nevertheless, may result in exclusion of people from a set of circumstances.

Sen further distinguishes between 'constitutive relevance of exclusion' from that of 'instrumental importance'. In the former, exclusion and deprivation have an intrinsic importance of their own. For instance, being unable to relate to others and to take part in community life can directly impoverish an individual, in addition to further deprivation that it may generate. This is different from social exclusion of 'instrumental importance', in which the exclusion in itself is not impoverishing but can lead to impoverishment of human lives.

Thus, we saw above, how the concept of social exclusion/ inclusion figured prominently in the policy discourse in France in the mid-1970s and was later adopted by the European Union in the late 1980s, as a key concept in social policy and in many instances it replaced the concept of poverty. This concept which had appeared as a response to the crisis of the welfare State has now gained considerable currency over the last five years in both official and development discourses in India. The debates surrounding inclusion/exclusion have ascended to conspicuous importance in the present political transition in India with several groups such as Dalit,[1] women, ethnic communities, voicing their demands for an inclusive state by virtue of which, the issue has now come to be a part of the popular public discourse. However, what has to be borne in mind is that the concept lacks universality in the way it has been defined and employed. While some claim that social exclusion is more illuminating and holds the promise of understanding disadvantaged groups better, others argue that this concept is so evocative, ambiguous, multi-dimensional and elastic that it can be defined in many different ways and owing to its ambiguity in definition it may mean all things to all people.

Mechanisms of Exclusion

How do people become excluded, what are the mechanisms, and how are these mechanisms instrumental in causing social exclusion, all these need to be analysed carefully.

Scholarly work on social exclusion agrees that it can be analysed both as a state and as a process. Such analysis entails the various factors that lead to it, including social identities, resource allocation, power relations, and cultural and structural norms of societies.

As a condition or an outcome, it is a state where excluded individuals or groups are unable to participate fully in their society. Factors responsible for such a state or condition can be enumerated as follows:

(a) Social identity, such as race, ethnicity, caste, religion, gender and age,

(b) Social location, such as remote areas, stigmatised areas, war or conflict areas,

(c) Social status, including the health situation (disability, illness of HIV/AIDS and other stigmatising diseases), migrant status (including refugees), occupation and level of education.

As a multidimensional dynamic process, it is governed by social and political relations, and access to organisations and institutional sites of power. Within that context, social relations and organisational barriers block the following: (a) attainment of livelihoods (b) human development, and (c) equal citizenship.

Kabeer asserts that while institutional rules and norms spell out particular patterns of inclusion and exclusion, they cannot cause them to happen. (Kabeer, 2000). Specifically, it is social actors who 'make up these institutions, the collectivities they form and interactions between them, which provide the agency behind the patterns' of rules, norms and asset distributions, which together help to spell out people's membership of different kinds of social groups, thereby shaping identities and defining interests. (*Ibid*) In other words, people are excluded by institutions and behaviour that reflect, enforce and reproduce prevailing social attitudes and values, particularly those of powerful groups in society.

Kabeer's analysis, as well as other studies, distinguishes between three categories of such attitudes and social practices. These are based on whether they are conscious or unconscious, intended or unintended, explicit or informal, and are as follows:

(a) Mobilisation of institutional bias (rules of the game) whereby a 'predominant set of values, beliefs, rituals and institutional procedures that operate systematically and consistently to the benefit of certain persons and groups at the expense of others' and those who "benefit are placed in a preferred position to defend and promote their vested interests". (*Ibid*)

This mechanism operates without conscious decisions by those who represent the status quo.

(Social) Identity

Social exclusion may be understood in terms of identity. Individuals may experience social exclusion in terms of its consequences for their personal identity, while groups and communities may experience exclusion in terms of its consequences for the collective identity.

If interventions are designed to help excluded communities, based on an implicit assumption that the individuals in the community share an idea of what the community is i.e., share a collective identity, where no such shared identity exists, there is likely to be a poor outcome. Similarly, when interventions are designed to increase social capital in a target community, an assumption of community identity may or may not be justified. Some methods of intervention may need to begin with the aim of increasing the collective identity of a community before other strategies can be fully successful. (Sullivan, 2002)

Social Exclusion: An Indian Perspective

These developments in social science literature enable us to understand the meanings and manifestations of the concept of social exclusion and its applicability to caste and untouchability-based exclusion in India. Social Exclusion in common parlance, is defined as a process of socio-political and cultural denial and rejection. Certain communities have been excluded on the basis of caste, class religion etc. In India, exclusion is embedded in societal interrelations and institutions that exclude, discriminate, isolate and deprive some groups on the basis of groups identities like caste, ethnicity and religion. (Thorat and Louis, 2003). Historically, the caste system has regulated social, economic and political life not only of the Hindu society alone but also of other religions through carry forward and spell over effect of the caste system. The nature of exclusion revolving around the caste system particularly needs to be understood and conceptualised, in so far as caste-based exclusion form the basis for various anti-discriminatory policies in India for other social groups like tribal, women and religious groups. (Thorat, 2004)

Social exclusion in India cannot be captured by the Euro-centric approach and its labour market framework. The exclusion discourse in Indian society has to be understood against the backdrop of the caste system.

Divisions between different caste groups have evolved over time into increasingly entrenched and closed hiarerchies based on rules of marriage endogamy, occupational restriction, limited social interaction and segregated residential patterns. While there is considerable variation in the actual configuration of castes across the region, and in the rigidity with which the rules of caste are observed, the lowest position within each local caste hierarchy is occupied by the 'untouchable' castes or dalits. Historically, excluded from the ownership of land and key productive assets, dalits have been incorporated into the social system as providers of various kinds of labour and services that were considered to be polluting. It was members of these castes who had to carry out the removal of night soil and carcasses of dead animals. They continue to predominate in sweeping, leatherwork, manual scavenging and forced prostitution, all activities which are looked down upon by the rest of society.

In this context it can be reiterated that exclusion revolves around the societal interrelations and institutions that exclude, discriminate, isolate, and deprive some groups on the basis of group's identities like caste and ethnicity. Social Exclusion is used here to mean the systematic exclusion of individuals and groups from one or more dimensions of society, such as structures of power and privilege, opportunities and resources. Caste, traditional India's system of social ordering and control, is the most elaborate form of social stratification ever known. It has dominated the Indian sub-continent for about three millennia, and is also the most exhaustive and obnoxious of all exclusionary systems.

As discussed above it is this caste-based exclusion, which has formed the basis for various anti-discriminatory policies in India. Membership and status are determined by birth; there is a hierarchy of social precedence among the castes; there are restrictions on social and cultural intercourse between castes; castes are segregated and stratified with regard to civil and religious privileges, occupations are caste determined with relatively little choice allowed, restrictions on marriage outside one's sub-caste help maintain the system. (Ghurye, 1979). Theoretical formulations by economists recognised that in its essential form, caste as a system of social and economic governance or organisation (of production and distribution) is governed by certain customary rules and norms, which are unique and distinct. (Akerlof, 1976; Scoville, 1991; Lal, 1988; Ambedkar, 1936 and 1987). The organisational scheme of the caste system is based on the division of people in social groups (or castes) in which the civil, cultural, and economic rights of each individual caste are pre-determined or ascribed by birth and made hereditary. The assignment of civil, cultural, and economic rights is therefore, unequal and hierarchical. The most important feature of the caste system, however is that it provides for a regulatory mechanism to enforce the social and economic organisation through the instruments of social ostracism (or social and economic penalties), and reinforces it further with the justification and support from the philosophical elements in the Hindu religion. (Lal, 1988; Ambedkar 1936 and 1987)

The caste system's fundamental characteristics are fixed in relations to civil, cultural, and economic rights for each caste, with restrictions for change implies 'forced exclusion' of one caste from the rights of other caste, or from undertaking the occupations of other castes. Exclusion and discrimination in civil, cultural, and particularly in economic spheres such as occupation and labour employment, is therefore, internal to the system, and a necessary outcome of its governing principles. In the market economy framework, the occupational immobility would operate through restrictions in various markets such as land, labour, credit, other inputs, and services necessary for any economic activity. Labour being an integral part of the production process of any economic activity, would obviously become a part of market discrimination.

This premise entails that the caste system involves the denial of not only equality and freedom, but also of the basic human rights, particularly of the low castes untouchables which become an impediment for personal development. The principles of equality and freedom are not the governing principles of the caste system. Unlike many other human societies, the caste system does not recognise the individual and his/her distinctiveness as the center of the social purpose. In fact, for the purpose of rights and duties, the unit of the Hindu society is not an individual (even the family is not regarded as a unit in the Hindu society, except for the purposes of marriages and inheritance). The primary unit in the Hindu society is caste, and hence, the rights and privileges (or the lack of them) of individual are on account of him/her being a member of a particular caste (Ambedkar first published in 1987). Also, due to differential ranking, and the hierarchical nature of the caste system, the entitlements to various rights become narrower and narrower as one goes down in hierarchical ladder in the caste system. Various castes get artfully interlined and coupled with each other (in their rights and duties), in a manner such that the rights and privileges of the higher castes become the causative reasons for the disadvantage and disability for the lower castes, particularly the untouchables. In this sense, as

Ambedkar observed, a caste does not exist in a single number, but only in plural. Castes exist as a system of endogenous groups, which are interlinked with each other in unequal measure of rights and relations in all walks of life. Castes at the top of the order enjoy more rights, at the expense of those located at the bottom. Therefore, the untouchables located at the bottom of the caste hierarchy have much less economic and social rights.

Since the civil, cultural, and economic rights (particularly with respect to occupation and property rights) of each caste are ascribed, and are compulsory, the institution of caste necessarily involves forced exclusion of one caste from the other. The unequal and hierarchal assignment of economic and social rights by ascription obviously restricts the freedom of occupation and the human development.

Social Exclusion and its Historical Formulations in India

If we trace back in history we find that exclusion in India is very old, and still persists in different forms, at least three strands of exclusion discourse can be discerned, all directed against the discriminatory, oppressive, exploitative and exclusionary practices of the caste system (For an overview of this discourse, see Milton Singer and Bernard Cohn, 1968). Tracing a few of them are the protest movements that have been a feature of caste society since the sixth century B.C. when Buddhism and Jainism arose in opposition to Brahminism and the supremacy and socio-cultural hegemony of the Brahmins and related caste prejudices.

The Bhakti movements in different parts of the country throughout the Middle Ages, and Veerasaivism in twelfth century Karnataka challenged the established hierarchy of caste in the name of social equality. The Brahmo Samaj founded by Rammohan Roy in Calcutta in 1828 repudiated caste, and established a brotherhood of men irrespective of caste or creed. The Satya Shodak Samaj, or society of truth-seekers, was founded by Jotiba Phule in Poona in 1873, and blamed the Hindu religion for social inequality, and the Brahmins for fabricating 'sacred scriptures' to maintain their social dominance, they are segregated and stratified with regard to civil and religious privileges, occupations are caste determined with relatively little choice allowed, restrictions on marriage outside one's sub-caste help maintain the system. (Ghurye, 1979).

Caste exclusions are writ large in the *Manusmriti*, or Laws of Manu, the fundamental work of Hindu law. It defines the duties and occupations ordained for the four chief castes, or *Varnas*. In its 'dos' and "don'ts" it describes the treatment of women, mixed-castes and castes of "low origin," of which the most despised are *chandalas*, the lowest untouchables. The rules are most glaring in the practice of untouchability, and the treatment of certain castes as 'unapproachable' and 'unseeable.'

Then, from the second half of the 19th century the British administration also showed concern about various forms of exclusion in Indian society. This was mainly in the context of Brahmin dominance, Muslim alienation and the social isolation and backwardness of the lower castes and tribes. As a result, British educational and employment policies came to be characterised by concessions, communal representation and patronage politics.

Since the 1950s social exclusion in India has assumed a wider connotation, and the discourse on it has had greater significance in political rhetoric, and among academics, more recently in writings on women, Dalit and other deprived groups. It has been debated that the term Dalit does not refer to a caste. It symbolises unity of all those, who suffered at the hands of iniquitous Brahminism, which is the basis of Hindutva. It is a symbol of change and revolution.

As said and believed that the Dalits reject the existence of God, rebirth and soul, sacred books that teach discrimination and the concepts of hell and heaven, because all these have made them slaves. However, the term is usually seen today in a much narrower context of referring only to Untouchables (socially excluded) and *Adivasis* (geographically excluded) communities of the past.

Dalits today not only constitute numerically an important section of the Indian society but also represent a community still struggling to break out of the centuries of mental bondage of the oppressive and hegemonic Brahminical/Hindutva order and inhuman existence.

Social injustice, cultural and economic deprivation and exclusion of Scheduled Castes, Scheduled Tribes and Other Backward Classes have a historical legacy. According to the Hindu Caste System only the Upper Castes had the right to the sacred thread ceremony, which ensured their right to study and gaining knowledge. They also had special privileges and powers in cultural, economic, political, legal and administrative fields, which were sanctified by the religious scriptures. Right to education and gaining knowledge, right to vocation or choose employment and right to good habitations, which form three principal needs for human development, were officially denied to the Dalits and Adivasis. Such historical negation finds some reflection in popular stories of *Shambhuka Vadh* (Killing of Shmbhuka) and chopping of thumb of Adivasi child Eklavya indicate this denial. This denial resulted in the lack of not only human development among the Dalits and Adivasis, but also prevented any significant technological changes in the means of production involving the labouring classes. It is not surprising therefore, that till the advent of the British period there was hardly any social and occupational mobility amongst the *Shudras*, the *ati-Shudras* and the excluded.

Locating Gender[2] in Social Exclusion Debate/Gender and Social Exclusion Analysis

The exclusion based on caste is one example and patriarchy is another, which is systemic or constitutive exclusion. This takes analysis, from a gender perspective[3] a step further to include more in-depth of analysis about who the men, women and children are, who are affected by poverty, exclusion and opportunities for development. It goes beyond identifying which groups are excluded, though this is undoubtedly a good first step, to ask the kinds of questions that can help identify the processes and mechanisms that facilitate and entrench social exclusion, and prevent excluded groups from accessing development opportunities and basic human rights.

Like gender relations, social exclusion is relational and is about power. Gender and social exclusion analysis can help us to identify:

- Who is excluded, where they are and some of the characteristics of their exclusion.
- The processes that cause and perpetuate gender inequality, discrimination and deprivation.

Women have remained the most silent, most invisible lot throughout history. Forms of gender discrimination have been almost universal. The men have been always projected as 'productive', 'political', 'public' and 'rational'; women as 'non-political', 'non-productive', 'private', and 'emotional'. All socio-political and epistemological structures and institutions-the state, market, organisations of civil society and cultural institutions and knowledge system have been an instrument in reinforcing gender inequality.

It has been claimed by feminist thinkers that philosophers are using 'value hierarchical' thinking and 'normative dualism'. They give greater value to what is seen as higher. (for example, men, culture, minds, or reason) and lesser value to what is seen as lower (for example, women, nature, bodies, or emotion). This kind of valuation results in 'logic of domination', an attempt to justify the subordination of the group of 'lower value' by the dominant group of 'higher value'. Like value-hierarchical thinking, "normative dualism" is exhibited when philosophers always create binary distinctions as mind/body, reason/emotion, man/woman, and so on. Historically the principle of exclusion works on these grounds: Law, Rationality and Tradition.

Women are comparatively weak and due to the tyrannical social custom which subordinated them to men. Owing to this weakness and domination by men, women have to spend their lives in ignominy and subordination. The dominant male tyrannise over, and exploit them according as they like, and women have no alternative but to submit to the same and eke out their existence.

For India an answer to the 'woman question' is very urgent. We have been politically independent for nearly five decades and along with independence have achieved some political rights for women. But, socially and economically, Indian women have still a long way to go. Legislation from above is not of much help when the beneficiaries from below are slow or unable to take advantage of it. We should, therefore, take stock of the situation and ascertain where the fault lies—the task is complicated by the chequered course of India's development over a long period.

Exclusion within Exclusion (Epistemological Analysis)

On the levels of episteme there are evidences of exclusion within exclusion in the category of gender if we go through the written documents. Except for a few notable exceptions, reflections on the transcoding of caste in feminist discourse and practices have been rare. Most of these women now included in History are Hindu, upper caste and upper class. There has been some attention, but not nearly enough to non-elite women and regional patterns. *Towards Equality* argued for the inclusion of all women, from minority communities, marginalised groups, and the lower socio-economic strata in the nation's progress and its history. Studies of women's status and economic needs have been more attentive to these differences rather than have those by historians. For example, *Women in Modern India*, which drew on the published literature does not do justice to the history of Muslim women, Christian women, and women from other minority communities nor to Dalit or tribal women. The recognition of caste as not just a retrograde past but an oppressive past reproduced as forms of inequality in modern society requires therefore, the integration of questions of caste with those of class and gender.

Recognising differences, power and connections of class, caste and community means transforming subjectivities, politics and pedagogies. At the level of practice, for those of us who have been complicit in the power and privilege of caste, one of the first realisations is our lack of knowledge of cultures that have been marginalised.

India now has a six decades experience in dealing with sharp inequalities and disparities rooted in several millennia of its independence. Yet, we still see sharp inequalities of caste, creed, tribe, rural and urban divide. Gender[4] cuts across all these layers, making women and girls of the disadvantaged groups, the most deprived members of our society. Apartheid of gender continues to stare at us despite proactive policies and laws for girls and women and if you are poor then this apartheid becomes all the more acute. Gender disparities in educational and all other social and demographic indicators reflect the unequal position of girls and women in a highly sexist gender discriminatory social context. Discrimination is a process and disparity and inequality is its end product. The process of discrimination has been a historical process which varies with time and space (context specific). Discourses and attitudes also change within specific cultures overtime. Although social and institutional discourses and their related technologies formulate our subjectivity, they are themselves social effects and respond to changes in social practices. What is right or ethical in any given time/period is simply what fits the dominant episteme and is authorised by the discourses and institutions in which the practice is framed.

In a particular society, with which we are overwhelmingly concerned in theory or practice, certain customs and institutions impose limitations which all women face with regard to their rights and duties; the effect on men of these customs and institutions is entirely contrary. Usually, the social position of women is examined from this aspect only. It is necessary to examine how these customs and institutions function, why they were introduced in society, and what their total effects on women are. But this aspect gives only partial answer to the 'woman question'.

An examination of all these aspects is needed to ascertain the direction of changes in the position of women interfacing caste class religion, etc., in a society and the forces affecting these changes. Virtually, in every society there are characteristically different sets of rights and duties for different social groups. These groups may be classified as privileged or under privileged in the light of organisation and values prevailing in the society. Accordingly, the position of women belonging to the respective groups would be arranged hierarchically with reference to the social stratification. Unless we take this into account and analyse the societal role of women from this perspective also, we cannot make a comprehensive evaluation of 'woman's question'. 'Man' was constituted as the subject of historical processes, whereas questions about 'Woman' were framed in terms of their nature, which was, by definition, unchanging, and hence to some extent a historical. This disciplinary legacy is still with us.

Disparity in the social role of men and women is apparent in almost all the societies in the world with some variation in its genre.The persistence of inequality, disparity between women and men as a problem is sharper in Asia than any other continent in the world. It applies even to sex-related mortality rates with Asia providing the bulk of the estimated 'missing women' in the world (Sen, 1999; Bardhan and Klasen, 1999). It has been empirically noted that the neglect of the interest of women related closely to their being excluded from employment opportunities basic education and land ownership (Boserup, 1970; Bardhan, 1984; Sen, 1984, 1985, and 1990). These exclusions are, thus, of great instrumental importance. The disparity raises the 'woman question', but it cannot be answered by referring to women only. It draws our attention to deal with two important aspects: (1) Social structure at particular period of operation of the society in which distinctive groups are discriminated against differentially; (2) Social customs and institutions which affect women are directly and are the expression of a particular social system.

Analysing how women are excluded from social and symbolic domains has been central to feminist theory and political strategies for change. Feminist analysis arguing that women's exclusion was embedded in power relationships was never integrated into mainstream policy discourses about exclusion. Instead policy discourses about groups, who are marginalised in society concentrate on individual rather than systemic change.

As we know social exclusion has become a dominant discourse of disadvantaged, marginalised almost all over the world and is increasingly adopted as a part of social policy approaches in development agencies. It offers an integrated framework for analysing social disadvantage, including gender as a form of exclusion.

Feminist Analysis of Exclusion

Exclusion has long been a central idea in feminist[5] Feminism itself is an ideology, an oppositional ideology to patriarchy. The concept of patriarchy and its use has been extensively debated by feminists (Rowbotham, 1981; Barret, 1980; Beechy, 1987) The dominance and control of the males are operationalised through many devices such as patrilineal descent, patrilocality, control of women's sexuality, ownership and inheritance of property, denial of educational, political and religious participation. (Thiruchandran, 1997)

The concept of ideology for feminist discourse is relevant considering the fact that male dominance is justified and legitimised through institutions like the family, church, and the State analysis. For feminists exclusion was a way of understanding women's social situation and a basis for political mobilisation. Feminists refer exclusion not just in terms of the absence, marginalisation or subordination of women in different social spheres but women's opposition *vis-a-vis* power relations in the public, private and symbolic domains.

The interplay of power and identities in the social processes of institutions give rise to gender and other disparities. Because gender identities are always cross cut by economic status, ethnicity religion, disability, etc., it becomes an entry point for intervention to interrupt these systems and address multiple disparities.

Feminism claims that same standards of equality applied universally to all women irrespective of where they come from is not relevant which mean that context-specific negotiation and translation must be taken for different groups of women in reality. The recognition of difference does not imply accommodation with specific cultural articulations of female roles and entitlements that treat women as inferior. Finally, and for the reasons discussed, feminism rejects appeals to culture and tradition that legitimise female subjugation. Most importantly, by stressing equality and the rights of the individual over group or cultural rights, it asserts that ascribed relations should not define women's entitlements. But let us see what the actual reality is.

Focussing on how gender exclusions operate in social contexts, an attempt has been made to deal with identities, social relations[6], power relations and processes.

Drawing attention to and taking action to rectify the uneven gender-based distribution of power and influence in society is thus one of the most important aspects of the gender perspective.

This cannot possibly be achieved without the systematic inclusion of the gender dimension. Indeed, gender is a core element of social relationships because it expresses a set of psychological and cultural characteristics and the functions and roles that a given society assigns to men and women according to which their activities are valued and appreciated.

This means that gender is an instrument of analysis that shows people as conditioned by society; it reveals relationships and the distribution of power and resources among men and women. Therefore, it is a foundation dimension on the basis of which, other dimensions, generators of differences act, ethnic origin, educational level, income, rural or urban condition, etc. By this, it is meant that the pauses and transformations in gender influence other social conditions and *vice versa*.

Socially excluded people are also likely to be least able to contribute to and benefit from development. In the same way that analysis is critical to understanding the ways in which women and men experience different conditions and opportunities in life, as a direct result of their gender. Social exclusion is also a social and cultural construct that determines a group's position in the social order and access to development opportunities. Social exclusion is complex and multi-dimensional, usually demonstrated by more than one factor of exclusion and liable to inter-generational determination.

We need to know more about which groups are poor and excluded and what forms of exclusion is take(ing) place today. We need to know more about how to reach excluded groups and how to facilitate the empowerment of disadvantaged and marginalised people in decision-making processes.

Identities

To start with identities it can be stated here that established institutional structures and traditions of practice are extremely powerful in framing how we understand ourselves as people, our place in our communities, our cultures and identities. Individuals can and do have multiple identities that are complementary, ethnicity, caste race, gender, religion etc. A sense of identity and belonging to a group with shared values and other bonds of culture[7] is important for individuals. But each individual can identify with many groups. We have assumed[8] and ascribed[9] identities.

Gender is widely described as social construction and in addition to biological sex this signifies the importance of social life for everyone's sense of their own gender identity. Our gender identities are then more than the obvious and natural consequence of our biological sex at birth. As a social construction, our gender identities are formed through our interactions within our social contexts throughout the life course. This distinction between sex and gender is highly important and in principle it is broadly understood.

Understanding gender as a social construction entails the acknowledgement that we learn about our gender identities as we meet and interact with others. Identities are relational, that is way they are worked out with respect to others who we regard as similar and different to ourselves. It is not a one-off occurrence; rather we continually act out our gender identities throughout our lives in a diverse institutions and contexts (Butler, 1990). As such our gender identities are accomplished rather than given; we are active in producing our gender identities. In this respect we need to think carefully about framing girls as docile subjects, without agency and as victims (Mohanty, 1991; Kapur, 2002; Saunders, 2002; Lazreg, 2005; Dunne, Humphreys and Leach, 2006; Leach and Humphreys, 2007; Dunne, 2007). The idea of individual agency or the active personal engagement in the production of gender identities is a central in the social construction of identity. This process of gender identity formation applies equally to our ethnic, religious and other aspects of our identities.

As Chandra Mohanty Comments (1991)

To define feminism purely in gendered terms assumes that our consciousness of being 'women' has nothing to do with race, class, nation or sexuality, just with gender. But no one 'becomes a woman' (in Simone de Beauvoir's sense) purely because they are female. Ideologies of womanhood have as much to do with class and race as they have to do with sex.

Identities then are never singular; we are never simply a 'man' or a 'woman'. Our gender identities are always intersected by, for example, ethnicity, religion, socio-economic status etc. As multiple, fluid and dynamic (Butler, 1990; Hall, 1996) identities are performed differently and with different emphasis in different contexts and times. Unless we recognise the multiplicity and contingency of identity, we will find it difficult to understand social life and its multiple disparities. It is thus important to consider how gender has been connected to other identities as without such understandings.

Identities are always cross cut by caste, class, gender, ethnicity, religion, disability etc. It is linked to multiple disparities experienced by marginalised groups. As such gender becomes an entry point into the analysis of the ways that exclusions are produced in the every day enactments of identity and power in social institutions. These processes are often normalised in ways that sustain the social, political and economic power dynamics of the status quo. Individual agency and our interrelations with others however, are framed within social contexts. The way we construct our gender identities is influenced by gender norms and traditions (the gender regime) of social and institutional contexts. Most social institutions (e.g., families, schools, and the workplace) have gender regimes in which males and females have particular roles and/or are expected to behave in specific ways according to their gender. The rules and structures of these social organisations interact with individual agency to shape identities (Giddens, 1991). As such expressions of our identities are shaped by our context and are variable. Gender identity performances differ across contexts, for example, a male wearing a *sulu* (skirt) would be less remarkable at a social gathering in Suva, Fiji than in Liverpool, England. The wide range of global social contexts in which individuals shape their gendered selves suggests that there are multiple ways of acting out and expressing our gender identities.

The above theorisations of enactments of identity provide crucial distinctions between sex and gender that highlight the significance of social interactions in different contexts. Building on this, further conceptual development has considered the significance of sexuality to an understanding of gender relations. And in the case of India, the gender identities interface with caste, religion, etc., which puts *dalit* women on the lowest hierarchy makes them speak differently as compared to the women higher social groups. Guru located the need for dalit women to talk differently in a discourse of descent against the middle class women's movement by dalit men. (Guru, 2001; Rege, 1998)

There are differences in the social, economic, political and cultural conditions of women of other castes and dalit women. Dalit women in rural areas work as daily wage labours. Apart from working in other fields, the dalit women have to do all the household chores. Dalit women in general have more freedom than women of tradition bound higher Hindu castes. Traditionally, dalit women were free in their economic and religious sphere. Unlike the upper caste women, who used to remain at home, the dalit women had to work for their bread mostly outside their home. Hence, dalit women are more economically independent than the upper caste women of Hindu society.

Dalit women's life pattern itself speaks volumes on dalitism. Dalit women have all the capacity, power and potential to govern the world but they are denied the opportunity to realise and express these potentials.

Dalit women are discriminated against and suffer disadvantages in social, political and economic opportunities because of their cultural identity. Socio-economic injustices and inequalities in income, education and health outcomes have been the defining feature of multi-cultural and pluralistic societies with marginal groups. These exclusions reflect long historical roots of conquest and colonisation as well as entrenched structures of hierarchy, such as caste systems.

We find identity politics of various hues abound in India, the most spectacular however, are those based on language, religion, caste ethnicity or tribal identity. But having said this it would be wrong on our part to assume that each of these identity markers operate autonomously, independent of the overlapping influence of the other makers. Caste-based discrimination and oppression have been a pernicious feature of Indian society.

The identification of a member of the group on the basis of sharing common attributes on the basis of all or some of the attributes, language, gender, religion, culture, ethnicity, etc., indicates the existence or formation of identities.

Notion of identities and the way that it can help us to understand gender exclusions and can open the way to understanding how gender intersects with other social characteristics (class, ethnicity etc.) in the lives of marginalised people. Besides how power and social processes contribute to these identities formation, it illustrates, using gender examples, how identities are acted out in a social context and how in turn the context shapes identities. Interactions and processes within the social institutions in any context are central to identity formation and to inclusion/exclusion.

Gender and sexual norms of institutions family, community, etc., are the context in which individuals construct their identities. There are multiple examples; mothers teaching their daughters how to sit, dress, serve and listen; the invitation for boys to take up space, speak and act publicly, rites of passage from boyhood to manhood etc. To a large extent this gender/sexual regulation is taken for granted as part of normal everyday life. For those who resist or do not conform there are explicit forms of social regulation usually enacted by others (mothers, fathers, siblings, peers) in the same social context. In many cases transgressions of the gender/sexual norms are met with social regulation ranging from verbal abuse that casts doubt on a person's heterosexuality to physical violence. These forms of social regulation impose the dominant social order and gender/ sexual power hierarchies. In this sense, they are exclusionary and deeply impinge on identity formation. These conditions for identity formation make normative gender roles and position appear natural. Gender mainstreaming is one strategy of disrupting the gender order which needs to be further extending across social institutions paying attention to the details of everyday life. Efforts to breakdown gender and other cultural stereotypes have been made in reviews and revisions of curriculum texts. Balancing representations and the inclusion of both females and males engaged in non-stereotypical activities acts to disrupt gender assumptions. Offering multiple ways to act out gender identities, masculinities and feminities breaks down the stereotypes that deterministically (though perhaps unintentionally) connect biology at birth with naturalised inequalities in education and all spheres of social life.

Power Relations

A social exclusion analysis focusses on who is being excluded and who is doing the excluding, and why. For example, social exclusion can be the result of deliberate discrimination, exploitation and/or an attempt to protect privilege.

Social exclusion can occur in different sites and spaces. These include state institutions, access to services and markets. Exclusion can also occur in the market place (e.g., social norms can exclude women in traditional societies from participating in the physical space where buying and selling takes place); through community norms; and within the family. A person can be denied access completely or given only unequal access-both can constitute exclusion.

Exclusion can result from the power relations that shape these spaces. Caste has added to the complexity of the Indian social system, which is very much stratified and is based on dominance. Dominance is based on wealth, that is, control over land, which also gives the dominant caste access to political power. An important aspect of the caste system is that those who have dominated the means of production have also tried to dominate the means of symbolic production. The symbolic hegemony then allows them to control the very standards by which their rule is evaluated, so that the perspective of the lower castes has no place in it. (Kapadia, 1996). But those at the bottom end have not always accepted this position and have found ways to interpret their own identities differently from the way the upper castes have constructed them.

Women who suffer from inequality in every society also face more complex problems and abnormal atrocities (exclusion) when their society is hierarchically divided. For a variety of reasons, women in upper caste (*Grihysutras* bound) families suffered more inequalities and more subtle forms of oppression than the women of the working class/castes suffered at the hands of their own men. This is not to claim that working class/caste women do not suffer; wife beating, for example might be more prevalent among working class/castes than the upper class/castes but the difference is that the working class/caste women have an outlet. (Ilaiah, 2007), He further says, that a dalit bahujan women within her caste/class existence is very much a political being, a social being and an economic being, where as an upper caste woman is not (Ilaiah, 2005).

The irony of the situation comes out quite clearly, if we examine the upper caste male attitude towards lower caste women. Women's sexuality is doubly defined by them. Sexuality defined for upper caste women is very much different from the sexuality of Dalit women which is very much governed by the caste relations. What does that imply? In other words, their body is untouchable but their sexuality is not.

The honour and respectability of upper caste men are regarded as protected and preserved by women, who therefore must be closely guarded and whose sexuality is stringently monitored. Upper caste women are regarded as the gateways-literally points of entrance into the caste system. The lower caste male whose sexuality is a threat to upper caste purity has to be institutionally prevented from having sexual access to the women of the higher castes through an effective system of surveillance and seclusion. (Chakravarty, 2006)

Social Relation, Power and Social Process

How social relations are governed by caste relations it is a matter to be analysed carefully. The mechanism of controls operated on women through three devices and three levels. The first was ideology; the second was the right discipline and keep women under control granted to their kinsmen; and the third was the power of the king to discipline and punish them for their errant behaviour. The ideological level of effectuating the control of women in *stridharma* or *patidharma*; wifely codes were internalised by women who attempted to live up to the idealised notions of *Pativrata* constructed by the ideologies of society. In the upper caste Hindu society, the design of the patriarchal class-caste structure was mapped out by the *Brahmans*. *Pativrata* the specific *dharma* of the so-called upper caste Hindu wife, then become the ideology which women accepted, and even aspired to chastity and wifely fidelity as the highest expression of their selfhood. This device was to ensure the social control of women; it was an ideological mechanism for controlling the biological aspects of women. (Chakravarty, 2006)

Now coming to second mechanism by which a women's sexuality is controllled, the brahminical scripture says that it is the highest duty of all husbands; even weak man must strive to guard the wife. The structure of social rules provided for a third level of control to ensure the perpetuation of the patriarchal structures: the king was vested with the authority to punish errant wives.

In keeping with the requirements of a caste-based society, the most reprehensible cases of adultery are when women have sexual relations with men of lower castes. The purity of women ensured the purity of caste and thus the social order itself, not just in the existing society but into future too. The archaic state was both a class/caste state and a patriarchal state: a close linkage existed between caste, class, the state and patriarchy. Together they provided the structural framework of institutions within which gender relations were organised. Thus, the structure of social relations that shaped the dominant/ hegemonic model of gender, and of caste, in early India was consolidated and reproduced by achieving compliance of women *(Ibid)*. While the total control of the sexuality of women was never fully achieved in practice, at the ideological and normative level of theoretical premises of brahminical patriarchy[10] have been accepted widely. Brahminical codes for women differ according to the status of the caste group in the hierarchy of castes with the most stringent control over sexuality reserved as a privilege for the highest castes. Finally, it incorporates both an ideology of chaste wives and *Pativrata* women who are valorised and a structure of rules and institutions by which caste hierarchy and gender inequality are maintained through both the production of consent and the application of coercion. In a nutshell, brahminical patriarchy implies the model of patriarchy outlined in brahminical prescriptive texts, to be enforced by the coercive power of the king, or those who act on behalf of the king.

Patriarchal formulations for women of the high castes and women of the lower caste were structurally integrated into the ideology and the material relations of the social system but this varies on caste lines. Class and caste ideology interact at very pertinent levels in gender relations, they are also in interplay shaping social relations as evident from the above analysis. Dalit women and girls are especially vulnerable, experiencing not only the discrimination of caste, but also of class and gender—'triple discrimination' as it's called here in India—leaving them in a vicious cycle of marginalisation and exploitation.

Vivek Kumar locates dalit women on the basis of their structural positioning, occupations performed and the societal treatment. He argues the specificity of dalit women. Dalit in general are treated in an inhumane ways and dalit women are marginalised even further in three folds on the basis of Caste, Class and Patriarchy. Dalit women are raped, beaten up and paraded naked to break the morale of the whole community. This inter-sectionality of caste-based patriarchy makes dalit women, dalit within dalits.

Kancha Ilaiah has pointed out that the possession or non-possession of material resources, in particular, in the form of property makes for fundamental differences between lower caste women and upper caste women. Since the lower caste by and large do not own property, all dalit families have to lower; this includes women and even children. These in built structures, according to Ilaiah, shape the manner in which dalit women are thoroughly integrated into labour systems and have a strong work ethics. Upper caste women on the other hand have no function outside reproduction and are thus reduced to the single axis of providing sexual labour.

Dalit women experience patriarchal oppressions in unique as well as in shared ways which according to Ilaiah is termed as *Dalit Patriarchy.* Given that the oppressions of both caste and patriarchy control the lives of dalit women in particular ways, it is not surprising that this situation has led dalit women to take the position that they need their women's organisation. In furtherance of this objective the Dalit Women's Federation, a national-level organisation was set up in 1990s.

Processes of becoming gendered are critical to understandings of multiple exclusions. Acknowledging gender as a process of accomplishment (a becoming) in which individual agency interacts with institutional norms, draws attention to the contextual and local in the formation of gender identities and structure daily life of social institutions. Even though daily life goes on in a taken for granted way, these daily activities are often enacted to passively or actively exclude specific groups. Institutional[11] processes (family, community, religion etc.) of domination and subordination are fundamental to social hierarchies that link power, identity and disadvantage.

Gender expectations and stereotypes inform individual gendered behaviour and interpretations of the gendered behaviour of others in ways that entrench and solidify organisational practices and associated gender myths. For girls, lower expectations of their educational performance have a fundamental bearing on their access to quality education. Strategies to improve educational outcomes for girls have included broadening forms of educational assessment. These include changes in the examination questions and blending formal tests with classroom assessment. Attention to language issues and references to the experiences of girls have been part of these reform strategies (USAID, 2008). Observations in schools show boys performing their dominance over the girls by their attempts to control the physical and verbal space of the classroom. They usually are seen to sit at the back and the sides of the class surrounding the girls and they often jeer and discouraged girls from answering questions in class. On most occasions, the teachers did not intervene in this 'natural' gender order. Through these informal social practices the male power in the school was reinstated and used to regulate male and female gender performances in the interests of the more powerful males. Attempts to transgress this gender order would be to risk the danger of public ridicule and humiliation.

Family is a key site, in which gender and sexual identities are formed and performed, power relations and hierarchy regulate each other and is central to how identities are negotiated and hold power interfacing with age and gender relations.

Like family, religion also operates and confers privilege on the dominant and excludes those who do not or cannot comply. While the main discussion has been on how gender and sexuality structure the disadvantage experienced by girls, the same constructs of power, process and identity can be used also to explain intersecting multiple forms of exclusion.

These two are only part of the social landscape in which gender and sexual identities are formed and inequalities prevail. Limited horizons and hetero-normative social practices are sustained also through customs like early marriage through which the social and educational disadvantage of women is sustained inter-generationally. Kinship, marriage and intimate sexual relations are all expressions of masculinity and femininity which on the whole work to regulate and subordinate females.

Insights into the processes of exclusion related to gender and sexual identities have much to offer an understanding of the exclusion of marginalised groups and the ways that these interact with gender.

However, these processes are necessarily contextually constructed as people in different contexts do not have access to the same range of possibilities (Gubrium and Holstein, 2000). This implies the importance of recognising multiple gender configurations.

Identities then are never singular; we are never simply a 'man' or a 'woman'. Our gender identities are always intersected by, for example, ethnicity, religion, socio-economic status etc. As multiple, fluid and dynamic (Butler, 1990; Hall, 1996) identities are performed differently and with different emphasis in different contexts and times. Unless we recognise the multiplicity and contingency of identity we will find it difficult to understand social life and its multiple disparities. It is thus important to consider how gender has been connected to other identities as without such understandings it is unlikely that EFA goals can be realised. Gender and poverty have been inter-related and discussed in terms of female disadvantages with respect to, for example, economics, literacy, education and health. Similarly, religion has been associated with specific forms of subordinated femininity although it might be argued that this is again a manifestation of male power in a specific country located gender regime.

The coming of patriarchal Hinduism and its caste system into India institutionalised the oppression of the outcaste dalits and this had a particularly deleterious effect on women. The control on women's sexuality was essential for the development of a patriarchal caste hierarchy, both for the maintenance of caste and for the legitimation and control of inheritance. Restrictions of time, place and space were therefore imposed on women to ensure the purity of caste by avoiding the danger of inter-caste 'pollution'. There was a stream of resistance against the rigidity of patriarchal Brahminism. There was a resurgence of mother goddess cults and fertility worship. The *Shakti* cult representing the female power principle became strong. The *Bhakti* cult, a strong non-Aryan southern movement, brought in anti-caste, anti-patriarchy challenges to Hinduism.

The problems of women vary from one social stratum to another, one cultural group to another and also from one economic stratum to another. Undeniably, those who are involved in women's studies as well as who are activists have looked at the intricacies of the above mentioned problem. However, it can be said that not enough attention has been focussed so far on the life condition and problems of women belonging to the Scheduled Castes and Tribes.

Further, it is argued that dalit women are placed at the absolute bottom of the social hierarchy as they face systemic and structural discrimination threefold: as dalits, as poor, and as women.

The dalit women subjected to severe exploitation at the work place also suffer on caste ground and gang rape from upper castes, while at the same time they may be beaten up in their own houses as well. In addition to this, the process of rural development has played a decisive role in forced migration of dalit women from rural to urban areas. Although the state sponsored development activities have brought some awareness to dalit women, it has led to overburdening and self-exploitation.

Thus, the institutions that shape the opportunity, structures within which individuals and groups must act include both formal and informal institutions. Formal institutions have written rules encoded in law and thus are ultimately backed by the power of the state. Central to our analysis is the idea that individuals and groups are defined and define themselves—in terms of multiple layers of institutions that surround them.

Exclusion and disempowerment takes place at various levels. One is within the individual and involves internalisation of a negative definition of his or her own identity. To a large extent the rules/norms/beliefs and behaviours laid down by the surrounding institutions define who the individual is, how they are valued by society and what they can or cannot do. In India, since these institutions have been primarily defined by the dominant male (patriarchy) high caste group (brahmanical), they can be very disempowering for an individual woman, Dalit or for a member of a linguistic or religious minority. In most of the world today and certainly in India—we encounter inequitable institutions. The distributional rules of the game vary for diverse individuals and groups on the basis of their social identity. This may sound discouraging; but our knowledge of the reciprocal relationship between people and their institutions gives us hope. People are born at a certain time and place into the complex web of institutions that not only determine their initial asset endowments, but also shape their thinking and behaviour—and even how they think of themselves and the kind of future they are able to "imagine" for themselves and their children.

Yet, these same institutions have themselves been created by people—and are continually contested by other people. The fluidity of the situation is what opens the way for human agency and change. Many of these overlapping institutions reinforce each other—sometimes in negative ways. However, institutions can also compete with each other for legitimacy and power thus, opening up space for structural change. Individuals and groups who are disadvantaged in some way by the prevailing distributional rules under one institution continually use these competing institutions selectively to negotiate ways to meet their own needs and aspirations. Because they are socially constructed, institutions are dynamic and this means that inequitable distributional rules established by one or even a set of inter-locking institutions, can be negotiated and changed. Taking note of this philosophy the approach to social inclusion requires a shift from an institutional environment which gives some individuals and groups more opportunity to realise their agency than others to one where the political system, and the rule of law support equal agency for all (discussed in the later chapters).

Review of Literature

Whatever literature are available on social exclusion and inclusion, they include findings of conceptual and empirical research at international and national level which have contributed to the understanding of both the theory and practice from a conceptual, social policy, deprivation point of view. Very few works have been done on the discourse of social exclusion and inclusion from a gender perspective. Though many books, articles and reports are published every year, but very few of these publications explains and analyses the exclusion and inclusion of dalit women in specific.

Conceptual Analysis

Study of Silver, H on 'Social Exclusion and Social Solidarity: Three Paradigms' 1994, tells as to how are we to understand the new social problems that have arisen as a result of the economic restructuring of advanced capitalist democracies since the mid-1970s? This International Labour Review article identifies three conflicting paradigms within which different meanings of social exclusion are embedded—solidarity, specialisation and monopoly. These derive from the political ideologies of Republicanism, liberalism and social democracy. While the idea of exclusion may help to focus attention on certain social categories, it may also distract attention from general rises in inequality and undermine universal approaches to social protection.

Levitas, R. (1998) in her work, 'The Inclusive Society: Social Exclusion and New Labour' develops an inclusive model which identifies three different approaches to tackle Social Exclusion for an inclusive society, which includes redistributive justice, social integration discourse and moral underclass discourse.

Bhalla, A and Lapeyre, F. (1997), "Social Exclusion: Towards an Analytical and Operational Framework, asks questions like what is the difference between poverty and social exclusion? How can the concept of social exclusion be used as a tool for policy-making? This paper argues that social exclusion overlaps with poverty but goes beyond it by explicitly embracing the relational as well as the distributional aspects of poverty. The concept has universal validity although it has not gained much attention in developing countries. An analytical framework should establish the interrelationships between the social, economic and political dimensions of exclusion.

Article by de Haan, A., 'Social Exclusion: Towards a Holistic Understanding of Deprivation' (1999) examines the usefulness of the social exclusion framework for understanding deprivation. It is divided into seven main sections which include: defining what is meant by social exclusion; comparing social exclusion with poverty; discussing whether social exclusion can be measured; and drawing out the implications for social integration policies and the way forward. He also discusses the genealogy of social exclusion, the importance of focussing on social relations rather than bounded groups, and the role of agency in terms of choosing exclusion in the context of rights and entitlements. Furthermore, overlaps between social exclusion and definitions of poverty (in particular the capabilities approach of Sen) are identified with implications for moving beyond mapping and monitoring deprivations, towards identifying the processes that lead to and cause deprivations.

Study by David Byrne on' Social Exclusion', (2008) in four volumes extensively discusses about the concept Social exclusion and its key issues. Volume One reviews the nature and history of the term 'social exclusion' and examines ways in which the idea has been used in social research. Volume Two covers income distribution; the nature of class in post-industrial societies and the related dimensions of inequality in relation to gender, ethnicity and age; social exclusion in the changing city; and the general political context of post-democracy with special reference to partnership and participation. Volume three explores the use of the term 'social exclusion' and programmes of social inclusion in specific policy areas including taxation and cash benefits, urban regeneration, health, education, housing, and transport. The final volume in the collection gathers together material to examine programmes specifically directed towards countering social exclusion, with particular reference to community development, and 'joined-up' government policy. It also considers radical alternatives to those policies.

Burchardt T., Le Grand T., and Piachaud D., 2002, "Introduction" in Hills, J., Le Grand, J. and Piachaud, D, 'Understanding Social Exclusion', categorically mentioned as to what are the different approaches to analysing and understanding social exclusion? There are three main approaches to social exclusion and these emphasise the roles of: individuals; institutions and systems; and discrimination and lack of enforced rights. Given the complexity of influences on individuals, however, a broad perspective is most helpful.

Article by Kabeer, N. on 'Social Exclusion, Poverty and Discrimination: Towards an Analytical Framework' (2000) examines the concept of social exclusion, and its transferability to developing country contexts. It asks what added value the concept brings, and how it can be understood in relation to mass poverty, justice and 'good' versus 'bad' exclusion. Overall, the author is in favour of retaining the concept for social policy analysis, and uses this article to develop a framework within which this can be done.

Work on 'Dimensions of Social Exclusion: Ethnographic Explorations' by K.M. Ziyauddin and Eswarappa Kasi (2009) discusses about dimensions of social exclusion and focusses largely on social exclusion in the context of communities and social groups, who have or have not been considered in discussing the benefits of mainstream inclusive society or development. It emphasises the social aspects of concerns such as housing, health, employment, education, participation in social activities and festivities, social interaction and social intercourse through social arrangements, normative value systems and customs. Apart from talking about exclusion based on caste, he also mentions about exclusion base on gender caused by patriarchy, which is a form of systemic or constitutive exclusion.

Study on 'B.R. Ambedkar: Perspectives on Social Exclusion and Inclusive Policies' by Sukhadeo Thorat and Narender Kumar reviews the current debate on equal opportunity policies of social inclusion. It discusses Ambedkar's contribution to the development of inclusive policies during the British Rule and its culmination into the policy of reservation in the Constituent Assembly. It also discuss problems of caste, discrimination, and untouchability as understood by Ambedkar and his suggested remedies and actions compares India's experience of affirmative action with the USA and underscores the international relevance of inclusive powers like reservation.

From A Gender Perspective

In recent years various studies on women have appeared with focal point ranging from 'abortions of female foetuses' to 'bride-burning' and 'ideology of *sati*'. Most of the women's studies concentrate on the middle class women among whom there are very few dalits. In fact, in the general literature of women, no special attention is paid to the problems of dalit women.

DFID, 2008, "Gender and Social Exclusion Analysis, How to Note", A Practice Paper, in its guidance note, suggests a structure, methodology and analytical framework for a Gender and Social Exclusion Analysis (GSEA). A GSEA, examines who is excluded, plus the processes, impacts and implications of gender inequality and social exclusion. DFID country offices should carry out a GSEA before preparing a Country Governance Analysis and as part of the country planning process. The GSEA should inform the analysis, issues and choices stages of the country planning process.

Article by Cecile Jackson on 'Study on Social exclusion and Gender: Does one size fit all?', (1999) enquires into the gender implications of some of the core elements of social exclusion paradigms, questions whether an integrated approach works for gender, and argues that feminist research and gender analysis offer both better situated understandings of the character and experience of marginality, and useful insights for the emerging applications of social exclusion frameworks to developing countries. This discussion is contextualised with a brief account of how feminists have analysed marginality and integration in the South, in a tradition which has paralleled but not crossed into European social exclusion discourses.

Work by Uma Chakravarty on 'Gendering Caste: Through A Feminist Lens', (2006) examines the linkages between caste and gender and states that the subordination of women and the control of female sexuality are crucial to the maintenance of the caste system, creating what feminist scholars have termed brahminical patriarchy. She discusses the range of patriarchal practices within the larger framework of sexuality, labour and access to material resources and also focusses on the centrality of endogamous marriages that maintain the system.

Going further it has also been found that historians have also done some study with focus on minority women like they have begun to write the history of Muslim women in South Asia. To name a few works like Shahida Lateef's Muslim Women in India (1990), Zoya Hasan's edited Forging Identities (1994) and Azra Asghar Ali's 'The Emergence of Feminism Among Indian Muslim Women', 1920-47 focus on women's entry into public life and introduce key questions for Muslim women's history (Azra, 2000).

Sonia Nishat Amin's the World of Muslim Women in Colonial Bengal: 1876-1939 and Gail Minault's Secluded Scholars: Women's Education and Muslim Social Reform in Colonial India are comprehensive works on Muslim women's education, family life and literary activity in colonial Bengal, and North India respectively. (Amin, 1999) although the chronicles informs us that Muslim women played important political roles, only a few historians have written about powerful women. Ellison Findley on Nur Jahan, and Shaharyar M. Khan and Claudia Preckel on the Begums of Bhopal (Ellison1993). Barbara Metcalf's Perfecting Women (Metcalfe1992), a partial translation and commentary of an important document for reformist Islam, and Syeda Saiydain Hameed's Hali's Musaddas on the rise and fall of Islamic civilisation by 'Urdu's first feminist poet' are of value to feminist historians.

Current research, for example that of Siobhan Lambert-Hurley, promises more analysis of powerful women, while Ph.D candidate Bilkis Rahman[12] mines the archives for documents such as the memoir of Bibi Kusum, the second wife of the renowned novelist Mir Musharraf Hussain. The work of these young historians is encouraging but there is still much to be done. In addition to retrieval projects, to collect and archive writings, memoirs, letters and diaries, photographs, and oral histories of Muslim women, we need to know more about women's response to modernising trends and efforts to change their lives. There are a few histories of women in pre-independence radical movements, for example, 'We are making history...' About the Telangana movement, and Peter Custers' Women in Tebhaga Uprising. Dalit women have been discussed in relation to male reformers, especially Phule and Ambedkar, but are only now being addressed as a separate group needing a history (For example, see Uma Chakravarty,' Reconceptualising Gender Phule, Brahamanism and Brahamanical Patriarchy', in Women in Indian History: Social, Economic, Political and Cultural Perspectives, ed. Kiran Pawar, Patiala and New Delhi: Vision and Venture, 1996) Anupama Rao's Gender and Caste: Contemporary Issues in Indian Feminism (Rao: 2003), and monograph, The Caste Question: Untouchable Struggles for Civil Rights and Recognition, with books such as The Silken Swing: The Cultural Universe of Dalit Women (Franco and Macwan: 2000) are step in the right direction. All these studies reflect a historical perception.

But in the past decades a few studies (Barnard, 1981; Brydon and Chant, 1989; UNDP, 1995; Chauhan, 1996) have come out dealing with socio-economic status of women and the problem of gender gap. The overwhelming evidence so far is that virtually no society in the world provides women equal status with men (Giele, 1977). Although India's Constitution provides equality of sex, women are still discriminated against in the social and economic areas (Apputhmurthuy, 1990). It is a well accepted fact that women in India enjoy a much lower status as compared to men in all spheres of life. At the same time considerable variations in the socio-economic status of women are found across different states of the country as several studies bring out (Kumar, Naresh 1993; Chauhan, 1996; Kumar, Shiva, 1996; Dreze and Gazdar, 1997).

In the early years, in the social sciences too, the inter-connection between caste and gender was not brought to the fore and category of 'dalit women' figured neither in women's studies nor in caste studies.

What may be drawn from the above discussions is that there is a significant lack of knowledge about the gender aspect of social exclusion. These works do not claim to have covered all significant issues related to the main theme. A survey of literature shows the necessity of deeper probe into how gender as a category forms the issue of social been exclusion at the level of pedagogy and practice, therefore still remains. For instance, an attempt has yet to be made to: (a) ascertain the reasons for the introduction of these factors in society, (b) analyse how and through which institutions and customs these overt cause expressed themselves, (c) examine whether any other societal factor had a role to play in this context, and finally, (d) explain the cumulative effect of all these factors on the position of women in society on the one hand and discuss the process of inclusion on the other. The present study is a modest attempt to fill in the gaps by analysing the theoretical formulations of exclusion and the process of inclusion within historical and contemporary framework through a gender perspective.

Objectives

The broad objectives are as follows:

- To give a historical review (including recent history).

- To analyse the different agencies which have subordinated and discriminated distinctive groups differentially.
- To examine the various streams of thought towards the issues of gender, exclusion and inclusive development.
- To highlight the emerging problems and necessary interventions through policy of inclusiveness.

Methodology

The study focusses on Social Exclusion and Inclusion from a gender perspective from ancient to present times. It examines as to how throughout the different periods of history the knowledge system has been male-centric and elitist in character.

Caste has impinged on women lives. Besides, it is a well accepted fact that women in India enjoy a much lower status as compared to men in all spheres of life. At the same time considerable variations in the socio-economic status of women are found across different states of the country as several studies bring out. The present study focusses on the exclusion of women in general and dalit[13] women in specific in India as a whole and Uttar Pradesh in particular, based on primary as well as secondary sources including books, journals, various government reports and newspaper articles, etc., collected from different libraries of the country. The method adopted in the work is historical and analytical. An effort here has been made to deal with the conceptual and theoretical aspects of social exclusion and inclusion. Moreover, the exclusion of women, both non-dalit and dalit women and their inclusion by the State forms the core of the study.

The study comprises six chapters including Introduction and Conclusion. The chapter Introduction describes how the discourse of social exclusion and inclusion can be conceptualised and theorised in Indian context. It further discusses about different dimensions and mechanisms of social exclusion. In this chapter, the focus has been on exploration of the gendered nature of social exclusion which have been mapped along the lines of identities, identity formation at the institutional level like family, religion, schools as well as power relations, social relations and social processes. If we look at women today their lives are located at the intersection of caste, class and patriarchy/ies. In many areas they face exclusion, discriminations and remain on the margins. To understand (dalit) women exclusion, marginalisation and discrimination, it is necessary to delineate both internal and external (structural/ institutional) factors that have bearing on their lives.

The first chapter on **Situating Social Exclusion within Phule, Periyar and Ambedkar Discourse** is an exercise of historically locating the 'different voice' of dalit women in their struggles, tracing the lineage through the Satyashodhak and Ambedkarite movements tries to show how the chapter further projects how the feminist philosophy tries to construct a new methodology, epistemology and ontology that incorporates the female perspective.

The second chapter of the project on **Dalit (Women's Question) Struggle from the Perspective of Movement: From Alienation to Assertion** not merely attempts to explain the narrative but also analysing and situating dalit (women) movement's in history. There is a compelling necessity to discover and reclaim the hidden and buried history of dalit to get clue from past to achieve (self-esteem by recognising) dalit solidarity by staging a successful movement. Analyses the contributions of some of the third chapter on **Contemporary Status of Dalit Women in India** analyses at depth the current positional aspects of dalit women in India in general and the state of Uttar Pradesh in particular. The significant part of this chapter is that it ends up with view that there is an urgent need to rethink over these aspects and devise some alternative strategies to reposition dalit women the most marginalised lot so that a vision of a just society could be realised.

The fourth chapter on **Process of Inclusion : Concepts and Trends** tries to define and trace the process of social inclusion in Indian context and whether something has been done for the inclusion of these excluded groups at the level of pedagogy and praxis over these years? In actual how far these efforts have been instrumental in translating these attempts into a reality. All these need to be examined carefully and seriously. Further, the chapter analyses at depth the contribution made by feminist sociologists, who challenged the long standing established theories of stratification and socialisation etc.

The last chapter on **'Conclusion'** summarises all the debates related to gendering social exclusion and inclusion with its limitations in the Indian context and a few interventions that there is a need for new approach and theoretical perspective for the study of all Indian social reality of crucial issues concerning exclusion of dalit women. It is time now to call the academy into question, and to engage with systems and processes that produce such colonised knowledge. And by providing alternative paradigms of knowledge, theory and understanding, through decolonising the epistemological and pedagogical base and asserting their legitimacy within the academy can be a way forward.

References

1. This has been quoted in Smith Peter J., 2008. From Beijing 1995 to the Hague 2006—The Transnational Activism of the Dalit Women's Movement, Canadian Political Science Association, British Columbia, June 2008.
2. The word dalit has its origin in Pali, a pre-Sanskrit language and it means the deprived. This term is used as an act of confident assertion, rejecting nomenclature of Harijan, the 'children of God'. Dalit Panthers, a radical movement of dalit youth in the seventies used this term for the first time for those who were Scheduled Castes and Scheduled Tribes, neo-Buddhist, the working-people, the land-less and poor peasants, women, and all those who are being exploited politically, socially, economically, and in the name of religion.
3. Gender is a social construct, they are made the way they are, by social norms and practices by the institutions and discourses that regulate our behaviour and by the way we regulate ourselves. It changes with time and space in history and culture.
4. The gender perspective is: An instrument to better analyse the current reality and questioning the relationships of power that that can be found between males and women and at the core of all social relationships in general. The gender perspective helps to perceive how the human groups, starting from biological differences, build the concepts of masculinity and femininity, attributing to them a range of symbolical competencies, performance possibilities and different evaluation points both to women and to men. When these socially built " naturalisations" become visible, this socially built methodology contributes to interpret the other mechanisms responsible for discrimination or social exclusion which by acting together, give power to those other ones related to gender (age, educational level, poverty, violence, etc.).

5. Gender is a social construct, they are made the way they are, by social norms and practices by the institutions and discourses that regulate our behaviour and by the way we regulate ourselves. It changes with time and space in history and culture.
6. Feminism itself is an ideology, an oppositional ideology to patriarchy. The concept of patriarchy and its use has been extensively debated by feminists (Rowbotham,1981; Barret, 1980; Beechy, 1987). The dominance and control of the males are operationalised through many devices such as patrilineal descent, patrilocality, control of women's sexuality, ownership and inheritance of property, denial of educational, political and religious participation (Thiruchandran, 1997). The concept of ideology for feminist discourse is relevant considering the fact that male dominance is justified and legitimised through institutions like the family, church, and the State.
7. It uncovers differences between women, divided by other aspects of social differentiation such as class, race and ethnicity. The aim is to understand the dynamics of gender relations in different institutional contexts and thereby to identify women's bargaining position and formulate strategies to improve this. It has proved challenging to adopt this approach in operational work.
8. The distinctive patterns of ideas, beliefs, and norms which characterise the way of life and relations of a society or group within a society. Culture is not a frozen set of values and practices. It is constantly recreated as people question, adapt and redefine their values and practices to changing realities and exchanges of ideas. Culturally determined gender ideologies define rights and responsibilities and what is 'appropriate' behaviour for women and men. They also influence access to and control over resources, and participation in decision-making. These gender ideologies often reinforce male power and the idea of women's inferiority. Culture is sometimes interpreted narrowly as 'custom' or 'tradition', and assumed to be natural and unchangeable. Despite these assumptions, culture is fluid and enduring. Dominant cultures reinforce the position of those with economic, political and social power, and therefore tend to reinforce male power.
9. Internalisation of ascription leads to the emergence of another identity which is the assumed identity. The dominant groups have barraged the dalits with an uninterrupted creation of myths first, about its own purity, valour, spirituality,

superiority etc., second, about the weakness, impurity, untounchability, lack of intelligence etc.

10. Characteristics ascribed to the dalits that ultimately went to establish an identity which was not theirs abound in the Vedas and the two epics. The contextualisation of an ascribed identity to the dalits cannot be ignored. While ascribing low and mean characters to the dalits Brahminism contextualised its mean efforts by simultaneously ascribing qualities of superiority to itself. The centrality of ascription on dalits is around an uncivilised but carefully crafted discourse of impurity, low origin, servitude, lack of civilisation etc.

11. It is a set of rules and institutions in which caste and gender are linked, each shaping the other and where women are crucial in maintaining the boundaries between castes. Patriarchal Codes in this structure ensure that the caste system can be reproduced without violating the hierarchical order of closed endogamous circles, each distinct from and higher and lower than others. This set of norms has shaped the ideology of the upper castes in particular extant even today amongst these castes and is often emulated by the lower castes especially when seeking upward mobility.

12. The existence of "a predominant set of values, beliefs, rituals and institutional procedures that operate systematically and consistently to the benefit of certain persons and groups at the expense of others". This mechanism operates without conscious decisions by those who represent the status quo.

13. Bilkis Rehman is a Ph.D. candidate in History at Dhaka University.

14. The term dalit has been derived from Sanskrit which means broken and down-trodden. B.R. Ambedkar often described the untouchables as broken people. The dalits are socially and economically weak, culturally backward and politically powerless. Thus, the word Dalit describes a condition of being under-privileged and deprived of basic rights and refers to people who are suppressed on grounds of their low birth.The term dalit here is used for the Scheduled Caste.

Bibliography

Ambedkar, B.R. 1987. 'Philosophy of Hinduism' in Vasant Moon(ed) *Dr Babasaheb Ambedkar: Writings and Speeches*, Vol. 3, Education Department, Govt of Maharashtra (first published in 1936).

Ambedkar, B.R. 1979. 'Annihilation of Caste' in Vasant Moon(ed) *Dr*

Babasaheb Ambedkar: Writings and Speeches, Vol. 1. Education Department, Govt. of Maharashtra, (first published in 1935).

Bhalla, A. and Lapeyre, F. 1997. 'Social Exclusion: Towards an Analytical and Operational Framework', *Development and Change,* Volume 28, pp. 413-433.

Burchardt T., Le Grand T., and Piachaud D., 2002. 'Introduction' in Hills, J., Le Grand, J. and Piachaud, D.,Understanding Social Exclusion, Oxford: Oxford University Press.

Butler, J. 1990. Gender Trouble: Feminism and the Subversion of Identity. London: Routledge.

Butler, J. 1990. Gender Trouble: Feminism and the Subversion of Identity. London: Routledge.

Cecile Jackson 1999. Social exclusion and gender: Does one size fit all? *The European Journal of Development Research*, Vol. 11, Issue 1. June 1999, pp. 125-146.

DFID, 2005. 'Reducing Poverty by Tackling Social Exclusion: A DFID Policy Paper', p. 3.

DFID, 2008. 'Gender and Social Exclusion Analysis, How to Note', A Practice Paper, UK.

Dunne, M. Akyeampong, A., and Humphreys, S. 2007. School processes, local governance and community participation: Understanding access. (CREATE Pathways to Access Research Monograph No. 6.). Falmer, UK: Centre for International Education, University of Sussex. Retrieved December 20, 2007, from www.create-rpc.org/publications/pathwaystoaccesspapers.shtml.

Dunne, M., S. Humphreys and F. Leach. 2006. Gender Violence in Schools in 'Developing' Countries, *Gender and Education*, Vol. 18, No. 1, pp. 75-98.

Giddens, A. 1991. Modernity and Self-Identity, Self and Society in the Late Modern Age. Cambrige: Polity Press/Blackwell.

Hall, S. 1996. Introduction: Who needs 'identity'? In S. Hall and P. du Gay. (eds.) Questions of Cultural Identity. London: Sage.

Hobsson, Barbara, Jane Levis Birte Siim. 2002. Contested Concepts in Gender and Social Politics, US/UK: Edward Elgar Publishing.

Ilaiah, Kancha. 2005. Why I Am Not A Hindu: A Shudra Critique of Hindutva Philosophy, Culture and Political Economy, Kolkata: Samya. (Second edition).

Ilaiah, Kancha 2007. Buffalo Nationalism: A Critique of Spiritual Fascism, (second rpt), Kolkata: Samya.

J. Beall and L.H. Piron. 2005. 'DFID Social Exclusion Review' (Department for International Development (DFID), May 2005.

J. Estivill. 2003. "Concepts and strategies for combating social exclusion: An overview" International Labour Office.

Jackson, C. 1999. 'Social Exclusion and Gender: Does One Size Fit All?' in *The European Journal of Development Research 11(1),* pp. 125-146.

Kabeer, N. 2000. Social Exclusion, Poverty and Discrimination: Towards An Analytical Framework *IDS Bulletin* 31(4): pp. 83-97.

Kabeer, N. ed. 2005. Inclusive Citizenship: Meanings and Expressions. New Delhi: Zuban.

Kapur, R. 2002. The Tragedy of Victimisation Rhetoric: Resurrecting the 'native' subject in international/post-colonial feminist legal politics. *Harvard Human Rights Journal,* 15(2), pp. 1-38. Retrieved March 1, 2004 from www.law.harvard.edu/students/org/hrj/iss15 /index.html.

Karin Kapadia. 1996. Siva and Her Sisters, New Delhi: Oxford University Press.

Lal Deepak.1988. "Hindu Equilibrium", Cultural Stability and Economic Stagnation, Vol. I. Oxford: Carendor Press.

Lazreg, M. 2005. Decolonising feminism. In O. Oyewumi (ed.) African gender studies: A reader. New York: Palgrave McMillan.

Leach, F. and S. Humphreys. 2007. Gender violence in schools, Taking the 'girls-as-victims' Discourse forward. *Gender and Development,* 15, 1, pp. 51-64.

Levitas, R. 1998. The Inclusive Society: Social Exclusion and New Labour, Basingstoke: Macmillan. d.ca/event/inclusion/papers/ index &http://www.radstats.org.uk/no071/article2.htm).

Mohanty, C.T. 1991. Introduction: Cartographies of struggle: Third World women and the politics of feminism. In C.T. Mohanty, A. Russo, and L. Torres (eds.) Third World women and the politics of feminism. Indiana: Indiana University Press.

Mohanty, C.T. 1991. Under Western eyes: Feminist scholarship and colonial discourses. In C.T. Mohanty, A. Russo, and L. Torres (eds.) Third World women and the politics of feminism. Indiana: Indiana University Press.

Molyneux, M. and S. Razavi. 2002 'Introduction' in M. Molyneux and S. Razavi, ed. *Gender Justice, Development, and Rights,* London, Oxford: University Press.

Mukhopadhyay, M. 1998. Legally Dispossessed: Gender, Identity and the Process of Law, Calcutta: Stree.

Mukhopadhyay, M. and S. Meer 2004. Creating Voice and Carving Space: Redefining Governance from a Gender Perspective: Amsterdam: KIT Publishers.

Peace Robin 2001. Social Exclusion: A Concept in Need of Definition? Social Policy, *Journal of New Zealand,* 16, July: pp. 78-90.

Saunders, K. 2002. Introduction: Towards a deconstructive post-development criticism. In K. Saunders (Ed.) Feminist post-development thought: Rethinking modernity, postcolonialism and representation. London: Zed Books.

Selvy Thiruchandran. 1997. Ideology, Caste, Class and Gender, New Delhi: Vikas Publishing House Pvt. Ltd.

Sen, A. 2000. 'Social Exclusion: Concept, Application and Scrutiny' in Social *Development Paper No. 1,* Asian Development Bank.

Silver, H. 1994. 'Social Exclusion and Social Solidarity: Three Paradigms' in *International Labour Review,133 (5-6)* pp. 531-578.

Spicker, Paul, 2007. The Idea of Poverty New Delhi: Rawat Publications.

Smith Peter J., 2008. From Beijing 1995 to the Hague 2006—The Transnational Activism of the Dalit Women's Movement, Canadian Political Science Association, British Columbia, June 2008.

Thiruchandran, Selvy, 1997. Ideology, Caste, Class and Gender, New Delhi: Vikas Publishing House Pvt. Ltd.

Thorat Sukhdeo and Narender Kumar. 2008 B.R. Ambedkar: Perspectives on Social Exclusion and Inclusive Policies, New Delhi: Oxford University Press.

Townsend Peter, 1979. Poverty in the United Kingdom: A Survey of Household Resources and Standards of Living, Harmondsworth: Penguin Books.

Ziyauddin K.M. and Eswarappa Kasi. 2009. Dimensions of Social Exclusion: Ethnographic Explorations, UK: Cambridge Scholars Publishing.

1 Situating Social Exclusion within Phule, Periyar and Ambedkar Discourse

In India as discussed earlier social exclusion in the form of caste-based iniquitous social order has been a constant source of discrimination, deprivation and exclusion. Certain groups like ex-untouchables, tribals, women, etc., are excluded historically for generations. These groups socially and economically positioned in such a way that they lack access to land, capital, gainful employment, adequate access to social needs like civic amenities, education, health and housing and as a result, many of their economic, civil, and cultural rights remain notional in character. The deprivation and discrimination thus get institutionalised through caste, class, gender, religious and ethnic status.

The struggle against such unjust social order goes back to the period of Buddha, who tried to reform the Indian society on the principles of liberty equality fraternity and compassion. It was followed by several social and religious reform movements, particularly the Bhakti movement, covering from the 8th century to the 11th to 16th century in north and south of India. More recently in the 19th and 20th centuries, several attempts were made to address the oppression of untouchables, women and others.

It can be said that afew individuals who ignite the intellectual ferment in a particular era are the products of situation and provide intellectual stimulation by redefining and revitalising social relations through their articulate acumen and sagacity. Thus, in order to know how change or transformation occurred in the Indian society we must understand their role (intellectuals) the ideas and philosophy in effecting such a change in the society.

It is essential to inquire why one or two persons emerged as the crusaders of the caste evil in India, and why not others. The reality is that, everybody in the society experience the ill-treatment, the discrimination mooted against them, through their conscience. This consciousness in experiencing wrong is found in everybody's mind. But all do not possess courage/ qualities to make this phenomena shared by each human being with communities at a large to make a meaningful change in the living. In this context, Gramscian idea can be best remembered. He wrote that all men are intellectuals but not all men have in society the function of intellectuals. What he meant by this was that, every one has an intellect and uses it but not all are intellectuals by social functions.

To speak in common parlance, it happens that objectively the masses need a certain change, but subjectively they are not yet conscious of the need, not yet willing or determined to make the change. In such situation, intellectuals help to analyse the events, rationalise their arguments who have the clarity of thought and vision. Among those who devoted their intellectual and socio-political efforts and were instrumental in fighting caste-based exclusion and effecting social change in India Phule, Periyar and Ambedkar occupies an important place.

As we all aware that history has been witness to the fate of Phule, Periyar and Ambedkar. Phule in spite of being a great social reformer was kept under the carpet of history for several decades. Ambedkar in spite of having the best mind and the best possible training to write English was certainly not discovered by the brahmanical forces of India. The marginalisation of the non-brahmanical perspectives and experiences in the institutional scholarship based on caste has blurred our understanding of the complete picture of the subaltern or marginal voice.

Writings on by Phule, Ambedkar, Periyar were not on the list of readings and most of us remained largely ignorant of the *abrahmani*[1] perspectives on caste. The *Satya Shodhak* and Ambedkar movements did not have a place in courses on social movements and the post-independence, dalit, tribals and women's movements, were cluttered into one module. The challenges posed in the last decade and more to the scholarship on caste, further underlined the now apparent disjuncture between academic knowledge systems and social practice of caste.

The ideology of the dalits for a just society has mainly been developed by these eminent personalities like Mahatma Jotirao Phule (1826-1890), E.V. Ramaswamy Periyar (1879-1973) and Babasaheb Bhimrao Ambedkar (1891-1956), with many others throughout India: Narayan Guru in Kerala, Achhutanand in Uttar Pradesh and Mangoo Ram in Punjab (Omvedt, 1995) they attacked the system of exploitation at all levels—cultural, economic, and political. They developed their vision of Indian society as an alternative to upper caste understanding of India. Thus, it is important to pay some attention to the historical context in which the egalitarian ideology to deal with society developed.

Mahatma Phule and Periyar Ramaswamy and Ambedkar, had a deep understanding of the cultural contradictions in our society and all three had tremendously contributed to the progress and development of SCs and other backward sections of our people. Here an attempt has been made to examine and contextualise the ideas and ideologies of these intellectuals one by one and situate them within social exclusion and inclusion discourse or *vice versa*.

The ideology (vision) of the dalits for a just society has mainly been developed by eminent personalities like Mahatma Jotirao Phule, E.V. Ramaswamy Periyar and Babasaheb Bhimrao Ambedkar, with many (others) (during the Indian freedom struggle phase) throughout India.

Social Exclusion within Phule's Discourse

Phule was the first Indian to launch a movement for the liberation of caste-oppressed, the common man, the downtrodden, men and women. It is believed that what Raja Ram Mohan Roy, Dayanand Saraswati and Vivekanand were to the elitist cultural nationalism. Phule was to the freedom struggle of India's long suppressed humanity. Based on this pionerring historical-materialist critique of caste and Brahminism, he spearheaded a multi-pronged struggle to reconstruct the society on the matrix of social equality, justice and reason. He found brahminism as the ideological and institutional mechanism of monopolising knowledge and power by a particular class which uses these to exclude, divide and dominate other groups in society. He argued that 'even before trying to overturn the material power of the upper castes over the lower castes, and over their own women, it was necessary to step out of the ideologies of Brahminism for which acess to knowledge was an essential prerequisite, to some extent similar to what Ambedkar addressed as education, that is one had to understand a system before one could dismantle it. (Chakravarty, 2002) He termed this understanding of knowledge as *tritiya ratna,* the 'third eye' which was the means to end brahminic hegemony and towards this end education, 'not mere alphabetical competence, but the power to see through hegemonic ideology', was to play a crucial role (*Ibid*).

First Theorist to Explain "Caste" (as a Process of Social Exclusion)

Phule was the first major theorist of caste and Brahmanism, who saw caste as the lynchpin of the most vicious slavery, more sinister than the worst colonialism. He argued in his 1873 revolutionary book Gulamgiri (Slavery) that the relationship between the so-called high castes and the low has essentially been the relationship of one between the colonisers and colonised. Caste system, Phule stressed, divides and degrades the productive majority into hundreds of mutually antagonistic castes in a hierarchical order that allows the upper castes to live off the labour of the lower. Caste, in Phule's analysis, was also responsible for the all-pervasive patriarchy and gender inequalities in Indian society. On this understanding, he wanted to smash the whole ideological and material matrix of caste for liberation of the lowered castes, women and all other oppressed people. This transformation, he insisted, would not come about without a struggle. But the struggle, he was emphatic, has to be based on unifying lower castes with a universal liberation ideology.

Phule is emerging as a prophetic figure among India's lower castes. The power and truth of Phule's fundamental points about power, culture, knowledge and exclusion remain highly relevant in today's India. Caste still remains the linchpin of India's political, social, and spiritual dynamics. The significance of Phule's social and spiritual war against caste cannot be overemphasised. He has authored a few significant books and one of the most outstanding contributions is **Gulamgiri** which remains Phule's most influential publication till date. The title itself suggests Phule's approach to the subject of caste. Phule considered caste and caste laws as form of slavery. Interestingly the sub-title of the book is "In the civilised British Government under the Cloak of Brahmanism". Further the page of dedication in the original book reads:

Dedicated to the good people of the United States as token of admiration for their sublime disinterested and self-sacrificing devotion in the cause of Negro slavery and with an earnest desire, that my countrymen may take their noble example as their guide in the emancipation of their Sudra Brethren from the trammels of Brahmin thralldom.

Now, if we analyse the sub-title and the dedication (**of Phule Work "Gulamgiri"**) two very important points are reflected:

(a) Phule considered caste as a form of slavery perpetuated by the Brahmins and that it flourished even under the British Government despite its claim to a civilised government.

(b) The emancipation of the Shudra's and Ati Shudra can only come about by a social movement and by the people themselves. Consequently, there was a need to awaken the people against the social domination of the Brahmins. Phule compares the caste system to slavery. Slavery, as we all know is an extremely inhuman system. A slave is stripped off all dignity and humanity.

By equating slavery with the suffering of the Shudras, Phule tried to give a very powerful social message. At the same time, Phule was aware that it was much more difficult to free people of mental slavery than physical slavery. The Shudra's were kept ignorant by denying education. And the Brahmins, predictably told them of a divine system which had ordained that the Brahmins were God's favourites and that the Shudra's duty was to serve the Brahmins.

Such a system of beliefs could only be countered by providing an alternate picture of the past. Thus, Phule's writing provided an alternate account of the past and tries to overturn the *Daivya/Daitya* hierarchy. He tries to show that neither the Brahmins were Devas nor the Sudras were Daityas.

He tries to prove that these Brahmin stories are not only far-fetched but also a proof of them being cunning. The Brahmin managed to convince the Shudra that he was inferior because the Shudra was uneducated. Hence, it is only through education that the Shudra can see through the cunning of the Brahmins. But the Shudra must not be educated by the Brahmins because the Brahmins have not been inclined to discard the notions of their own superiority. The Sudra's must be taught by the Shudra's so that he is able to recognise himself as an equal of the Brahmin. However, this is only possible if the government changed its attitude towards the education of the masses. Instead of spending time and resources on higher education which benefits the Brahmins, the Government must spend time and resources on the education of the masses. If the masses are educated then the society will be free of the repugnant caste laws and there will be more harmony and peace in society. It is only then that the country can hope to progress and prosper. Phule simply reversed this notion, arguing that low castes, whom he sometimes called 'Shudras and Ati-shudras' were the original inhabitants of the country, enslaved and exploited by conquering Aryans who had formulated a caste-based Hinduism as a means of deceiving the teeming masses and legitimised their own power.

Phule's attack on Brahminism was uncompromising. He realised that the seeds of Brahmin' power supremacy and privileges lay in their scriptures and puranas; and these works and the caste system were created to exploit the lower classes (O' Hanlon, 1985). Phule also reinterpreted sacred religious literature. He attacked the brahmanical scriptures and Puranas, revolted against priesthood and also against the caste system to set a stage for initiating a social movement for the liberation of the Shudras and women.

Explaining His Vision of Society by Using Symbolism from History

Phule realised that the strongest hold of religious tradition on the people derived from the extensive integration of Hindu religious literature into the popular culture and oral traditions. Phule's answer to this was to provide alternative accounts of the texts, myths and stories most common in popular Hinduism. He linked these with important symbols and structures from contemporary Maharashtrian society in order to convey the real community of culture and interest that united all lower castes against their historical and cultural adversaries, the Brahmins. (Michael, 2007)

He realised that the seeds of the Brahmin's power, supremacy and privileges lay in their scriptures and Puranas and these works and the caste system were created to exploit the lower classes (O' Hanlon, 1985). Phule reinterpreted sacred religious literature. To give an example, Phule did so by reading the nine *avatars* of Vishnu as stages of Aryan conquest and used king Bali as a counter symbol to the elite's use of Ram, Ganpati and Kali (Keer, 1964; O' Hanlon, 1985). Thus, Phule attacked the Brahmanical scriptures and Puranas, revolted against priest craft and the caste system and set on foot a social movement for the liberation of the Shudras, Ati-shudras (untouchables) and women.

Phule understanding of the sub-continent's history, and his struggle for a just, casteless and inclusive society was centered on the symbol of Bali Raj. In Phule's reconfiguration of the myth, Bali Raja was the original king of Maharashtra, reigning over an ideal state of beneficence, castelessness and prosperity, with the popular gods of the regions, (Khandoba, Jotiba, Naikba, etc.) depicted as officials.[2] (Omvedt, 2006) Phule retrieved the real meaning of this ancient fable and infused it with vision for a new society. In the brahmanical lores, Bali was a *rakshas*, a demon king, whom the Brahman-Vaman hoodwinked into a false position and crushed him to death. King Bali, however, in popular legend, was the noble indigenous king, an embodiment of a just and kind ruler, who bravely warded off the attack of Aryan invaders.

Phule took the story of Bali and made it into a sub-versive symbol, giving it a historical interpretation in terms of conflicts between the Aryan-brahman and indigenous people. He re-narrated the story to underline how the Aryan-brahman established caste and a pseudo-religion based on caste and enslaved the native peoples of the land.

Weber (1958) has rightly said, all human history takes its meaning from the struggle. And we find this concern in intellectual and reformer like Phule, who strove hard to locate the struggle of the lower castes within history, to transform myth into history and establish a diachronic relation between present and past oppression. His use of symbols like king Bali is reflective of how Phule's perception of human history strengthened his scheme more generally on the mass level history become purposive (O' Hanlon, 1985).

Advocated the Relationship between Knowledge/Power

Phule was also the pioneer who pointed to the close relationship between knowledge and power. He stressed the need for education of the oppressed, which alone would enable them to see through the socio-cultural machinery of domination, ultimately leading them to launch their freedom struggle. A cultural revolution-based on mass education was at the heart of Phule's freedom struggle.

According to G.P. Despande, Phule was the first Indian System builder... (the) first to attempt at transforming plural categories of history into singular or universal... (he) talked about knowledge and power much before Foucault did. In Foucault's post-modernist analysis came at a time when European has literally seen an end to history, where as Phule's efforts were to change the world/society with the weapon of knowledge.

His Idea of Inclusion through Equality and Education

Phule for instance was a great thinker and philosopher, who identified the sociological origins of exclusion in India and strived to establish an 'Inclusive society'. He was a firm believer in enlightenment and he chose 'education' as the right tool to empower the excluded lot. He made education the focal point of his movement, with the belief that knowledge would generate forces that would sound the death knell of the old order and emancipate the subjugated. Phule's anti-caste movement developed an image of womanhood-based on the identities and symbols of low caste dalits and peasants. To fulfill his life's ambition to establish a casteless society. Phule formed Satya Shodhak Samaj (Society of Seekers of Truth) in 1873, a group whose main aim was to liberate women, shudra and untouchable castes from exploitation and oppression. The Samaj actively encouraged marriages without Brahmin priests, negated the very principle upon which he hoped a community of the lower castes would be based. It was this faith that the Samaj under him and his wife Savitri Phule started the first schools for girls in India in 1848. Between 1848 and 1852, Phule set up 18 schools. The 1860's saw Phule actively campaigning for widow remarriage and banning the practice of child marriage. In 1863, he set up a home for widows, who were often forced to abort or kill their children because they lacked social legitimacy[3]. Phule's decision to establish an orphanage to save the widows and prevent infanticide picked on 'one of the most vulnerable spots in Brahminism, the linchpin of upper caste gender codes, enforced widowhood and its consequences' (Chakravarty, 1998). Phule and Savitribai gave protection to frightened widows and assured them that the orphanage would take care of their children. In fact, Phule himself adopted the son of a Brahmin widow as his own in this orphanage.

He believed that revolutionary thought has to be backed by revolutionary praxis. And he tried to eliminate the stigma of social untouchability surrounding the lower castes by opening his house and the use of his well to the members of the lower castes. He further played an active role in the remarriage of a Saraswat Brahman widow in 1864. The brahmanical practice then was that widows were made to shave off their heads. Phule organised a barber's strike against inhuman custom.

Thus, Phule was the first social scientist to theorise social exclusion-based on the caste, gender, community and commensality. In other words, Phule evolved a path to proclaim the rights of those men and women, who were condemned to live in subjugation simply because the Hindu scriptures ordained it that way.

In Gramscian sense Phule and Ambedkar both were original thinkers and organic intellectuals but their theories and practices were neither noticed nor discussed in the mainstream discourses like other social reformers and intellectuals. There is a criticism that Phule and Ambedkar's contributions, in this sense had not been analysed as much as they deserve to have been. A section of serious minded scholars consider that Phule was the first systematic theorist of caste and the most radical opponent of the caste system; he desired nothing less than a complete smashing up of its oppressive structure. Phule's Bali Raj an ideal of caste-free society—was to be built through struggle, education, and rational thinking. Importantly, he also employed the image of Bali by recalling the Christian vision of a coming Redeemer, and the Judeo-Christian paradigm of all human history as the working out of a battle between good and evil. Phule also identified Jesus as the coming King Bali in many of his writings—sometimes directly, sometimes indirectly, seeing caste and Brahmanism as an embodiment of evil and the biggest stumbling block in the establishment of the Kingdom of God in the subcontinent.

In many ways, *dharma* and caste are at the centre of Phule's thought. His opposition to Brahmanism did not relate only to the *Varna* system. It also related to almost everything within the Hindu system. Phule rarely uses the term Hindu or Hinduism. (Deshpande, 2002)

Jyotiba Phule is taken to be the founding father of not only dalit and anti-caste movement in India but as also the founder of the women's movement in Maharashtra. He looked his goal as the liberation of the 'shudras' (peasant castes) and 'ati-shudras' (untouchables or dalits) from the slavery of Brahminism. To him the Indian National Congress was only a propaganda organ of the Brahmins. He asked the question: How could India, so divided by caste and language, with its people so enthralled in superstition, be considered as a nation? (Omvedt, 1993). His writings were focussed on the liberation of the Dalits, the peasantry and women. Phule's liberation theory reversed the Aryan theory and gave a version of history in which aggression, violence and conquest played a major role. His works drew on non-Aryan identity and based on regional, adivasi and peasant heroes as opposed to the nationalist narrative which fed on the Aryan identity (Omvedt, 1993).

Phule and Women Liberation: An Inclusionary Mission

Phule's movement along with the caste hierarchy challenged women's enslavement, since women were considered as ati-shudras (at par with dalits), within the caste hierarchy and denied any rights. The Brahminical system he argued, treats all women-irrespective of caste as inferior creatures; the Dharmashastras like Manusmriti invariably club them together with shudras or dasas. Therefore, he included women, all women, in his notion of the oppressed, or shudra ati-shudra, and contended that the subordination of women and toiling castes and denying them right to education were the main causes of the unspeakable backwardness of Indian society.

Like the elitist reformers, Phule was also a forerunner of female education and women's rights but he was unique in asserting equality between the sexes. As he saw subjugation of women as a part of the larger hegemonic design inherent in the ideology of caste, his critique necessarily implied the view that the end of the brahmanical system would ensure the end of patriarchy as well. According to Uma Chakravarty, while interpreting the past and exploring caste as a cultural hegemonic system, Phule emerges as a sharp critic of brahmanical patriarchy.

He alone, among nineteenth century social reformers, was able to stand outside Brahminical patriarchy and although gender was not a central factor in his analysis of caste and the reproduction of inequality, his rejection of the caste system and of brahminic Hinduism enabled him to adopt a more radical approach to gender inequality than any of his contemporaries.

Believing in gender equality Phule did not think of women's problem in terms of Brahman or shudra ati-shudra. Going deeper into his philosophy and ideology over gender issues we find that in the context of widowhood and *sati,* he says that when a husband dies, it is the woman who leads a life of suffering, if not burnt on the funeral pyer with husband,[4] and become sati. But ' has anyone ever heard of a man burning himself alive if his wife dies, and become *sata*?' (2002). *Sata* was of course an ironical coinage by Phule to suggest a male *sati.* He wanted that the traditional family and marriage system be analysed on the grounds of reason and gender justice.

In his *Sarvajanik Satya Dharma Pustak*, he talks of '*sarva ekandar stree-purush*', by which he meant dealing the problem together with a difference. Within this alternative framework women resisted their oppression and developed a new self-identity. His writings assimilated women into his general theory of conquest and violence. Scholars like Gail Omvedt has pointed out that Phule does not use the common word *'manus'* (human being), but insists on using *'stree purush',* thus emphasising gender differentiation, while pleading for equal and common human rights for women and men. He was the first to do so in India.

He took a stronger position describing male patriarchal power as a specific form of exploitation. The "double standard" which oppressed women was prevalent he argued, not only as seen in the pitiable conditions of Brahmin widows, but also in the patriarchy of Shudra households in which the woman was expected to remain a loyal *pativrata* while the man was free to have as many women as he wanted. While Phule was sensitive to gender problems faced by all women, he was also conscious of crucial differences among women-based on caste and their place in the system of production. In Shetkaryacha Asud (The Cultivator's Whipcord), Phule has shown how the women of toiling castes had to labour at home and in the fields, where as the Brahmin women work only at home and lead a relatively comfortable life. Thus, 'the brahman women are subject only to the power of the brahmin men, while the labouring women are doubly exploited as they are dominated by both the upper caste men and the men of their own families'.

Later, however, Phule's understanding of women's oppression changed somewhat as he tried to relate subordination of women with a structure of relations that might be recognised as akin to patriarchy. (Chakravarty, 1998) Phule perceived an interface of caste and gender hierarchies, the highly restricted movements of women or even though female seclusion. This understanding got reflected in his defence of feminist radical pioneers like Pandita Ramabai and Tarabai Shinde, against attacks from male orthodoxies of all streaks.

Phule was the only person, who came forward to support Pandita Ramabai's[5] struggle against Hinduism. He applauded her efforts for education among high caste women. In his booklet, Satsar (The Essence of Truth) Phule argued that Ramabai, as a truly educated woman, had seen herself the discriminatory orientation of *shastras* against lowered caste masses and women and therefore rightly decided to break away from the 'tyrannical' religion. He was the only one who raised his voice against the near-hysterical reaction to Tarabai Shinde, who had published in 1882 *Stree Purush Tulana*[6] (A Comparison Between Women and Men) a feminist treatise of its kind, talked against the patriarchal order. This book was a scathing criticism of the way that men depicted women and excluded them from power which met criticisms from many radical satya-sodhak activists, who were calmed by Phule's rational intervention.

It would be no exaggeration to say Phule rejected this pseudo-religion along with the texts that upheld it. And this rejection was very clearly reflected in his writings Phule was not interested in manipulating with this or that aspect of the brahmanical structure to make it a little more humane. He argued for its complete rejection and destruction.

For Phule, Brahmanism was historical, constructed over time, and since it was the ideology of oppression and dominance, it had to be opposed and ultimately smashed. The bulk of Phule's writings on religion therefore consist of a fierce polemic against Brahminism.

However, Phule did not look upon Brahman orthodoxy or brahminical religion as 'the ultimate cause of the deprivations of lower castes'. This remained 'a matter of private disagreement between himself and his colleague'. This point is made by Rosalind O' Hanlon, who analyses Phule's play *Tritiya Ratna* (The Third Eye) to conclude that 'he rejected decisively the view that the sufferings of lower castes were the product of a social system supported by all except untouchable castes. (O'Hanlon, 1985)

Emphasising the bipolarity of the *Varna* system had two other implications. One, it meant that Phule was not looking at it as a system of endlessly regressing hierarchy, where there is always someone, somewhere, who is lower than the lowest. In other words, his main emphasis is to demonstrate the basis on which the oppressed can come together and unite rather than on the divisions and schisms amongst them. Two, he rejects the centrality of the pollution principle. This does not of course mean that Phule was blind or indifferent to the pollution principle. His attack on brahminical *dharma* necessarily involved rejection of the notions of *pavitra* and *apavitra* (pure and polluted respectively), *sprishya* and *aprishya* (touchable and untouchable respectively), and so on. On these scores his attack on Brahmin hypocrisy is unforgiving. But the main thrust of his attack is on the exploitative and oppressive nature of Brahminism. Here he was very much close to Marx, who in his analysis of capitalism, emphasise the bipolarity of modern society between proletariat and bourgeoisie.

Recognised as a First Shudra Thinker [Explained Social-Exclusion]

Phule is the first shudra thinker as he would have liked to be described to have thought about gender exclusion, no doubt a great feminist thinker of his time. The reformers of the so-called Indian Renaissance were content to take basically humanist view of the problem. Their approach was liberal, progressive, and historically necessary. But their upper-caste biases were apparent in much of what they did or advocated. In this respect, again Phule is more radical than his contemporaries.

Phule's reconstruction of the past and linking it to the oppressive present was one aspect of the attempt to fight the inegalitarian system and brahmanical ideology. A more essential and enduring way to change the existing power structure was through education. A staunch rationalist, he wanted to use knowledge as a weapon to bring about an attitudinal change leading to 'a kind of cultural revolution as well as a technological one'. For him, the acquisition of knowledge by the oppressed was emancipator and his pedagogy was informed by a clear understanding of knowledge and power. Above all, his emphasis on the oppressed to come together and unite rather than being on the divisions and schisms was the way toward inclusion as one can perceive.

E.V. Ramaswamy Periyar

E.V. Ramaswamy Naicker, better known for his Periyar's movement was against exclusion based on racialism. He considered that casteism and Hinduism were one and the same. Similar to Phule, Periyar also denounced the Aryan view of race, which according to him was the creation of elits as a mechanism to understand caste. As it was believed that the Brahmins, Kshatriyas and Vaishyas were to be descendents of the invading Aryans, while shudras and untouchables were believed to be the descendents of the native conquered inhabitants. Turning towards this racial consciousness, he sought to defend the rights of Dravidians against Aryan domination, considering Brahmins as agents of social Injustice (Devanand, 1960).

Periyar's View on Social Exclusion

If we situate Periyar within the framework of social exclusion discourse we find him vehemently opposing caste, race and religion for hierarchical oppressive social structure.

To Periyar, caste was simultaneously, (both) a system and an ideology, it comprised a complex set of social relations, as well as those principles which informed, sustained and justified these relations. As a system, caste served the interests of brahminisms, who were its favoured agents and existed chiefly to gratify and perpetrate their sense of their own superiority. As an ideology caste referred by Periyar as Brahminism, *Varna-dharma* and Hinduism worked to ensure that notions of 'high' and 'low' birth.

Writing in September 1971, two years before his death, Periyar observed:

> Though I have endeavoured all along to abolish caste, as far as this country is concerned this has meant I carry out propaganda for the abolition of god, Religion, the *Shastras*

> and Brahmins. For caste will disappear only when these four disappear. Even one of these were to remain, caste will not be abolished in its entirety... because caste has been constructed out of these four... Only after man had been made a slave and a fool would, caste has thus been imposed on society. One cannot abolish caste without instilling a taste for freedom and knowledge (in the people). God, religion, the *shastras* and brahmins make for the growth and spread of slavery and folly and strengthen the existence of caste (Anaimuthu, 1974).

The movement's central agenda was to restore self-worth, pride and dignity to the long-humiliated men and women similar.

Periyar aimed at bringing about a cultural revolution on the basis of casteless egalitarianism and rationalism. Stressing egalitarian social relations across caste, community and gender lines, Periyar advocated the overthrow of caste and instituted non-brahmanic forms of marriage celebrating the equality of woman and her right to choose life partner and other such practices designed to give a death blow to the brahmanical order. Presenting a radical critique of the religious beliefs and practices in a variety of ways, Periyar wanted to demolish the whole brahminic structure of society which he saw as the root cause of the degradation and subordination of women and non-brahman populace.

Periyar's Idea of Women Exclusion

Periyar's idea of women exclusion was very much similar to feminist perspective. He compared the depressed status of women and outcastes and said '...at about the same time when a community of depressed classes was created and denied access to the means of knowledge, women were also prevented from acquiring, learning and thereby oppressed and consigned to servitude.'

He refuted the notion that men and women were innately different and remarked, though women get pregnant and carry children in their wombs for ten months this does not make them different from men. With respect to qualities such as courage, anger, the prowess to command and the will to violence women are like men (that is they too possess these qualities/ attributes)... on the other hand, just because men do not bear children it cannot be said they differ from women in respect of love, peace and the ability to nurture.

He argues that masculinity is merely an expression of brute male power and which poses a greatest obstacle to female freedom. Periyar is particularly critical of sexual standards which excuse, legitimise and even celebrate male promiscuity, while condemning women to either a life of limited monogamy or wretched widowhood. He undertakes an exhaustive critique of chastity and its converse, female promiscuity. Arguing that the chaste wife and the prostitute mirror each other, he suggests that one connotes life-long sexual slavery to one man, while the other sells herself to several men. In either case, femininity is condemned to servitude. (Geetha, 2001)

Periyar warned, unless masculinity and its obverse feminity (which always implied subservience) were destroyed there could be no genuine freedom for women. For this women must consent to rethink their roles, must give up thinking that they could not even live without men.

He insisted that men too deserved to be judged in their conduct by standards of chastity. He encouraged women to prove that they were as capable of earning money and taking on familial responsibility.

Theorising Brahminical Patriarchy

Periyar's ideas on brahminical patriarchy drew sustenance from his original and robust rejection of the conventional feminine ideal of chastity. Linking up the pressure on women to remain chaste with social imperative which held she must prove fertile and reproductive. Periyar enunciated a theory of motherhood in caste society. He then went on to describe and interrogate those values and ideologies which valorised motherhood and those material processes which ensured the reproduction of motherhood and mothering.

Periyar did not confuse biological difference with gender roles. He did not imagine that because men's bodies were different from women's bodies, men and women were different in their attributes and temperament.

To make strength, anger and ruling ability solely male attributes calm, patience and ability to nurture life, female ones is to say that bravery, strength and ruling prowess are characteristic of the tiger while the ability to care characterises the lamb. (Anaimuthu, 1974)

Such worth pieces of fiction, reasoned Periyar not only misplaced in their intent but arbitrary in their choice of attributes for masculine and feminine qualities were in realities produced by acts of history and practices of culture. Therefore, male and female roles were in changeable: we maintain that while it is the case women possess the attributes of bearing a child in their womb for ten months and eventually giving birth to it, this in itself does not make them different from men with respect to (qualities such as) anger, ruling prowess and strength. Likewise, we think that though men do not possess the (biological) means to get pregnant, it cannot be said that they possess qualities different from women in respect of love, calm and the power of nurture. If we are to value true equality—if there exists true love between man and woman, it is certain that all responsibilities except that of bearing a child should be considered common to both (*Ibid*).

By making parenthood rather than motherhood the decisive factor in the nurture and care of human life, Periyar liberated the female body from the oppressive and suffocating realm of eternal fertility and thus granted the female person a will and subjecthood.

Periyar's narrative of the history of women's subordination possessed a further dimension in that he placed the logic of reproduction in the context on Hindu caste society, presided over by Brahmin priesthood. He noted that desire to have children for inheritance one's name and wealth would not have assumed such immense significance in Hindu society, if it had not been for the religious and cultural reasons that were advanced in justification of this desire.

After, it had become the norm for people to want children to safeguard property, Brahmins who had invented fictions of heaven and hell to keep the poor from stealing from the wealthy and to secure some of that wealth for themselves now sought to argue that... man must have a (male) child who would keep alive his name after death and perform his last obsequies. (Anaimuthu, 1974)

Thus, even as the real reason for wanting children faded into the recesses of community memory, the fictitious reasons invented by Brahmin came to take hold of the Hindu male imagination. Women were now to bear children not only to produce heirs but also to facilitate the passage of the mortal soul from this world to the next. Motherhood came under increasing pressure for now it was significant for the reproduction of the patriarchal caste order in this world and also for its existence in the next as well.

Periyar thus demonstrated how private property, sexuality and caste were invariably inter-linked so as to form a structure of which they were the constituents. To him not one of these constituents could be detached from the structure and considered the basis of an oppressive system for it was in and through their interaction so manifest in the realm of conjugality that the social and sexual order reproduced itself.

The year 1928-29, seems to have marked a new beginning, for through out this time, we find Periyar and others writing, remonstrating, arguing, persuading and compelling their readers to heed gender concerns.

Periyar observed, if women had written the *dharmashastras,* they would, perhaps, have not defined chastity in those terms, that were common place in the present world. However, this may be given the unequal world of the sexes that we inhabit today concluded Periyar. Women had been coerced and persuaded, in turn, to accept their bondage, consent to an idea that stifled their desire and distorted their very being. Periyar also pointed out that women had come to assent to this state of affairs convinced that they were chattels of men and wary of provoking their husband's anger. This was not to be wondered at, considering that in Hindu society for centuries now a set of communities had come to view themselves as low and outcaste, had in fact accepted their own subordination. Women too had come to consent to their oppression in a like manner and to practice as mortification of their slaves all on account of false ideal (Anaimuthu, 1974).

His Idea of Inclusion

Periyar organised 'Self Respect Movement' for Dravidian people which represented not only the radical phase of the non-brahman movement but also a response to the 'politics of piety' as espoused by Gandhi (Geetha and Rajadurai, 1998).

The Self Respect League that he formed in 1926 bore a striking similarity in its objectives—so that of Phule's Satyasodhak Samaj, calling for annihilation of caste, opposing brahminical hegemony and championing the liberation of subjugated class and women. A trenchant critic of caste hierarchy, ritualism and idolatry. Periyar-like Phule and Ambedkar-conflated Hinduism and casteism and Brahmanism and condemned Hindu Laws and institutions as inhuman instruments of 'brahminic', 'male' and Aryan exploitation.

The 'Self Respect Movement' of Periyar was 'fundamentally opposed to the holy alliance of religion, caste and nationalism, an alliance which it understood as embodying a social and political order that was inherently inegalitarian. (*ibid*) His 'Self Respect Movement', was designed as a way to uplift Dravidians, seeking to expose Brahmin tyranny and the deceptive methods by which they controlled all spheres of Hindu life. He publicly ridiculed the *Puranas* as fairy tales, not only imaginary and irrational but grossly immoral as well. He attacked the Hindu religion as the tool of Brahmin domination.

His movement took a turn toward racial consciousness and became a "Dravidian" movement, seeking to defend the rights of Dravidian against Aryan domination. It blamed the Aryans for introducing an unjust and oppressive system in the country (Hardgrave, 1965). Periyar realised that the important feature of all new ideologies of the elite was the 'Aryan view of race". The Aryan view was adopted enthusiastically by the Indian elite as a new model for understanding caste. That is , Brahmins, Kshatriys and Vaishyas were held almost as a matter of definition to be the descendents of invading Aryans, where as Shudras and Untouchables were those of the native conquered inhabitants. Periyars' movement sought to defend the rights of the Dravidians against Aryan domination. He saw in the Brahmins the representatives of Hindu arrogance and the stronghold of social injustice.

The Self Respect came to question and challenge the gendered nature of caste and the Brahminical basis of patriarchy in Hindu caste society.

Periyar saw motherhood as a carefully and ingeniously designed idea that had historically been used to secure women's bodies with their reproductive capabilities as the natural property of men. Periyar traced the valourisation of motherhood to those early historical times when private property first came into existence… First women was brought into the male household as a protector of property and soon enough she, herself came to be viewed as a Man's property.

Periyar rejected brahminical rituals such as *kanyadan*—the giving away of the bride as gift, because it reduced women as mere objects and denied their autonomy and subjectivity. Besides, he said that the *purohits* Sanskrit *mantras* were degrading. Periyar wondered how a woman sense of herself could be enhanced, if her sexuality was thus refined and displaced from her being on to rites of which she understood nothing.

Implicit in Periyar's rejection of marriage was his rejection of what he perceived as a brahminical system of values which negated female self-hood on the one hand, even as they obfuscated and confused non-brahmins on the other. As he remarked 'just as how Brahminism condemns a large portion of the working population to shudrahood, so it has condemned women to the servitude of marriage… To the extent that women live up to the norms of a chaste and ideal wife to that extent she accepts and revels in her slavery' (Anaimuthu, 1974).

How was woman to be liberated from brahminical patriarchy? Periyar saw his self-respect marriage as part of the solution and in his several speeches at such marriages outlined its theories of conjugality, love, marriage and divorce.

Apart from his strong views against Brahminism, Periyar's writing on women are not only fascinating but revealing. In fact, as a feminist would call him far ahead of his time and a human right defender of women. He said that, we need to create a social and cultural movement of revolt—against, caste, Brahminism, religion and rule of men over women. He talked of female self-hood or female as an identity and not as object. He believed that valourisation of motherhood has enslaved women's body and mind. Women needs to be freed from Braminical colonisation to be treated as human being.

Thus, Periyar was not just a political ideologue, his forte was his linkages with masses. He not only blamed Brahminical system for all the evils related to caste in our society but also provided alternatives. His self-respect marriages was one such progressive idea that helped change the marriage system a lot in Tamil Nadu.

Periyar was a revolutionary, who felt that social empowerment and cultural changes should precede any political process.

Babasaheb Bhimrao Ambedkar[7]

Similarly, Dr. Ambedkar was also 'excluded' from the mainstream discourse for several years. Although Ambedkar proved himself to be a genius and was known as a great thinker, philosopher, revolutionary, jurist par excellence, prolific writer, social activist and critic and stood like colossus in the Indian socio-political scene unto his death, his thought never received adequate attention in the generality of Indian society just because he was born as an untouchable. It is indeed impossible to understand the caste-based social exclusion in India without understanding the ideas of Ambedkar. Ambedkar interpreted Phule's theory of Hinduism, untouchability and caste-based exclusion and extended the debate to logical end.

Ambedkar attacked two central features of the Indian order: culturally enforced inequality and economic inequality. Ambedkar's attempts all the way in his life can be considered as the attempts for the establishment of an inclusive society. Ambedkar's ideas on freedom to the oppressed, rights for Hindu women in the form of Hindu Code Bill, affirmative action and positive discrimination are the most important steps towards the liberation of the oppressed.

Ambedkar and the Social Exclusion Discourse

For Ambedkar understanding the nature of the institutions of caste and untouchability were essential for recognising the consequences for the excluded groups. It is therefore necessary to discuss Ambedkar's interpretation of caste system and untouchability which served as basis for his inclusionary ideas and approach.

Ambedkar on Caste System and Inequalities

Ambedkar went on to prove through a series of writings that the degrading and dehumanising caste system has been the chief factor responsible for horrifying forms of bondage, deprivation, ignorance, and ultimate enslavement of millions of people relegated as 'low' caste.

To begin with, Ambedkar said that caste system is based on the division of people into social groups or castes in which the civil, cultural, religious and economic rights of each individual caste are pre-determined or ascribed by birth and made hereditary. The caste system's fundamental characteristic of fixed civil, cultural and economic rights for each caste, with restriction for change implies 'forced exclusion' of one caste from the rights of the other castes. In his work *Castes in India: Their Mechanism, Genesis and Development*, he observed, endogamy is the only characteristic that is peculiar to caste. The super imposition of endogamy on exogamy means the creation of caste, and castes are enclosed class. (Ambedkar, 1979)

He further said that the system also provides for regulatory mechanism of social ostracism and reinforces it further with justification from the philosophical elements in the Hindu religion to maintain its social order. (Ambedkar, 1916 and 1987) Ambedkar's view the doctrine of inequality is the core of the Hindu social order.

Isolation and exclusion (social and physical) of the Untouchables is also a unique feature of the Hindu social order. Ambedkar observed:

Classes or social groups are common to all societies, but as long as the classes or social groups do not practice isolation or exclusiveness, they are only non-social in their relations towards one another. Isolation and exclusiveness makes them anti-social and inimical to one another. (Ambedkar, 1987)

Being a severe critic of brahminical social ideology and religion, he referred the 'sacred law books' as 'lawless books (Mani, 2005) and tried to summarise them as follows:

- Graded inequality between different classes,
- Complete disarmament of the shudras and the untouchables,
- Complete prohibition of the education of the shudras and the untouchables,
- Ban on the shudras and the untouchables occupying places of power and authority,
- Ban on the shudras and the untouchables acquiring property,
- Complete subjugation and suppression of women (BAWS,1945).

The caste system also governed by the principle of rank and gradation, in so far as the rights increase in ascending order from the Untouchable to the Brahmin, which he termed as *graded inequality.* In the case of untouchables exclusion leads to deprivation and poverty in so far as they are denied of all sources of livelihood, except manual labour which consists of assigned occupations considered to be polluting and inferior and service to the caste above them. Therefore, their exclusion has multiple dimensions and is simultaneously comprehenshive and results in severe deprivation as a social group. Besides, the untouchables also suffer from social and residential separation, isolation due to the practice of untouchability. The concept of purity/pollution brings in an additional dimension to their discrimination and exlusion and, in more respects than one, further segregates them from the human capability and capacity building processes. (Thorat and Kumar, 2008)

The practice of caste-based exclusion and discrimination thus necessarily involves a failure of entitlement, not only to economic rights, but also to civil, cultural and political rights. It involves what has been described as living mode exclusion, exclusion from political participation and exclusion and disadvantage in social and economic opportunities. (United Nations, 2004)

Ambedkar spoke up not against mainstream nationalism but also against upper caste programme for lower caste progress. In 1926, he mobilised his supporters to struggle to break the ban on 'untouchables' from drinking water from the town tank in Mahad in the Konkan.

In his historic Mahad speech on December 25th, 1927, Ambedkar declared that the issue at stake was not merely to enable the untouchables to drink water from the prohibited lake (that water was not nector that would make us immortal, he jibed but to 'assert that we too are human beings like others'. The real reason why the upper castes, was not because they would pollute it, but to show that castes declared inferior by the sacred tradition of *shastras* were not their equals. The struggle, therefore, was to set up the norm of equality. This could not be accomplished unless the edifice that supported the whole hierarchical and ascriptive structure was brought down (Dangle, 1992). Ambedkar emphasised that the issue was not merely to remove untouchability but to radically reorganise

Indian society on the principles of equality, fraternity and liberty. We need to pull away the nails which hold the framework of caste-bound Hindu society together, such as those of the prohibition of intermarriage down to the prohibition of social intercourse, so that Hindu society becomes all of one caste. Otherwise untouchability cannot be removed nor can equality be established (Dangle, 1992).

As Gore has observed, in Ambedkar's ideology, identity was subordinate to human dignity. Advocating a way out to resistance to upper caste high handedness and assertion of one's human rights, he said, "We do not value Hinduism, we value human dignity" (Gore, 1993). Elsewhere, he reiterated the same point, "We want equal rights in society. We will achieve them as far as possible while remaining within the Hindu fold, or if necessary, by kickng away this worthless Hindu identity" (*Ibid*).

The Mahad Satyagraha, often called the 'first untouchable liberation struggle' did not succeed in getting water for the untouchables, but did conclude with the public burning of the Manusmriti, the most die-hard text among the *dharmashastras*. It was this juncture that the dalit movement found itself at a crossroad, turn between contending accommodationist, 'upper caste' approach on the one hand and Ambedkar's antagonistic 'lower caste' approach towards the problem of how to deal with Hindu caste society, on the other. What the dalits needed, they feel, was primarily a strategy of their own. By the year 1929, Ambedkar had emerged as most articulate dalit leader not only of Maharashtra but of India as a whole with small resistance effort taking off in different parts of the country on the lines of *Mahad satyagrahas*, an all India dalit movement seemed finally to be in the making. It was natural that Ambedkar, the inspirational figure behind this development should be called to represent the 'Depressed classes of India 'at the Round Table Congress with India leaders, invited by the British government between 1930 and 1933. The purpose of all such Congress was to work out the modalities closed with Gandhi and the representatives of the Indian National Congress over the issue of an Indian award of separate electorate to 'untouchable'. In 1932, Gandhi went on fast against the award ending his fast only when the award of separate electorates to "untouchable" was annulled, and combined electorates with some electoral constituents received only for "untouchable" candidates was proposed. Ambedkar was to oversee the compromise and interrogated Gandhi's sincerity on safeguarding interests of the dalits. However, under pressure from the nationalists and from his own followers, he later relented and went along with the common consensus on this issue, but though, Ambedkar agreed to this proposal in the so-called Poona Pact between different functions of Indian leadership, he felt disillusioned with the reformist tendencies of the mainstream Indian movements on social concepts.

His sense of disappointment inaugurated his revolutionary phase which leads to an announcement in 1935, that he was unborn a Hindu but would not die a Hindu and in 1936, he founded an Independent Labour Party (ILP), by amalgating proletarian peasant party with a red flag (as a symbol) along with the radical economic agenda of the ILP. A, purely Marxist agenda. In fact, Ambedkar undoubtedly hoped to compensate for the 1930's tactical retreat by radically modernising character of the Constitution that he was drafting. On November 4, 1948, in his capacity as the president of the 'Drafting Committee', he set out the constitutional project much of which he had written. If none of its articles abolished caste, they did outlaw discrimination, based on religion, race, caste, sex, and place of birth given the paramount importance of the right to equality, which was to become Article 15 of the 1950 Constitution.

Ambedkar advanced a cultural programme of demystification of the 'superior achievements of Hinduism' culturally as much as economically, he felt the Hindus had always subjugated the dalits. In the 1950s, he led a mass exodus of 500,000 of his followers from the fold of Hinduism to the fold of Buddhism in a final repudiation of caste society.

Ambedkar on Exclusion and Women

On the issues of exclusion and women, Ambedkar had the belief that women were the victims of the oppressive, caste-based and rigid hierarchical social system. He believed that socio-cultural forces artificially construct gender relations, especially by Manusmriti and Hindu religion. As Simone De Beauvoir observed, "Women are made, they are not born", so Ambedkar also critically commented that Manusmriti had made women subservient.

He raised questions as to why Manu degraded her (woman)? In his works, *The Riddle of the Woman, The Women and the*

Counter Revolution, The Rise and Fall of Hindu Women, Castes in India: Their Mechanism, Genesis and Development and through the issue of his journals, *Mook Nayak (1920) and Bahishkruit Bharat (1927),* he tries to show how gender relations and differences are constructed by Hindu Brahminical order which conditions women to conform a stereotype feminine behaviour requiring them to be passive and submissive. Indian patriarchy is based on caste and endogamy, and *shastras* resulting into the institutional colonisation of Hindu women. Why killing of women is treated as drinking of liquor and equated with killing of Shudras. Manu suggests that a man can not sit in a lonely place with his own sister, daughter or even mother. A woman is dependent all throughout her life on a man at different stages of life.

Ambedkar in his volumes such as *The Revolution and Counter Revolution, The Buddha and his Dhamma, Annihilation of Caste* exposed how *varna* system prioritised 'birth' instead of 'worth'.

He also made it very clear in his article titled *The Rise and Fall of Hindu Woman* that the root cause of suffering for women in India are the '*religious scriptures*'. It not only justifies the treatment of dalit women as a 'sex object' and promotes child marriage, but also justifies a number of violent atrocities on women as can be seen in the following verses: A man, aged thirty years, shall marry a maiden of twelve who pleases him. Or a man of twenty-four a girl of eight years of age. If (the performance of) his duties would otherwise be impeded, he must marry sooner. (*Manusmitri* IX. 94)

By a girl, by a young woman, or even by an aged one, nothing must be done independently, even in her own house." (*Manusmriti* V. 147) Her father protects (her) in childhood, her husband protects (her) in youth, and her sons protect (her) in old age; a woman is never fit for independence (*Manusmriti* IX. 3). Women have no right to study the Vedas. That is why their Sanskaras are performed without Veda *mantras*. Women have no knowledge of religion because they have no right to know the Vedas. The uttering of the Vedas *mantras* is useful for removing sin. As women cannot utter the Veda Mantras, they are as unclean as the untruth (*Manusmriti* IX. 18). A Brahman, Kshatriya, or Vaishya Man can sexually exploit any Shudra woman (*Manusmitri* IX. 25). Even the killing of a dalit woman is explicitly justified as a minor offence for the Brahmins: Equal to the killing of an animal (*Manusmitri*). If the killing of an untouchable was justified as a minor offence, you can imagine the treatment women received throughout their lives.

Regarding inheriting property a wife was degraded by Manu just as a slave. Manu instructs women, "Though destitute or virtuous are seeking pleasure elsewhere, or devoid of good qualities, yet a husband must be constantly worshipped as a god by a faithful wife... She must always be cheerful, clever in management of her household affairs, careful in cleaning her utensils, and economic in expenditure". Ambedkar cites evidences of higher status of women in the pre-Manu days. She was free and equal partner of man and had the right to education, divorce, remarriage and economic freedom. The story of public debate between *Janaka* and *Sulabha*, *Yajnavalkya* and *Maitrei*, *Yajnavalkya* and *Gargi*, and *Sankaracharya* and *Vidyadhari* show that Indian women in the pre-Manu period could rise to the highest pinnacle of learning and education. Ambedkar pointed out at the way Manu treated women. He referred to the laws of Manu governing the status of women are very significant in shaping and influencing the Hindu attitude and perspective towards women perpetuated and maintained through Hindu personal laws based on *Shastras*, caste system and endogamy, (i.e., the core of features of Indian *patriarchy*). He attacked Manusmriti, which legitimises the denial of freedom, self-respect, right to education, property, divorce etc. He observed that Manu equals women with Shudra.

Since Ambedkar himself was the victim of oppression and discrimination in all its severity, his views about women's oppression and equal rights are most significant than anybody else's theory-based on mere observation for the feminist movement to strengthen its strategy for approaching the systemic challenges and contradictions in a more pragmatic way to bring women to the mainstream.

Apart from his academic writings when Dr Ambedkar headed in public life, women were the major force in all his struggles. In historic Mahad Satyagraha there were about 500 women took active part in this procession. On July 18, 1927, Dr Ambedkar addressed a meeting of about three thousand women of the depressed classes, where he said that 'I measure the progress of community by the degree of progress which women had achieved' and said to the women. 'Never regard yourself as untouchables, live a clean life. Dress yourselves as touchable ladies. Never mind, if your dress is full of patches, but see that it is clean. None can restrict your freedom in the choice of your garments. Attend more to the cultivation of the mind and spirit of self-help.' Then with a little fall in voice he said, "But do not feed in any case your spouse and sons if they are drunkards. Send your children to schools. Education is as necessary for females as it is for males. If you know how to read and write, there would be much progress. As you are, so your children will be." Dalit women too responded very positively to Dr Ambedkar's advice and to the surprise of all the women left early in the morning with wonderful change in the fashion of their *sarees* as ordained by Babasaheb.

Further, Ambedkar said to women 'Learn to be clean. Keep away from vices. Give education to your children. Instill ambition into them. Inculcate in their minds that they are destined to be great. Remove from them all inferiority complexes.' On marriage he remarked, 'Do not be in a hurry to marry. Marriage is liability. You should not impose it upon your children unless they are financially able to meet the liabilities arising from marriage. Those who will marry will have to keep in mind that to have too many children is a crime. The paternal duty lies in giving each child a better start than its parents had. Above all, let every girl who marries stand by her husband, claim to be her husband's friend and equal, and refuse to his slave. I am sure if you follow this advice, you will bring honour and glory to yourselves.'

His main observations include,'endogamy is the only characteristic that is peculiar to caste', ...the superposition of endogamy on exogamy means the creation of caste; a caste is an enclosed class'. (Ambedkar, 1987). Ambedkar saw binaries through the prism of caste in Indian history as Karl Marx saw the binaries in the West through the prism of class.

The numerical sexual disparity in marriage, he observes as 'the problem of caste, then, ultimately resolves itself into one of repairing the disparity between the marriageable units of the two sexes within it'. When women and man become a surplus, woman (widow) and a surplus man (widower) due to spouse's death their existence was seen as a menace. To regulate them the methods practiced in the mechanism of caste presents three singular uxorial customs, namely: (i) *Sati* or the burning of the widow on the funeral pyre of her deceased husband; (ii) Enforced widowhood by which a widow is not allowed to remarry; (iii) Girl marriage (Ambedkar 1987). Since man has traditional domination over woman his wishes have always been his privileges. On the contrary, woman has been an easy prey to all kinds of iniquitous injunctions, religious, social or economic that is man made. According to Ambedkar, society must be based on reason and not an atrocious tradition of caste system. Therefore, in *Annihilation of Caste,* he suggests annihilation of caste as a means, which is reinforced through *Shastra.* Like every man and woman, free from the thralldom of the *Shastra* cleanse their minds of the pernicious notions founded on the Shastra and he or she will inter dine and inter marry. He found education, inter caste marriage and inter dine as methods, to eliminate castes and patriarchy, which is maintained through endogamy.

Ambedkar also subscribed to JS Mill's ideas on women and liberty, who expressed in the subjection of women, the legal subordination of one sex to the other is wrong in itself and one of the chief hindrances to human development, and ought to be replaced by a principle of perfect equality, admitting no privilege or power on the one side, nor disability on the other. He was firmly committed to the ideas of equality, liberty and fraternity.

Ambedkar pointed out the direct relationship between caste and gender and observed that gender could not be seen in isolation from caste. Thus, much before the Indian feminist school, Dr Ambedkar had expressed and accepted this fact.

Dalit Emanicipation (His Inclusive Policy)

It can be rightly observed that Ambedkar gradually emerged not merely as a champion of the dalits or Scheduled Castes-which he definitely was—but 'a national leader of all marginalised classes with an alternative vision of society, nation, culture and politics'. His commitment and struggle made him a hero in the eyes of the deprived and the voiceless, who expected him to lead them in their battle for a life of dignity under the emerging civil society. As such, Ambedkar's alternative ideology of Indian culture and nationalism was not only his own but reflected the viewpoints of the entire spectrum of disadvantaged and marginalised classes (Aloysius, 1997). Ambedkar thought deeply about the problems of casteism, untouchability, inequality and deprived. He showed how they were inter-linked, and in turn responsible for social strife, which hindered emotional integration and economic development.

Ambedkar's crusade for the greatest happiness of the greatest number-*bahujan hitaya bahujan sukhaya* (the famous spiritual precepts of Buddha which he tried to practice)—as the foundation of all morals and legislations set him apart as a radical action philosopher (Mani, 2005). And this was his philosophical discourse for the marginalised and the socially excluded people. For Ambedkar social and cultural emancipation of men and women was as important as political and economic empowerment. It is unfortunate that in the abashed pursuit of political power today the politic vision of Ambedkar is completely forgotten and the pernicious strength of caste and patriarchal mentalities in our society is not seriously combated (Jaiswal, 2007).

He categorically wrote, 'abolition of sub-caste only help to strengthen the caste and make them more powerful and therefore mischievous. (Ambedkar, 1990) He argued for the annihilation of caste for which he thought the real remedy lies in inter-caste marriages. The fact that he thought the dalit communities self-respect would be recognised only when they organised them (selves) for collective political action. This does not mean that he wanted to nurture caste identities.

If we position Ambedkar within the discourse of social exclusion of women from a feminist lens we find that the interface of caste class and gender in feminist political discourses makes Ambedkar's views on women's oppression, social democracy, caste and Hindu social order and philosophy significant to modern Indian feminist thinking.

Ambedkar and His Vision for Inclusion (Social Democracy) of Dalit

He used term like social democracy. In his speech delivered in the Constituent Assembly on November, 25 1949, he said 'Political democracy cannot last unless there lies at the base of its social democracy'. By social democracy he means a way of life which recognises liberty equality and fraternity as principles of life.

Ambedkar's defence for women as the Law Minister of free India, appeared in the form of the Hindu Code Bill in Parliament on April 11, 1947 which invited strong opposition from the Hindu orthodoxy in post-independent India. The Bill provided for several basic rights to women.

Ambedkar said in his speech delivered in the Constituent Assembly on November 25, 1949, 'Political democracy cannot last unless there lies at the base of it social democracy.' By social democracy he means a way of life, which recognises liberty, equality and fraternity as principles of life. He further said: "On 26th January 1950, 'We are going to enter into a life of contradictions. In politics we will have equality and in social and economic life we will have inequality. In politics, we will be recognising the principle of one man one vote and one vote one value. In our social and economic life, we shall, by reason of our social and economic structure, continue to deny the principle of one man one value. How long shall we continue this life of contradictions? How long shall we continue to deny equality in our social and economic life? If we continue to deny it for long, we will do so only by putting our political democracy in peril. We must remove this contradiction at the earliest possible moment or else those who suffer from inequality will blow up the structure of political democracy which this Assembly has so laboriously built up.' The new social movements emerged especially from dalits, women and peasants, to assert democratic rights and urged for a new path of development which legitimises this warning of the Father of the Indian Constitution, when he submitted it to the nation.

Ambedkar has given equal status to women at par with men by providing many provisions in the Constitution. "The Constitution quickened by social conscience has added invincible legal missiles for women's liberation' (Iyer, 1996). Our Constitution forbids sexual discrimination and guarantees social and economic justice for women.

Inclusion through Constitutional Ways

In the early years during the pre-independence days Ambedkar once again raised the women's issue as Member of Legislative Council during his debate in Bombay Legislative Assembly on 10th November 1938. He strongly advocated family planning measures and said that besides many other problems giving birth to many children negatively affects mother's health. Later in the year 1942, Ambedkar also introduced Maternity Benefit Bill during his tenure as Labour Minister in Governor General's Executive Council.

Since Ambedkar was well-convinced about the status of women, as the Chairman of the Drafting Committee he tried an adequate inclusion of women's rights within political vocabulary and Constitution of India. Therefore, considering women equality both informal and substantial senses, he included special provisions for women while in all other general provisions are applicable to them, as to men. Hence, there are Articles like 15(3), 51(A) and so on. His key work in the preparation of Indian Constitution made it to be known as New Charter of Human Rights. He looked upon law as an instrument of creating a same social order in which the development of individual should be in harmony with the growth of society. He incorporated the values of liberty, equality and fraternity in the Indian Constitution.

Ambedkar Effort for Inclusion of Women (Legal Measures)

Besides, providing Constitutional guarantee, Ambedkar introduced and got passed four Acts which strengthened the position of women in the society. These were incorporated in the Hindu Code Bill. They were:

- The Hindu Marriage Act, 1955;
- The Hindu Succession Act, 1956;
- The Hindu Minority and Guardianship Act, 1956 and
- The Adoption and Maintenance Act, 1956.

One of the main considerations which led to the codification of Hindu laws pertaining to women is that some of them placed women at advantage as compared to men.

The Hindu Marriage Act, 1955, which was amended in 1976 made the following provisions for women:

- The legitimisation of illegitimate children (Section 16);
- Punishment-bigamy (Section 26);
- Custody of Children (Section 26);
- Marriageable Age of females raised to 18 years;
- Provision for alimony (Section 25). The Act abolishes the difference between a maiden and a widow.

Under the Hindu Succession Act, 1956:

- A widow has a right to adopt a son or a daughter which not there in the Hindu law.

- It also provided an opportunity to be independent and dispose of her property by will as she wishes and desires (Section 14).
- A uniform scheme of succession to the property of a Hindu female, who dies, intestate after commencement of the act, was made in Section 15. Previously, under the uncodified law the succession to *stridhan* varied according to the marital status of a woman.

Under the Hindu Minority and Guardianship Act, 1956:

- The mother is empowered to change the guardian, appointed by the father and may appoint a new guardian by will.
- The father's right to appoint a guardian for the minor by will during the life time of the minor's mother is prohibited under this Act.

The Adoption and Maintenance Act, 1956:

- This Act accepts adoption of a male and a female child without any difference, whereas under the uncodified law, a daughter could not be adopted.
- This Act permits a wife to adopt a child on her own right even during her husband's life time. She had no such right prior to this enactment.
- In the codified laws a spinster or a widow had no right to adopt whereas this Act grants them the right to adopt.
- Under the old Hindu law a wife need not be consulted while adopting a child or while giving a child for adoption, where as this Act made it essential to consult her in both the cases.
- Section 11 lays down that, a father should adopt a daughter at least 21 years younger to him.

But the Caste Hindus who considered this move as an attempt to attack the sanctity of Hinduism opposed this revolutionary Bill. It was opposed both inside as well outside the House, not only by leading members of Hindu Mahasabha but also by large number of caste-Hindu (upper caste) women protested against this. In his vigorous defence to this Bill, Dr Ambedkar alleged that the ideals enshrined in this Bill are derived from the Constitution of India, which is based on liberty, equality and fraternity. He observed that 'the sacramental marriage does not satisfy the ideal of liberty or equality'. And described 'sacramental marriages as polygamy for the men and perpetual slavery for the women because under no circumstances within that system woman got liberty from her husband however bad he may be, however undesirable he may be'. But unfortunately this revolutionary Bill couldn't see the light of the day as in face of growing opposition Pt Nehru, then Prime Minister decided to drop this Bill.

Ambedkar was so disgusted with this that he resigned from Nehru's cabinet. He said, "it (The Hindu Code Bill) was killed and buried, unwept and unsung". Thus, Ambedkar practiced what he preached. Ambedkar's influence on Women is still visible especially in the Maharashtrian Buddhist women, who are not only empowered but often criticise mainstream Feminist movement as the Brahmin Women Movement.

Ambedkar Philosophy and Feminist the Movement in Post-Independent India

Ambedkar's views on women's oppression, social democracy, caste and Hindu social order and philosophy, are significant to modern Indian feminist thinking. Ambedkar provides a powerful source of inspiration to formulate a feminist political agenda which simultaneously addresses the issues of class, caste and gender in the contemporary socio-political set up, which still keeps conservative and reactionary values in many respects, particularly on gender relations. The Writings and Speeches of Ambedkar show what values India should develop and how they would modernise its social and political institutions with changing time and space.

It was mainly the Hindu culture and social customs, which stood in the headway of women's empowerment. As a great fighter for dalit human rights, indeed for all human rights, Ambedkar began to seek answers in Buddhism. His conviction, born out by his own experience, the continuing atrocities on dalits, and his studies of Indian history, was that caste in Indian society was the major factor responsible for the denial of rights, and that it was indissolubly linked to Brahmanism. As he puts it, Brahmanism itself was nothing but the denial of human rights, the denial of liberty, equality and fraternity.

Regarding his policy of inclusion of the dalits and women he suggests Buddhism, which can provide emancipation from oppression. He found the dalits and women emancipation in Buddhist values, which promotes equality, self-respect and education. Ambedkar believes that Buddha treated women with respect and love, and never tried to degrade them like Manu did. He taught women Buddha Dharma and religious philosophy. Ambedkar cites women like Visnakha, Amrapali of Vaisali, Gautami, Rani Mallika, queen of Prasenajith who approached Buddha, as evidences of Buddha's treatment of women as equals. (Paul, 1993)

Adhering to Ambedkar's ideologies, The National Policy for the Empowerment of Women 2001, also admits, "The underlying causes of gender inequality are related to social and economic structure... and practices. Consequently, the access of women, particularly those belonging to weaker sections including Scheduled Castes/Tribes Other Backward Classes and Minorities... to education, health, and productive resources, among others is inadequate. Therefore, they remain largely marginalised, poor and socially excluded" (GoI, 2001).

Moreover, feminist scholars also realised the importance of caste in contemporary India. Many feminist scholars, especially after the Women Reservation Bill debate, agree that one cannot analyse Indian society without taking note of caste. Though patriarchy is pervasive in India, it varies in degree depending on the religion, region, caste, community and social group, maintained and perpetuated through endogamy. The contemporary situation cautions feminists to work for the emancipation of women-based on the ground realities as experienced by all sections of oppressed and discriminated women, within the framework of the Indian context. Since Ambedkar himself was a victim of oppression and discrimination in all its severity, his views about women's oppression and equal rights are more useful than anybody else's theory-based on mere observation for the feminist movement to strengthen its strategy for approaching the systemic challenges and contradictions in a more pragmatic way to bring women to the mainstream. To understand Ambedkar's arguments and the ideals for which he stood, it is necessary to know some of his bitter and better life experiences that he underwent at the outset of the socio-political awakening from the time of his birth.

Scholars have tried to analyse Ambedkar's perspective on gender indifferently. Nalini traces Ambedkar's presentation as an 'innovative argument' on the relationship between the rise of the caste system and the decline of the status of women. Here Ambedkar's argument is combined with that of Engles (Malini, 1993). Scholar like Dietrich arguing on Ambedkar's views on women say that Ambedkar, though aware of women's position in general, has not integrated his analysis of caste with an analysis of patriarchy. (Dietrich, 1992)

Overall, it can be said that the inclusive policy proposed by Ambedkar has four components which include creating an egalitarian economic structure, which will provide a base for equal economic and social opportunities for the poor, including discriminated groups; equal opportunity policy in terms of reservation for discriminated groups with adequate legal safeguards against discrimination; the participation of discriminated groups in governance through a fair share in Legislature, Executive and Administration involving decision-making and monitoring processes; and finally responsibility on the State to undertake such policies with a clear provision in the Constitution and in other statutory forms.

Thus, the pioneers like Phule, Periyar and Ambedkar, who worked for the liberation of the dalits and women, propagated the idea of the need for a cultural revolution or a total transformation of Indian society. They rejected the vision of the upper castes, which identified the Indian nation as basically Hindu, deriving from Vedic times, and fundamentally a creation of the Aryan people. While rejecting the ideals of the upper caste notion of Indian society-based on the ideas of values of Manu and *Varna vyavastha*, they propagated the Principles of equality, justice, liberty and rationality. This broad-based standpoint is widely accepted among the dalits.

To sum up, it can be said that the trio not only spent a considerable part of their intellectual energies on the task of recovering and developing the non-brahmanic tradition, but also strived to link it to their contemporary struggle for casteless, democratic society. The socio-cultural struggle that Phule Ambedkar and Periyar started remains a challenge to all, who are on the side of justice and equity, who are part of the ongoing struggle for the abolition of caste, for the equality of women and for the economic emancipation of the poor, under privileged and the excluded. Their vision of Indian past or Indian history and culture was thus, radically different. In a paradigm shift from the elitist approach, they tried to understand the past by the present and *vice-versa.* Their understanding of history, in other words, was animated by contemporary social and personal experiences. Thus, it would be no exaggeration to consider these scholars the crusaders of social exclusion and architects of inclusive policy in India.

References

1. Non-brahmanical perspectives
2. The puranic myth in which the Brahman boy Woman asks three boons of Bali and then steps on his chest to send him down to hell is taken by Phule as a story of deception and conquest by invading Aryans. This interpretation had a strong resonance with popular culture in Maharashra where Bali is seen as a popular and 'peasant' king and is remembered with the Marathi saying, *ida pida javo, Balica rajyo yevo* (*lets trouble and sorrows go and the kingdom of Bali come*').
3. As O' Hanlon (1985), and Chakravarty (1998) have shown, the material and sexual consequences of enforced widowhood were responsible for large number of young Brahmin women becoming pregnant. Faced with the fear of excommunication or even worse, many of them resorted to abortions or threw their illegitimate children to their cruel fate.
4. Earlier the women burnt themselves or were forced to be burnt alive with their husbands on the the same funeral pyers, by their family members and relatives and become *sati.*
5. Pandita Ramabai was the first Indian women to declare on the basis of her study of the *shastras,* that 'the Sanskritic core of Hinduism was irrevocably and essentially anti-women'.
6. A Comparison between Women and Men by Tarabai Shinde, translated and edited by Rosalind O'Hanlon, Oxford University Press, 1994.
7. The Hindus wanted the Vedas and they sent Vyas, who was not a caste Hindu. The Hindus wanted an Epic and they sent Valmiki who was an untouchable. The Hindus wanted a Constitution and they sent me.

Bibliography

Agarwal, S. 1999. Genocide of women in Hinduism, Jabalpur: Sudrashan Books. India.

Aloysius, G. 1997. Natonalism without a Nation in India, Delhi Oxford University Press.

Arya, Sudha. 2000. Women Gender Equality and the State, New Delhi: Deep and Deep Publications. Available online: http://www.dalitstan.org/books/.

B.R. Ambedkar,1990. Annihilation of Caste: An Undelivered Speech, edited by Mulk Raj Anand, New Delhi: Arnold Publications.

Baxi, Upendra. 1994. Emancipation as Justice: Babasaheb Ambedkar's Legacy and Vision in Ambedkar and Social Justice, Vol. I, edited and Published by Ministry of Information and Broadcasting, Government of India, Delhi.

Dangle, Arjun ed., 1992. Poisoned Bread: Modern Marathi Dalit Literature, Bombay: Orient Longman.

Gabriele, Dietrich. 1992. Dalit Movements and Women's Movements, in Reflection on the Women's Movement in India, New Delhi: Horizon India Books.

Geetha, V . 2009. Gender, Stree: Kolkata.

Geetha, V. and S.V. Rajadurai. 1998 Towards a Non-brahmin Millennium: From Iyothee Thass to Periyar, Calcutta: Samya.

Gopal Guru, 1995. 'Dalit Women Task Differently' *Economic and Political Weekly,* 14-21 October, 1995, pp. 2548-50.

Government of India, 2001. The National Policy for the Empowerment Of Women, 2001, New Delhi, Department of Women and Child Development, Ministry of Human Resource Development.

Heywood, Andrew, 1998. Political Ideologies: An Introduction, London Macmillan: Press.

Keer Dhananjay, 1964. Mahatma Jotirao Phooley, Father of Indian Social Revolution, Bombay: Popular Prakashan.

Limaye, Champa: 1999. Women: Power and Progress, New Delhi: B.R. Publishing Corporation.

Malini, M. 1993. Caste and Patriarchy: Ambedkar's Insight into the Status of Women, in K.S. Chalam. (ed) Relevance of Ambedkarism in India, Jaipur: Rawat Publications.

Mathew, Thomas, 1991. Ambedkar: Reform or Revolution, Segment Books: New Delhi.

Naicker Ramaswamy, E.V. 1959. The Ramayana: A True Reading, Madras: Rationalist Publications.

O' Hanlon, Rosalind. 1985. Caste, Conflict and Ideology: Mahatma Jotirao Phule and Low Caste Protest in Nineteenth century Western India, Cambridge: Cambridge University Press in association with Orient Longman Ltd.

Omvedt, Gail, 1976. Cultural Revolt in a Colonial Society: The Non-brahmin Movement in Western India, 1873 to 1930, Pune: Scientific Socialist Education Trust.

Phule, Jotirao, 2002. Selected Writings, ed., G.P. Deshpande, includes *Slavery* (*Gulamgiri* 1873), Cultivator's Whipcord (Shetkaryacha Asud 1883), Delhi: Left Word.

Phule, Jotirao, 1996, Mahatma Jotiba Phule Rachnawali, in Hindi, ed., L.G. Meshram Vimalkirti, includes Tritiya Ratna (1855), Sarvajanik Satya Dharma Pustak (1890), Delhi: Radha Krishnan Prakashan.

Thind, G.S. (n.d). Our Indian Sub-continent Heritage British Columbia, Canada: Crosstown Press.

V. Geetha, 1998. Periyar, Women and an Ethic of Citizenship, *Economic and Political Weekly* Vol. 33, Issue No.17, April 25, 1998.

Zelliot, Eleanor. 1992. From Untouchable to Dalit: Essays on the Ambedkar Movement, Delhi: Manohar.

years of age, (ii) universal participation till they complete the primary stage through formal or non-formal education programmes; and (iii) universal achievement at least of the minimum levels of learning.

Provision of continuing education and skill development programmes for youth.

Making suggestions for greater gender equality in education and female empowerment.

Making necessary interventions to provide equal educational opportunity to children belonging to the Scheduled Castes, Scheduled Tribes and the poorest sections of society.

Laying special emphasis on all educational activities on culture and communication; science and environment and inculcation of a sense of social justice.

The district primary education programme-II was started in 1997 in 22 districts of the state, which ended in 2003. Moreover, DPEP-III was started in 32 districts of the state in 2000, and has ended on 31 March, 2006.

Janshala project was implemented in district Lucknow during 2000-03.

Sarva Shiksha Abhiyan was started in the state in 16 districts in 2001-02 and now covers all 70 districts of the state.

Background

Prior to 1972, the primary and upper primary schools in Uttar Pradesh were run, maintained and controlled by District Boards and municipalities including municipal corporations, etc., constituted under various acts related to management of local bodies, i.e.,

UP Kshetra Samiti and Zila Parishad Adhiniyam, 1961
UP Municipalities Act, 1916
UP Nagar Mahapalika Adhiniyam, 1959

Considering urgent need to improve literacy in the state, it was felt that education needed planned interventions from the State government. In this background, the Government of Uttar Pradesh passed the Uttar Pradesh Basic Education Act, 1972 (UP Act No. 34 of 1972).

The main objective of this act is to organise, co-ordinate and control imparting of basic education in schools other than high schools or intermediate colleges. By this Act, an Autonomous Body named "Uttar Pradesh Board of Basic Education" was constituted under chairmanship of the Director, Basic Education. All schools which were managed and controlled by local bodies have since then been transferred to the Board. The Board of Basic Education controls

2 Dalit (Women's Question) Struggle from the Perspective of Movement: From Alienation to Assertion

History suggests that consolidated mobilisation and continued assertion efforts of deprived/excluded masses with increasing level of consciousness created by the intellectuals emerged as consequential force which took the form of movement and led to the development of the concept of egalitarian authority. In other words, 'a social movement is an organised attempt on the part of one section of society through collective mobilisation-based on an ideology' (Rao, 1978) for achieving a goal. The most essential pre-requisite for an organised attempt of a collectivity through its mobilisation is its multiple forms of deprivations—be these powers, wealth and privilege or all of them.

That is, movements are conscious efforts on the part of men to mitigate their deprivation and secure justice... Thus, movements emerge when men committed to a specified set of goals participate in protest-oriented, purposive collection actions'. (Oommen, 1990) And the excluded lot comprising women and the dalits have become more assertive both collectively as well as individually. All this has become possible due to the aforesaid assertion, which in the words of Bourdieu (1973) may be termed their 'cultural capital' or even 'social capital' (Ram 2008).

Here attempt has been made not merely to explain the narrative but analysing and situating dalit (women) movement's in history. There is a compelling necessity to discover and reclaim the hidden and buried history of dalit to get clue from the past to achieve (self-esteem by recognising) dalit solidarity by staging a successful movement.

Dalit Struggle: Glimpses from History

There has been a long tradition of intellectual reconstruction of the Dalit identity in India since earlier times which has not been properly documented as academic records. Dalit movement has a rich history of rationalism and humanism. In fact, the historical evolution took place with Buddha's revolt against *varnashram dharma*. Buddha not only rejected supremacy of Brahmins but also of the *Shastras*. After Buddha, Mahavir Swami rejected the notion of caste and violence in the brahmanical structure. Let us trace the movement in early historical period.

First Phase of Dalit Struggle: Bhakti Period and Struggle for Philosophical Base of Equality

The eminent activists who contributed to the process include, Phule Periyar and Ambedkar, among others. Before them, the *Bhakti* saints like Ramanand and Raidas in the North, Chaitnaya and Chandidasa in the East, Ekanath, Chokamela, Tukaram and Narsinh Mehta in the West and Ramanujan, Nimbarka and Basava in the South, who made remarkable contribution in the form of questioning the Brahmanical hegemony. Their contribution to the anti-brahmin thought lies in opposing caste distinctions and asserting equality before God. They questioned restrictions on worship during the 10th and 13th centuries, because of which the *Bhakti* movement became popular among the shudras and the ati-shudras. In fact, we find reactions and responses against untouchability and inequality which came in the form of the *Bhakti* cult. The *Bhakti* cult which originated in the 12th century was an antithesis of the vedantic philosophy propounded by Sankaracharya, who believed in *dhyan* and *karma* as the only two ways to achieve salvation. But despite the protest of saints, Chokamela and Kanaka (the untouchable saint) was not allowed to enter the temple of Vithal at Pandharpur and the temple of Krishna at Udupi respectively. In the 15th century Kabir talked of rejection of caste system and one God. He attacked rituals and *shastras* and talked of a society based on equality. Yet the brahmanical system continued. The brahmanical literature degraded dalits and talked about the pre-birth theory. It is a fact that *Bhakti* cult could create a philosophical base for social equality by launching a crusade against social inequality based on caste and gender. However, they could not bring about any substantial change in the existing social structure at that time as the rights of the untouchables to spiritual equality could not go beyond the singing of *Bhakti* songs. And we cannot negate the impact of the preachings of these saints of this period which had produced a considerable degree of social consciousness among the dalit masses which, in turn, led them to introspect/question their location in the societal arrangement and to find somewhat better position.

Second Phase of Dalit Struggle: Forming Organisation 1857-1920

Written accounts of Dalit movements organised before the era of social reform (later part of the nineteenth century up to the early decades of the Twentieth century) are not easily available. Yet, being inspired by social reform movements carried in different parts of the country, dalits had organised a number of movements against their religious discriminations and social degradation. In the pre-independence period, this anti-caste movement comprised strong non-brahmin movements in Maharashtra, Punjab, Western Uttar Pradesh , Bengal, Kerala Tamil Nadu coastal Andhra and Hyderabad. These region specific dalit movements were known as 'Adi-dharma', in Punjab, "Adi-Hindu' in UP and Hyderabad, "Adi-dravida, 'Adi-Andhra' and "Adi-Karnataka' in South India but having common claim of the dalits and the shudras being the original habitants of India. Gail Omvedt writes:

> It was in the 1920s, however, that dalits began to organise strongly and independently throughout many regions of India. The most important of the early Dalit movements were the Adi-Dharma movement in the Punjab in 1926; the movement under Ambedkar in Maharashtra, mainly based among Mahars which had its organisational beginnings in 1924, the Namashudra movement in Bengal, the Adi-Dravida movement in Tamil Nadu, the Adi-Karnataka movement, the Adi-Hindu movement mainly centered around Kanpur in UP and the organising of the Pulayas and Cherumans in Kerala (Patankar and Omvedt, 2007).
>
> So far Uttar Pradesh is concerned, the construction of dalit identity was initiated by Adi-Hindu Movement, under the leadership of Swami Acchutanand. Though Arya Samaj promised to facilitate the social uplift of lower castes, its intention of enslaving untouchables to Hinduism is criticised by ther Adi-Hindu leaders. Swami Acchutanand claimed in a speech, 'The Samaj aimed to make all Hindu slaves of the Vedas and the Brahmins'. (Goopt, 2016).

Acchutanand and Ram Charan constructed an identity which traces out the history of the original inhabitants of India. They outlined an idealised vision of social equality and of past power and glory of the untouchables. 'Self-assertion' was an important principle of Adi-Hindu movement. Exploring the identities of self-assertion and empowerment that Adi-movements espoused, Nandini Goopta states that the untouchables were the true masters of the land, the Adi-Hindu preachers cultivated a sense of entitlement to rights and power at the same time as they heightened an awareness of historical deprivation. The stress on *atmagyan* (self-knowledge) and introspection as the source of independent knowledge without higher caste impositions also enabled the exposition of a distinction, autonomous, proud and even defiant self-identity of the untouchables. (*Ibid*)

These movements, being aimed at the argument of the original inhabitants have a common tag 'Adi' which means original inhabitant and were significant in the formation of the Dalit identity. In addition there were non-Brahmin ideological trends elsewhere and weaker or unorganised dalit assertions in such areas as Mysore and Bihar. Preceded by the failures of movements for temple entry, these dalit movements were more clearly visible in the form of religious revivalism of *Bhakti* traditions of the medieval period, claiming their religion as *'adi'* (original) and distinct from the Hindu religion. The Adi-movement provided not only 'an ideology of radical equality' and 'a strategy for doing better in everyday life, but also 'a political culture for civil rights and organised protest' (Khare, 1984).

Dalit movements of this period also attacked the caste system and insisted on equality and dignity of human beings. These movements partially succeeded in sensitising and mobilising larger segments of dalits, but they could not transcend the rigid cementation of castes, and thus got culminated in sectional movements. Besides, they also got largely subjugated in the movements of dalits for sharing power and privileges, during the 1930s and 1940s in the later phase of the dalit movements. Needless to say that the challenges of dalit movements of this period were of diverse nature which were ably-handled under the leadership of Ambedkar.

While Mughal rule in India was a status quo one, the emergence of British power made a lot of difference upon the lives of downtrodden people. The first form of liberation for dalit started with Jyotiba Phule, who belonged to the Mali community of Maharashtra. It was Phule, who laid the foundation for the contemporary dalit movement, and who is also known as the father of the Indian social revolution (Keer, 1964). In Pune, Chitpawan Brahmin would not allow any dalit and backward to join schools. Women and particularly of dalit community could never dream of going to school. Phule realised that unless the community is educated, they would not be able to emancipate themselves. So, he started a massive work of education by starting various schools in and around Pune. The Brahmins opposed this education movement among dalits which they had denied for years. Phule appreciated Christian missionaries for their noble work in school education. It was such that some scholars consider Phule's era as the first phase of dalit struggle. Phule was the first low caste organiser, who founded Satyasodhok Ṣamaj in 1873, in order to strengthen the sentiments of low caste. He narrated the so-called pseudo-historical episodes bearing testimony of the traditional solidarity between the Mahars and Shudras and protested against the Brahmins stratagies for dividing the low caste. Gail Omvedt argues that 'The mobilisation of the oppressed and exploited sections of society, the peasants, dalit, women and low castes that Phule had spoken of as shudras and ati-shudras occurred on a large scale in the 1920's and 1930's, under varying leaderships and with varying ideologies' (Omvedt, 2006).

The second phase started during 1920s and 1930s and continued till 1950s. During the subsequent colonial period, the dalits witnessed mixed kind of treatment. As the alien rule proved to be instrumental in bringing the remaining autonomous native regimes not only in the federal structure of governance but also a nation in the political sense of the term, it even introduced the agenda of social change in Indian society.

The 1920's when the autonomous anti-caste tradition began to take shape, was a time of change. The Indian National Congress was on the rise across the country, not least because of Gandhi.

Following the mystics' and the social activists' attempts at crystallising the dalit identity, Ambedkar provided intellectual basis to the formation of the dalit identity. Following the early dalit movement, Ambedkar organised dalits socially, politically and intellectually through the process of which, the formation of the dalit identity assumed a definitive form.

Ambedkar launched many struggles during the 50 years of his social life. Ambedkar's Mahad Struggle for the untouchable's access to public water in 1927 was successful as a civil rights issue. Later on, he became the champion of human rights. Subsequently, Ambedkar fought for separate electorates. Ambedkar educated the dalits that their identity is different from that of the Hindus. In the late 1920s, Ambedkar for the first time raised the issue of equality, liberty and fraternity, and in a word, social justice to be accorded to the Untouchables or the then depressed classes. It was Ambedkar, who articulated their socio-political assertion, spear-headed their powerful movement for the purpose and took the same to the logical end by fighting on a number of occasions and with congress and demanded political and social space at par with other communities. The resultant impact was that the British government had to allow him to represent on behalf of the backward caste in the second round table conference to place his demand for the liberation of dalit. On the whole, the nature of colonial government's policy provided new opportunities to the lower strata or castes, including the Untouchables or the dalits to articulate afresh their social discrimination, oppression and subordination, and to make best use of a new site of avenues opened during this period.

Moreover, this social consciousness and assertion among dalits has also been aroused by a number of legislative measures enacted, after independence, for their welfare-now empowerment, protection and development. Although these measures as well as schemes have not produced the desired results in concrete terms, these have certainly increased their consciousness and the resultant agitations as well as their discontents and assertion, besides their agitational capacity and capability through several decades in the recent years.

Over the past few decades, social and political dalit movements, specifically the BSP-led dalit Bahujan Samaj movement, have placed the category of 'dalit' on the national and international agenda. Literally meaning 'poor and oppressed' in several Indian languages, the category of 'dalit' has been imbued with different meanings by dalit and non-dalit scholars and activists (Guru, 2001). Eleanor Zelliot defines the category as representing 'those who have been broken, ground down by social groups above them in a deliberate manner' (Zelliot, 2001). Ghanshyam Shah, write that dalit movements have been mainly confined to ex-untouchables, those, who are called Scheduled Castes (SCs) (Shah, 2001).

Development of dalit consciousness and the resulting movement during the early phase was the phase of Sanskritisation, when the depressed castes adopted Sanskritisation and emulated upper castes in order to rise in caste hierarchy/upward mobility. But in the 1940s, it got replaced by the renouncement of Sanskritisation—and entered the political arena in order to improve their socio-economic situation and obtain a share in power in the new independent order that was emerging.

From 1935 onwards, instead of the term *'Harijan'* the dalit leaders adopted the nomenclature of Scheduled Caste and in some places used *'Achhut'* which signified their pride in low caste identity. Realising that upward mobility through sanskritisation as a route (channel) was closed to castes below the ritual barrier of pollution, and that it led to a positional change and not a structural one, led the *'Achhuts'* to use political means to bring about change in the conditions of their community. The years between 1930 and 1936 were a 'turning point' in the history of dalit movement in India as it was a widespread social movement aiming at fundamental change of a system seen as exploitative and oppressive, part of a broader anti-caste movement, with growing ideologies and organisation of its own.

In the 1940s, there came a significant break when many educated dalit leaders in North India turned their attention to the National Movement and became interested in the activities of Ambedkar and his disagreements with Gandhi. Jurgensmeyer described this process of change as the Ambedkar Alternative (Jurgensmeyer, 1988), while Lynch called it a 'turning point' (Lynch, 1969).

Third Phase of Dalit Struggle: Protest and Political Agitation (1920's onwards)

The third phase of dalit movements roughly starts after political independence of the country to the present times. Dalit movements in the post-independence period have continued in one way or the other, their attack on the caste system and have resisted socio-religious discriminations practiced against the dalits. Besides their stress on sharing power and privileges, many dalit movements have been organised against the socio-economic exploitation of dalits in different parts of the country. Quite a few of these movements have also protested against physical and social violence or atrocities inflicted on dalit in villages. In a nutshell, it can be said that these movements have varied issues which are contextual and they manifest differently with their varying stress on one issue or the other. However, being inspired by Ambedkar's ideology, their latent objective is to achieve equality, freedom and justice for the dalit community as a whole.

Independent India saw two decades of quiescence for anti-caste struggles, then a renewed upsurge from the early 1970s, marked by the founding of dalit Panthers in 1972. The term 'dalit' as discussed earlier has its roots in Sanskrit means the 'oppressed' and 'exploited'. While the word has been used in Maharashtra for a long time particularly in the 1960's due to dalit Panthers in Uttar Pradesh and in many other parts of the country, it became current only in the 1980s. Ambedkar in his journal *Bahishkrut Bharat* defined 'dalithood' as 'a kind of life condition which characterises the exploitation, suppression and marginalisation of dalits by the social, economic, cultural and political domination of the upper caste Brahminical order. However, he did not use this category often in the colonial period, preferring different terms such as 'depressed classes' and 'Scheduled Castes' depending upon the changing political context, consciousness and movements was a significant feature of colonial India. The pace of change was, however, different in different regions of India leading to uneven development of the Dalit movement across the sub-continent in the post-independence period. While parts of southern and western India experienced strong movements demanding reservations and improved social status under important leaders such as B.R. Ambedkar and M.C. Rajah, these were conspicuous by their absence in larger parts of northern India.

Now, let us begin with the earlier trend, i.e., organised solidarity of the pre-independence period. As we have seen in the previous chapter that how a foundation for the awareness/ consciousness raising was led by the pioneers like Phule Ambedkar and Periyar which got translated into organised solidarity, taking shape of the movement.

The lack of consciousness or movements during the colonial period had greatly influenced the Dalit movement in the post-independence period. The society remained steeped in social inequality and the upper caste/class elite retained until fairly recently firm control over society, economy and polity. Extreme inequalities in political power excluded large sections of the population-including Dalits from effective participation in the democratic process.

Dalit assertion is also an important aspect of contemporary politics; in the seventies the Dalits were influenced by the 'Black movement' in the USA, especially by the radical Black Panther movement. At the cultural level, drawing from the experience of cultural oppression, the Dalit Panther movement of Western India has fore grounded the caste question and forced the attention of the liberal intelligentsia, and the academic community, especially in Maharashtra, to take cognisance of the issues they have raised. Both dalit women and men have written powerfully their experiences of caste oppression. In public debates, led by upper caste middle classes, the caste question is sought to be reduced to a battle over reservations. But at the level of people's movements and women's movement, the existence of caste-based oppression is now being recognised, at least to an extent, and attempts are being made to factor caste into conceptualising oppression.

In fact, Dalit movements are protest movements opposed to injustices committed on Dalits by certain social collectivities, groups, communities and so on. These are also opposed to the traditional social norms, value systems; and so on as these are considered to be inimical to the goals of equality, liberty and fraternity. The protests of Dalits' is also directed even against the government's attitude which, in their opinion, are passive and sometimes partial and partisan, especially on the issues like proper implementation of certain constitutional measures and protecting them from both social and physical violence committed on them by other (Rao, 1988).

Ideology of Dalit Movement

The ideology of Dalit movements is centred around the goals of achieving equality, fraternity and social justice—the core of Ambedkar's ideology, which is the main source of inspiration for the contemporary Dalit movements in India (Ram, 1995). Further, the ideology of protest which has wrongly been conceived of as Ambedkar's ideology (Gore, 1993) is in actuality a strategy of Ambedkar followed by the Dalits to protest against their exploitation, harassment and also against the caste system as a whole of which the unequal treatment to them is also a part. Thus, their movement is a social movement 'with wider social objectives, carried out by the Dalit themselves for their complete liberation from the stronghold of the caste system (Jogdand, 1991). Jogdand further says (1991) that the quest of the Dalit movement is the levelling up the status of people and it is the real manifestation of a new consciousness among them (the dalits).

The 1980s were marked by the newly-exploding caste identity and consciousness and theoretical and political issues involved in the debate on caste and its role in social transformation came to be debated (Kothari 1994). The Dalit movements from 1980s onwards aimed at fighting for Dalit assertion. The exploitation and discrimination of the Dalits on one hand and their protest and revolt on the other hand initiated the questions of self-assertion and consciousness among the Dalits. Through their revolt, Dalits provided a new identity for them. This identity strengthened its resolve to fight every form of discrimination and determine the path for liberation. Asserting themselves, the Dalits challenged the very foundation on which the Indian society and polity are based.

Uttar Pradesh had not responded much to the Dalit movement in the pre and early post-independence periods. The political consciousness and the participation of the Scheduled castes in Uttar Pradesh in the politics of state have traditionally been low in comparison to other regions of the country. UP did not witness anti-caste movements in the colonial period unlike the southern and western parts of India. (Pai, 2001) There were less dimunitive and less influential stream of lower caste agitations, not necessarily violent, during the colonial period in Uttar Pradesh (then united Provinces). It was hard for those agitations to keep alive and separate from the vast anti-colonial movement. The anti-colonial movement in the United Province came under the umbrella of the Congress, prominently under the leadership of Mahatma Gandhi. The Gandhian movements were accommodative and provided significant space for lower caste people though they were given minimum representation within the party. During the Civil Disobedience Movement, there was huge participation from the Dalit community. The emergence of Dalit leadership in Gandhian movement was enough for dalits to raise their voice against the atrocities meted on them by the upper castes and the Hindu religion. But dalit mobilisation, which was a part of the Independence Movement could not raise social issues along with political issues. The Gandhian movements were successful in associating dalits only with 'political' but not with social or economic concerns. However, during the late 70s and 80s, things changed dramatically and the state witnessed a resurgence of the dalit movement with a clear political agenda for social change. The movement had a leading objective to capture state power for the dalits. The objective was equipped with the expectation that once dalits get enough economic and political benefits using statepower, it would automatically improve their social status.

And it was found that in the 1980s after considerable acceleration of the process of democratisation, leading to the formation of movements and parties espousing the interests and demands of regional, sectional and oppressed groups, that Bahujan Samaj Party (BSP) was formed in 1984. The emergence of BSP, a dalit-based party has been one of the most significant developments in the society. Many scholars hailed it as a revolutionary movement, whose goal was to break the caste system and introduce social transformation. (Illaiah, 1994) Others argued that like the erstwhile Republican Party of India (RPI), it would prove to be a flash phenomenon, but it has survived and grown into a strong party and it is at crossroads today. On the one hand, it has constructed a strong dalit movement, based upon identity and consciousness, in a State which still has a rigid and conservative social structure. On the other hand, despite considerable politicisation of dalits in Uttar Pradesh by the 1980s and 1990s, the BSP has failed in its avowed goal of displacing *Manuvadi* (representing upper castes) forces and introducing social change (Pai, 2002). The BSP changed quite a lot in the 1990s. When the BSP started as a political party in early 1990s its agenda was based on 'self-respect'. Mayawati herself had asserted 'self-respect is more important the Dalits than material gains' and 'what we are fighting for is dignity and self-respect (Mayawati, 2001). This agenda pushed the BSP into an aggressive public dialogue against the political parties dominated by the upper castes (Pai, 2002).

But unfortunately due to BSP linear approach towards economic development, the broad vision of Ambedkar's thinking on the issue seemed blurred. The BSP translated Ambedkar's economic thinking into short-term social policies exclusively for the Scheduled Castes and did not respond to the economic development of the State. As stated above that capturing state power was a prime objective of the Dalit movement which got reflected in 1930 in Ambedkar's address to the first Round Table Conference, London.

'We are often reminded that the problem of depressed classes is a sociological problem and than its solution lies elsewhere than in politics. We take strong exception to this view. We hold that the problems of the depressed classes will never be solved unless they get political power in their hands. If this is true, then the problem of the depressed classes is, I submit, eminently a political problem and must be treated as such'. (Quoted in Jaffrelot, 2005)

But in keeping the political project, as it has been believed by some scholars, that the BSP has weakened the identity of the Dalit movement which Ambedkar maintained successfully, even though he had put all his efforts in making many political parties like the Indian Labour Party (ILP), Scheduled Caste Federation (SCF), and the Republican Party of India (RPI). But at the same it should be accepted that BSP has challenged values that historically put the SCs in invisible positions in relation to others. The BSP has given a face to SCs or Dalits in the public sphere.

Dalit Movement and Women

The early 1990s saw the assertion of autonomous dalit women's organisations at both regional and national levels. Such an assertion had thrown up several crucial theoretical and political challenges, besides underlining the Brahmanism of the feminist movement and the patriarchal practices of dalit politics.

Let us ponder on the gender dimension of dalit movements in India. Notwithstanding gender being embedded in social categories like caste, class, women have all along been asserting for their recognition of a social category and, in turn, claiming for gender equality. This being universally highlighted in recent years, the issues of dalit women have ironically not drawn attention of gender studies. Rather, we are immediately concerned with questions, whether gender, as a social category, is deciphered and subjugated in the caste-class paradigm of dalit movements, or whether the Dalit movements are patriarchal in terms of their followings and organisational leadership, or whether both Dalit men and women go hand in hand in their fight for human rights and dignity. It is true that dalit women are Dalit among Dalits. Their majority of lives are in villages where they work mostly as agricultural labourers by the side of their men. Even in urban areas, they are mostly illiterate and work in the unorganised sectors. In either of the cases, they face the brunt of misery similar to their men, though their agonies are more due to their vulnerable gender. Hence, they are equally agitated and assertive for their human rights and dignity.

If we go deeper into investigation to scrutinise their participation in Dalit movements, a few available evidences suggest that the peasant women in general and dalit women in particular fought vigorously against the feudal lords and police against socio-economic exploitation in the then existing social structure in numerous villages in West Bengal, the Telangana region in Andhra Pradesh, Bihar, Maharashtra and so on (Mencher, 1978; Omvedt, 1980; Sen, 1985).

Participatory Role of Dalit (Women) in Dalit Movement

The participation of Dalit women in Dalit movements has become more vigorous and widespread in the post-independence agrarian social structure. Except in few cases, where they had organised movements in support of their men under the banner of the left ideology (Omvedt, 1980), they have been fighting against their socio-economic exploitation and rejecting the hegemony of the Brahmanic social and religious traditions in South Indian villages (Delige, 1994; Kapadia, 1995). Since there are some visible socio-economic and cultural differences among Dalit women, like their men, compared to non-Dalit women, their participation in Dalit movements is also qualitatively different. Some educated and, in few cases employed Dalit women, mostly living in urban areas contribute to the Dalit movements through their writings and speeches and organising the poor and illiterate Dalit women. Even in such cases, they are actively supported by their men. Hence, an independent movement of Dalit women, either against caste Hindus-both men and women or their own men, is absent. But in both cases, they are inspired by the spirit and ideology of movements organised by Phule and Ambedkar during the pre-independence period.

But gradually in the post-independence period, the New Social Movements of the 1970s and the early 80s saw the emergence of several organisations and fronts such as the *Shramik Mukti Sanghathan*, Satyashodhak Communist Party, *Shramik Mukti Dal, Yuvak Kranti Dal*—all of whom did not limit dalit women to a token inclusion. Their revolutionary agenda, in different ways accorded them a central place.

Further, the Dalit Panthers made a significant contribution to the cultural revolt of the 1970s—but in both their writings and their programme—the Dalit women remained encapsulated firmly in the roles of the 'mother' and the 'victimised sexual being'.

Now coming to women's collective consciousness we find that the 1920s and 1930s witnessed the peak of the so-called first feminist consciousness. This was the period when women began to organise and mobilise on issues of social reform and civil and political rights. It was a phase of remarkable unity, albeit one achieved at the cost of major social and ideological exclusions. During these years women's organisations were able to draw both on the benefits of modernity, (from Colonil rulers and male Indian reformers), and from the idiom of "Indianness" constructed in the nationalist discourse. Female segregation and seclusion offered opportunities to build women's collectives that rejected male tutelage but accepted traditional patriarchal gender roles. This social feminism allowed a remarkable hegemony of elite women to speak for "all Indian women" from a united platform.

Movement and Exclusion of Dalit Women

But before we take up the issue we need to analyse the treatment about Dalit women. Two different opinions regarding this have emerged, which may be discussed as follows:

- Treatment of Dalit women as One/Monolithic/ Homogenous Category.
- Treatment of Dalit women as a Separate/Different Category.

Treatment of Dalit Women as One/Monolithic/ Homogenous Category

One strand of thought believes in treating Dalit women, not in isolation, instead treating all women subjugated by Manu's dicta, as on an equal footing for twin projects of emancipation of Dalits and emancipation of women. Thus, there is a need to combine Dalits and women, as both are the victims of the same system. Religion has ascribed both the groups the same status and both share similar disabilities. They are deprived of education, have no religious rights, neither social status. Likewise, women in India did not have equal openings in educational, religious or social spheres. Therefore, it is imperative that both join hands. If we confine to logic then the struggle for Dalit women is a struggle for emancipation of all women. And there is no need to distinguish between Dalit and women in general as women from upper most to lower most classes, i.e., all women fall under the same category. An upper class woman does not realise the subjugation. She is subjected to and suffers from the same predicament as Dalits do. If we go back to history, we see *Sita* an empress was also abandoned, *Draupadi* an empress was dragged in a royal court and disrobed. All great historical women were treated as nothing. They faced the same was misfortune and thus irrespective of *Varna* or caste, any women qualifies to be called Dalit. Hence, efforts for Dalit woman's emancipation mean efforts for emancipation of entire womanhood.

Treatment of Dalit Women as a Separate Category

The other strand says treating of woman as a separate category. They say that the social conditions prevailing in the country point to different nature of disabilities of upper caste women and Dalit women, the latter being at the lower rung. Upper caste women are an adjunct to a man, a dependent and a slave in the household. Dalit woman have additionally to face outside world necessitated by economic deprivation and an urgent need to earn for livelihood. Her subjugation is more acute (the case of the lower caste women the fact that their labour outside the family is crucial for the survival of the family, leads to the lack of stringent control on the labour, mobility and sexuality and this renders them 'impure or lacking in virtue'.

In several instances of the rape of dalit women, it may not be considered as rape at all because of the customary access that the upper caste men have had to dalit women's sexuality. Since lower caste women by the virtue of their double oppression have no 'honour' to speak of the right to redressal is often denied. In a recent incident at Birati in West Bengal, the police argued that since the women 'crying rape' were prostitutes the matter could be overlooked (Sarkar, 1992). Being dalit, she is treated with contempt by the upper caste women. There is a qualitative difference between the plights of non-dalit and dalit. Ambedkar realised this double bind of Dalit women and tried to restore human dignity to her. As per this position emancipation of Dalit women originates in the agitation launched by Ambedkar. A major reason for differentiation between an upper caste women and a dalit women is that the upper caste women has been ahead of Dalit women in education and other social spheres for the last many decades. These women never took Dalit women along with them in the movement.

It has been asserted that Dalit women are never included in agitations launched by these women, not even in their programmes. Upper caste women have never reached to Dalit women to empathise with them. They have neglected Dalit women. This line of thinking therefore, proposes a separate movement for emancipation of Dalit. Within the women's movement, the Dalit women feel discriminated against by the high-caste, women and sense that their issues are not taken up seriously for debate.

Indian Feminism and the Concerns

As already stated the women's movement that took shape during the nineteenth century, was closely connected with the Hindu caste reform movement, working for reform and betterment for women, but not interested in restructuring of society. A small group of elite women became the crucial beneficiaries of colonial modernity and were able to negotiate patriarchal (and class) spaces to access education and employment and to aspire to political leadership. Yet, the recasting of patriarchy in the image of high-caste and upper-class norms meant that most women were left out of the benefits of modernity and deprived of their traditional rights and freedoms. There was not only increasing divergence in the trajectories of upper caste/middle class urban women and the 'others', the very process that underlay the 'modernisation' of the first group became the foundation for further disempowering the poor, low caste and minority women. Thus, the new patriarchy was no less draconian or barbarous than the system it sought to civilise and replace.

It can be said that in the 1940s the growing involvement of women in diverse social and political movements broke down the essentialist construction of "Indian women". Neither women's organisations nor nationalists could continue to speak of (or for) "Indian women". The loss of hegemony hindered women's organisations' quest for equality but helped many other women seek new gender identities beyond narrow caste or class constituencies and the limitations of social feminism. The "petition politics" of the1930s had outlived its efficacy by the 1940s. After independence, female activists were marginalised because they avoided the political arena for behind-the-scenes activities. At the same time, the ideas that replaced social feminism had nothing to offer activist women—none of them even had an agenda against patriarchy. Thus, women's concerns and ideas were not incorporated into the various struggles they joined, either against the *Raj* or for social and economic justice before and after independence.

Further moving to the wave of feminism in later years which emerged in the late 1970s, and early 1980s, we find women's organisations set up at this time did not make a bid for hegemony. These were autonomous groups, joined not through the structure of formal association but through informal networking, local leaderships, an emerging feminist press, and an intensification of multi-voiced exchanges. This display of organisations represented women from all classes, castes, communities, and locales defined by, if anything, a common commitment and a language that is more leftist than liberal a situation not very different from that in most European feminist movements. This movement can make no singular claim to represent all Indian women, but it has, collectively, a national profile and presence. The various all-India campaigns launched by women engendered a cultural radicalism in which a broad range of issues and a multiplicity of voices could be articulated. This is an Indian women's movement with a difference. Thus, there is an urgent need to redefine feminist political agency—to allow for the possibility of secular political collectives to which women can belong not by ascription, but by voluntary participation.

In recent years, the euphoria of the 1970s and early 1980s, symbolised by street-level protests, campaigns in which groups mobilised at a national level, the sense of a commonality of experience cutting across class, caste, region and religion—all this seems to have gone, replaced by a more considered and complex response to issues. In many parts of India, women are no longer to be seen out on the streets protesting about this or that form of injustice. This apparent lack of a visible movement has led to the accusation that the women's movement is dead or dying.

The reality is somewhat different. While the participation of urban, middle class women is undeniable, it is not they who make up the backbone of the movement, or of the many, different campaigns that are generally seen as comprising the movement. The anti-alcohol agitation in Andhra Pradesh and similar campaigns in other parts of India were started and sustained by poor, low-caste, often working-class women. The movement to protect the environment was begun by poor women in a village called *Reni* in the Northern hill regions of India, and only after that did it spread to other parts of the country. It is truism that Dalit women have not been absent historically, although their history has been neglected until recently. From the 1920s, the Dalit women were active in autonomous anti-caste tradition, although they did not organise separately to the extent which has been seen since the middle of 1980s. With Ambedkar in the 1930s, women became even more aware and organised separate meetings and conferences:

> He saw to it that women's conferences were held simultaneously with those for men. By 1930, women had become so conscious that they started conducting their own meetings and conferences independently. (Moon and Pawar, 2006) The 1930s saw the organisation of independent meetings and conferences by dalit women in the Ambedkarite movement. This was an obvious consequence of Dr Ambedkar's practice of organising a women's conference along with every general meeting and Sabha that he called. In these *'parishads'* of the 1930s, dalit delegates passed resolutions against child marriage, enforced widowhood and dowry; critiquing these practices as brahmanical. Women's participation in the *Mahad Satyagraha*, their support to the Independent Labour Party and the Schedule Caste Federation has been well-

documented (Moon and Pawar, 1989). Women in large numbers supported *Dharmantar* as a need for a religion that would recognise their equal status. Women's participation in the Ambedkarite movement must be read in the context of the fact that in Ambedkar's theory of caste there is also a theory of the origins of sub-ordination of women and that he saw the two issues as intrinsically linked (Pardeshi, 1997).

When Ambedkar in Mahad in 1927 claimed the right of the 'untouchables' to take water from a public tank, women participated in the procession; equally important, they took part in the meetings when the resolutions were passed about demands for equal rights. They were also part of the movement in Nasik from 1930, when Ambedkar demanded temple entry for 'untouchables', up to 1935 when he declared that he had been born as a Hindu but would not die a Hindu..During this period the women conducted meetings and supported Ambedkar's claim for separate electorates (*Ibid*). It can be said that Dalit women began to organise separately from Dalit men from quite early times. They supported the claims of Ambedkar and consequently organised separately from women within the Hindu caste reform tradition at the time. Their activism moved from a phase of organising conferences and participating in *satyagrahas* to a more provocative one of criticising Brahmanical customs and patriarchy, making great strides in achieving political consciousness.

Infact, the revival of the women's movement in India came with the 'new women's movement in the 1970s, which Dalit women activists labelled as Hindu caste reform tradition, as these movements were said to focus in the same way as their predecessors on the problems of upper-or middle caste-based-discrimination to which the Dalit women were exposed. Dalit women activists also accuse the broader women's movement of not having taken the SC women along in the betterment they experienced since the 1970s, in education and in the social sphere. Dalit women also find the problems of the SCs to be very specific and not being highlighted by the broader women's movement (Dolas, 1995; Jondhale, 1995; Prabhavati, 1995).

Dalit Feminism: In Search for an Alternative

However in the second half of the 1980s, dalit women came to express a need for a separate platform within the broader women's movement. And this assertion of Dalit interests has posed new challenges for the women's movement in India and have criticised the women's movement for the lack of representation of women from marginalised communities[1], and for its lack of engagement with caste identity of women. (Menon, 2004, Morgan, 1970) have pointed out that as caste Hindu, middle class, urban educated women have been at the helm of the women's movement, this has resulted in their perspectives dominating the movement, often at the cost of women from marginalised communities (Balmiki 2005; Rao 2003; Thorat, 2001). The participation of women as factory workers, dalit women and urban poor are co-opted to make up the numbers. Overall, it has not been very successful in capturing the imagination of wider society, despite notable success in legal reform for women's rights, the provision of some supportive services and to a certain extent in the media—all areas of concern to the middle classes. Those involved in women's activism have now begun to acknowledge that women's issues are connected to identities other than gender. Dalit women are gradually becoming involved in women's activism and their concerns are being addressed by the women's movement. However, such engagement has confronted the movement with new dilemmas.

Women Movement and Issue of Caste

The issue of 'caste' continues to raise concerns for the women's movement in India. However, the nature of these concerns has changed as a result of the efforts made by state and non-state actors to include Dalit women and their interests in their work. Women activists-caste Hindu, Dalit or otherwise-carry their caste identity into their organisation and field of activism. Their experiences differ depending not only on their caste but also on the context in which they are operating.

In addition, Dalit women, activists, who had been marginalised in the women's movement, are beginning to use their 'caste' identity along with their identity derived from working as village level activists, in order to take their interests beyond the realm of social activism. By participating in local electoral politics, they are unquestionably also using their own agency and sense of empowerment derived from their involvement in women's activism.

On the contrary, the mainstream feminist argued by putting forth their stand that when feminist movement started (in the initial years) the category 'woman[2]' was conceived as collectively, based on their being oppressed by the fact of their womanhood. Since most of the vocal feminists of the 1970s were white, middle class and university educated—it was their experience which came to be universalised as 'Women's experience.' Thus, sweeping statements such as "All women are Niggers" were made (Rubin, 1969). The mainstream feminist movement very much subscribed to the idea of treating all women as 'monolithic' category as mentioned above that in a feminist discourse, the word 'woman' derives its meaning out of gender differentiation. Having this ideology they took up the cause collectively.

To some extent it may appear true that while for the Dalit 'caste' was contained in class, for the women the notion of 'sisterhood' was pivotal. All women came to be conceived as 'victims' and therefore 'Dalit'; so that what results is a classical exclusion. All 'Dalits' are assumed to be males and all women '*savarna*'. It may be argued that the categories of experience and personal politics were at the core of the epistemology and politics of the Dalit Panther movement and the women's movement. Such a position resulted into a universalisation of what was in reality the middle-class, upper caste women's experience or the Dalit male experience.

Theoretical debates came to centre on the theme of patriarchy, its material base, its persistence across modes of production and different levels within modes of production. Socialist feminists and radical feminists posed the issues in terms of capital needs vs. male control. The crux of the differences between them rested on their differential conceptualisation of the causes of women's oppression. Yet, there was a consensus between them, in that they believed in the search for fundamentals of social causation i.e., both the camps asked the question 'what is the original or founding cause of women's oppression?

But by the 1980s—this consensus had broken up and 'difference' came to the centre of feminist analysis. (Barrett and Philips, 1992). Several factors have played a constitutive role in the processes that brought the category of 'Difference' to the centre of feminist analyses. This has meant a focus on the language, culture and discourse to the exclusion of political economy, a rejection of universalism in favour of difference, an insistence on fluid and fragmented human subject rather than collectivities, a celebration of the marginal and denial of all causal analysis (Wood, 1996).

Thus, using the category of 'difference'-feminists came to celebrate the aspects of feminity that were previously looked down upon or the 'different voices' of women of different nationalities, races, classes, etc., came to celebrated and began the process of narratives and counter-narratives in history. Some scholars have pointed out that in the 19th century itself some women had been found vocal in their writings by harshly responding to 'brahmanical patriarchy' and we find the instances of "New Women" began to speak in the 1880s, questioning elements of their subordination. They found a voice in writing about their lives and the condition of women. In 1881 Vijayalakshmi, a young Brahmin child-widow was sentenced to death for killing her illegitimate child. Tarabai Shinde, a young woman, responded with a harsh critique of Brahminical patriarchy, *Stri-purush tulana* (A Comparison between Men and Women): "So is it true that only women's bodies are home to all the different kinds of recklessness and vice? Or have men got just the same faults as we find in women?" (O'Hanlon, 1991). And this process got accelerated in the 1920s when the second generation of "New Women" became more active. They articulated the needs of women, critiqued their society and foreign rulers, started associations, developed institutions, and sought to consolidate women's interests.

One of the most significant counter narratives was Jotiba Phule's mission for the liberation of the shudras, anti-shudras and women from the slavery of Brahminism. He conceptualised a Bali Rajya of equality of all men in opposition to Ram Rajya based on *Varna Ashrama Dharma*, thus reversing the Aryan theory and giving a liberatory vision of history as discussed in previous chapter. His contestation of Brahminical patriarchy stands in contestation with the recasting of patriarchies by upper caste brahminical male reformers. His recognition of the material and sexual consequences of enforced widowhood is apparent in the reformist work done by him.

Muktabai (a student in Phule's school), in an essay entitled 'About the Girls of Mangs and Mahars' drew attention to the deprivation of lower castes from their lands, the prohibition of knowledge imposed on them and the complex hierarchies wherein even the lower castes were stratified into more or less polluting. She then compared the experiences of birth for lower caste and Brahmin women, underlining the specificities of experiences of lower caste women (Chakravarti, 1998). Savitribai Phule's letters reveal an acute consciousness of the relationship between knowledge and power and crucial need for democratic access to knowledge for the shudras and women.

Tarabai Shinde's *'Stree Purush Tulana'* (1882), a text against women's subordination was written from within the Satyashodhak tradition. This text launched an attack not only on brahmanical patriarchy but also the patriarchies among the *'kunbi'* and other non-Brahmin castes. Going beyond—a mere comparison between men and women, Tarabai draws linkages between issues of de-industrialisaton, colonialism and the commodification of women's bodies (Bhagwat, 1997).

The Indian society is a combination of numerous types of social contradictions which are more distinctively visibly in the form of a number of corporate social categories, like caste, class and gender, besides, other social categories of tribals and minorities. These differ at the conceptual level and so also they wary in their social structural location and interest articulation. Gender for instance as an ordinate attribute, has not only demarcated the role domain of females but also put them in the most vulnerable condition in contemporary Indian society. Their problems have got aggravated especially when they hail from the lower caste and not class background. Whether such women have organised any independent movement or actively participated in movements organised by their men is a pungent question. Perception of the Dalit woman as the other is the distilled impact of centuries-long alienation generated by ingrained patriarchal and Brahminical values at all levels in society which in turn causes the high-level of exclusion, invisibility and structural and domestic violence which is the experience of Dalit women.

And to counter the mainstream women's movement emerged Dalit Feminist Standpoint.[3] Conflating 'non-brahminical renderings of feminism ' with the ' Dalit Feminist Standpoint' (DFS), Rege asserts by dissenting towards mainstream Indian feminism's idea that women can make common cause and speak together *across* castes, and emerges from a concern with the emphasis on 'differences' in feminist politics. Warning us about the 'narrowness' of authenticity-based identity politics. Rege claims that non-dalits can *reinvent* themselves as dalit feminists, which is to say that they can *transcend* their Non-dalitness. Such a standpoint refuses to realise that existing identities 'must be thoroughly understood before they can be either transformed or dismantled.' There is a need to realise that 'identities are not something to transcend or subvert but something we need to engage with and attend to (Moya, 2001).

Believing that the current fora do not speak for them, whether at the level of recognising the specific forms of oppression that Dalit women experience or the inability, or the tardiness, of the women's movement in giving the caste question its due, DFS has taken the initiative to set up the Dalit Women's Federation. This has forced the women's movement to address the caste. Further, Dalit feminists have formulated the position of the three-way oppression of dalit women:

- As subject to caste oppression at the hands of the upper castes.
- As labourers subject to the class-based oppression, also mainly at the hands of the upper and middle castes, who form the bulk of landowners.
- As women who experience patriarchal oppression at the hands of all men, including men of their caste.

The 1980s were marked by the newly-exploding caste identity and consciousness and theoretical and political issues involved in the debate on caste and its role in social transformation came to be debated (Kothari, 1994). The early 1990s saw the assertion of autonomous Dalit women's organisations at both regional and national levels. Such an assertion had thrown up several crucial theoretical and political challenges, besides underlining the Brahmanism of the feminist movement and the patriarchal practices of dalit politics (Rege, 1998).

Several associations of dalit women exist today, which have been nurturing and asserting dalit women's identity. Prominent among them are the dalit Mahila Sangathan and the National Federation of dalit Women. The emergence of autonomous dalit women's organisations led to a major debate at least in Maharashtra. As the dalit women become politically conscious they started speaking differently in terms of their double deprivation and their exclusion in the feminist discourse (Mangudkar, 1976). They also criticised the post-Ambedkar Dalit leadership for its cavalier approach towards their problems (*Ibid*). Thus, the Dalit feminists recognised the need to reformulate the feminist discourse.

A review of all these counter-narratives underlines the fact that the 'difference' or 'different voice' of the Dalit women is not an issue of identitarian politics; some 'authentic direct experience' but from a long lived history of lived struggles. Dalit women play a crucial role in transferring across generations, the oral repertoire of personalised yet very collective accounts of their family's interaction with Babasaheb or other leaders of the dalit movement. The question that emerges then is 'Why is this different voice of the women inaudible in the two major New Social Movements of the 1970s, namely the Dalit movement and the Women's movement.

Some scholars pointed out that the period marked by Chatterjee as the period of the 'resolution of woman's question' is the very period in which women's participation in the Ambedkarite movement was at its peak. But in Chatterjee's framework, such movements would be dismissed as Western-inspired, and orientalist, for they utilised aspects of colonial policies and western ideologies as resources. (Sarkar, 1997) If the 'difference' of dalit women's protest is to be historicised then these protests and struggles must be reinscribed; what has been excluded must be remapped and renamed.

The assertion of autonomous dalit women's organisations in the 1990s threw up several crucial theoretical and political challenges, besides underlining the brahmanism of the feminist movement and the patriarchal practices of dalit politics. (Rege, 1998) The apparent absence of a revisioning of feminist politics only suggests an ideological position of multiple/plural feminist standpoints. Within such a framework of 'difference' issues of caste become the sole responsibility of the Dalit women's organisations. (*Ibid*)

Independent Dalit (Women) Organisations in Late 1990s and their Role

All these efforts got culminated into several independent and autonomous assertions of dalit women's identity; a case in point—is the formation of the National Federation of Dalit Women and the All India Dalit Women's Forum. At the state level, the Maharashtra *Dalit Mahila Sanghatan* was formed in 1995, a year earlier, the women's wing of the Bharatiya Republican Party and the *Bahujan Mahila Sangh* had organised the *Bahujan Mahila Parishad*. In a historical happening, in December 1996, at Chandrapur a *'Vikas Vanchit Dalit Mahila Parishad'* was organised and a proposal for commemorating 25th December (the day Dr Ambedkar set the Manusmriti on flames) as Bharatiya Streemukti Divas was put forth. In 1997, the *Christi Mahila Sangharsh Sanghatan*, an organisation of dalit—Christian women was found. These different organisations have put forth varying non-Brahminical ideological positions and yet have come together on several issues such as the issue of *Bharatiya Stree Mukti Divas* and the issue of reservations for OBC women in parliamentary bodies.

Guru (1995) had argued that to understand the Dalit women's need to talk differently, it was necessary to delineate both internal and external factors that have a bearing on this phenomenon. Though Guru's argument is well-taken, and we agree that dalit women must name the difference, to privilege knowledge claims on the basis of direct experience on claims of authenticity may lead to a narrow identity politics. Such a narrow frame may in fact limit the emancipatory potential of the dalit women's organisations, and also their epistemological standpoints. It is apparent that the issues underlined by the new dalit women's movement go beyond naming of the 'difference' of dalit women and calls for a revolutionary epistemological shift to a dalit feminist standpoint (Harding, 1991).

What was clearly needed in its place is an articulation-based on the consciousness of the Dalit women themselves, their experiences of suffering, exclusion and *thrice-removedness*—isolation by virtue of gender, caste, and class—not to speak of religion.

Role of Dalit Women's Network for Solidarity (DAWNS)

In 2006, Dalit Women's Network for Solidarity (DAWNS) was set up and a new term Dalit Womanism, was coined, which explains the need for this new entity. In its Preamble, DAWNS states:

At a time when nascent movements of the marginalised are under siege in India from the forces of dominant ideologies including Brahminism, majoritarianism, and globalisation, we feel the need to affirm that the voices of the marginalised and their aspirations should be reflected in the rich tapestry that comprises the Indian nation. The voices of the women and children of the populations which are pushed to the margins are rarely heard—specifically, the Dalit women. This consultation dedicated itself to bringing to the mainstream discourse their voices, aspirations, and visions. As no one movement can effectively reflect the specific issues and situations of Dalit women whose situations vary widely across regions, states, languages and religions, we welcome the trend of a growing number of movements of dalit women to take up issues and work on their concerns.

Therefore, we have decided to come together as a Collective, termed the Dalitt Women's Network for Solidarity (DAWNS). It will work to strengthen the voices of Dalit Women through building knowledge working towards ideological clarity, and highlighting the values, visions and aspirations of Dalit Women. It will strive to put their agendas in the mainstream, thereby giving a new shape and direction to socio-political and cultural discourse. It is a conscious effort to break the existing stereotype of Dalit women as mainly activists (doers), who have little to contribute (as thinkers) to ideological discourses in society, politics, governance, ethics, economics, and development. To this end, it will network and dialogue with societal change agents including academic institutions, trainers, NGOs, government institutions, and development groups. It will provide a platform for solidarity on these issues to grassroots activists, students and other civil society actors with a vision of a gender-just, non-casteist and equitable society (Stephen, 2009).

In a nut shell, it can be said that the Dalit Feminism is not only trying to build and shape theory, it is also learning to mediate the spaces as well as build solidarity between itself and the existing Feminist and Womanist thought and theory. It is also trying to negotiate its differences with and build solidarity with men from Dalit and other subaltern and marginalised groups. Its efforts are to change the paradigms of society from a caste and patriarchy dominated ethos towards a more inclusive and equitable society.

V. Geetha (1991), has rightly pointed Dalit women are not seen as active historical agents making and remaking their lives and hence history.

Feminist scholars also agree that one cannot analyse Indian society without considering the caste factor. Though patriarchy is pervasive in India, it varies in degree, depending on the religion, region, caste community and social groups maintained and perpetuated through endogamy.

Whether the mainstream women's movement can accept the equal partnership, if not the leadership of women from grassroots Dalit (or adivasi or tribal) backgrounds is still a question. Have they really tried to groom capable younger women from the underprivileged, working class and Dalit and adivasis sections for leadership? If so, have these women and affirmed supported by those from more privileged backgrounds, and have they accepted their leadership? If not, are they justified in their claim to speak for all Indian women everywhere? Can they be exempted from the criticism that they are as guilty of discrimination against their sisters on the basis of caste and class as the society they are attempting to challenge and change?

> *Exclusion of Dalit women from the mainstream women's movement has caused them to start building their own praxis, identity and agency, and build effective working relationships and their own platforms.*

Since women are not monolithic group, any single frameworks will not be sufficient to capture the complexity and the different dimensions and particularities of their struggles. Dalit Women constitute almost half of India's 160 million Dalits; comprise about 16 per cent of India's total female population, and eight per cent of the total population. However, there is little understanding of the economic, religious, political and ideological isolation of Dalit women this is certainly true of their experience in the mainstream women's movements, where most of them feel disillusioned and alienated.

India is fragmented over issues of region (articulated whether as north/south or rural/urban or adivasi/non-adivasi) and religion, language, ethnicity, caste, class, and gender amongst other issues. This means that the context itself suggests a need for a plural expression of feminism around women's multiple oppressions, *viz.*, class, caste, ethnicity, gender, sexual preference, etc. Indeed the different fragmented contexts of struggle suggest that there can be no 'one' feminism in the "Indian' context or one way of understanding or locating women's oppression.

In the historical scheme of things, all of the above are notable but modest gains. Much more remains to be done, particularly in the material lives of dalit women. Yet, it must be acknowledged that dalit women are no longer invisible, they do have their organisations, and they are increasingly able to make their claims and to be heard nationally and internationally.

References

1. Prof Gopal Guru in an article "Theoretical Brahmin and Empirical Shudra", published in EPW many years ago, says feminism and feminists in India engaged with was far removed from the lived experiences of Dalit women. The agenda of feminism, as set by its very well-known, senior and experienced leaders, had little, if anything at all, to do with the lives of Dalit and other subaltern women. Prof Gopal Guru as "Theoretical Brahmin and Empirical Shudra", in an article published in EPW many years ago.
2. In a feminist discourse, the word 'woman' derives its meaning out of gender differentiation. Thus, the concept of gender is immanent to any feminist project without which there is no one gendered subject (female subject) to either act or to liberate. However, if we are problematising this category itself as Judith Butler' docs, then on what grounds can one use this category 'woman' without being essensialist and using it in such a way that does not have exclusionary implications? The above analysis then suggests that, critique of subject, when applied to feminist theories, means more than assuming the multiple and shifting identities of a unity called-woman'. As Butler says (1990:327),

   "The political critique of subject" questions "making a conception of identity into the ground of politics, however internally complicated", since "it prematurely forecloses the possible cultural articulations of subject-position" existing prior to its discursive articulation. The above critique of the subject thus forewarns us about giving the category 'woman' a foundationalist role even when we attribute to the category multiple and shifting subject positions.
3. Dalit Feminist Standpoint (DFS) is a counter discourse to women's movements overlooking the marginalisation of dalit women in social, economic and political relations. Ideologically, and organisationally, dalit feminism is closer to the dalit movement, and alienated from women's movements. DFS is a demand on mainstream feminists to engage with the realities of the caste dynamics of patriarchy and the specificities of dalit women's oppression.

Bibliography

Agnes, Flavia. 1994. Women's Movement within a Secular Framework, *Economic and Political Weekly*, 29 (19): pp. 1123-27.

Akerkar, Supriya. 1995. Theory and practice of women's movement in India. A discourse analysis, *Economic and Political Weekly, 30* (17): WS pp. 2-23.

Anveshi Law Committee. 1997. Is gender justice only a legal issue? Political stakes in UCC debate, *Economic and Political Weekly*, 32(9-10): pp. 453-58.

Bandyopadhyay, Jayanta. 1999. Chipko Movement: Of floated myths and flouted realities. *Economic and Political Weekly*, 34 (15): 880-82.

Bannerjee, Sumantha, 1989. Marginalisation of women's popular culture in Nineteenth Century Bengal, in Kumkum Sangari and Suresh Vaid, (ed.), Recasting women. Essays in colonial history, New Delhi: Kali for Women.

Basu, Amrita. 1992. Two faces of protest: Contrasting modes of women's activism in India. Berkeley: University of California Press.

Basu, Amrita, 1995. Introduction, in A. Basu (ed.). The Challenges of local feminisms: Women's movements in Global Perspectives, Boulder, CO: Westview.

Beal, l J., Hassim S., Todes A.1989. A bit on the side? Gender struggles in the politics of transformation in South Africa, *Feminist Review*, 33: pp. 30-56.

Bhambri, C.P. 1991. State and Communalism in India, 1947-87. New Delhi: Vikas Publishing House.

Bharat Patankar and Gail Omvedt. 2007. The Dalit Liberation Movement in Colonial Period, New Delhi: Critical Quest.

Chandhoke, Neera.1995. State and civil society: Exploration in political theory. New Delhi: Sage Publications.

Chatterjee, Partha. 1989. The nationalist resolution on the women's question, in recasting women. Essays in colonial history (eds) Kumkum Sangari and Suresh Vaid, New Delhi: Kali for women.

Chatterjee, Partha. 1997. Beyond the nation? Or within? *Economic and Political Weekly* 32(1): pp. 4-11.

Cynthia, Stephen. 2009. Feminism and in India by 16th November, 2009 Source: http://www.countercurrents.org/stephen161109.htm.

Dattar, Chayya. 1999. Non-brahmin renderings of feminism in Maharashtra: Is it a more emancipatory force? *Economic and Political Weekly*, 34 (41).

Dolas, Avinash. 1995. Dalit Women and the Women's Movement in India, in P.G. Jogdand (ed.) Dalit Women in India: Issues and Perspectives, New Delhi: Gyan Publishing House.

Forbes, Geraldine. 1996. Women in Modern India, Cambridge: Cambridge University Press.

Gandhi, Nandhita and Nandita Shah. 1992. The Issues at stake: Theory and Practice in Contemporary Women's Movement in India, New Delhi: Kali for Women.

Gail Omvedt. 2006. Dalit Visions: The anti-caste Movement and the Construction of an Indian Identity, New Delhi: Orient Longman.

Gore, M.S. 1993. Non-brahman Movement in Maharashtra, New Delhi: Segment Book Distributors.

Jalal, A. 1991. The Convenience of Subservience: Women and the State of Pakistan, in Women, Islam and the State (ed.). D. Kandiyoti, Philadelphia: PA. Temple University Press.

Jogdand, P.G. 1991. Dalit Movement in Maharashtra, New Delhi: Kanak Publications.

John, Mary. 2000. Alternate Modernities? Reservations and Women's Movements in 20th Century India' *Economic and Political Weekly*, 35 (43): WS22-WS29.

Jondhale Surendra, 1995. 'Theoretical Underpinning of Emancipation of Dalit Women' in P.G. Jogdand (ed.) Dalit Women in India: Issues and Perspectives, New Delhi: Gyan Publishing House.

Jurgensmyer, Mark. 1988. Religious Rebels in the Punjab: The Social Vision of Untouchables, Delhi: Ajanta Publications.

Khare, R.S. 1984, The Untouchable as Himself: Ideology, Identity and Pragmatism among the Lucknow Chamars, Cambridge.

Kapur, Ratna, and Brenda Cossman. 1993. Communalising gender/ engendering community. Women, Legal Discourse and saffron agenda, *Economic and Political Weekly*, 28 (17):WS35-WS44.

Katzenstein Mary, Smithu Kothari, and Uday Mehta. 2001. 'Social Movement Politics in India: Institutions, Interests and Identities', in The success of India's democracy, Atul Kohli (ed.) Cambridge: Cambridge University Press.

Keer, Dhananjay. 1964. Mahatma Jotirao Phooley: Father of Indian Social Revolution, Bombay: Popular Prakashan.

Kishwar, M. 1986. Pro-women or anti-Muslim? The Shah Bano Controversy, *Manushi* 32:4-13.

Krishnaraj, M. 2003. Challenges before women's movement in a changing context, *Economic and Political Weekly*, Vol. 38 (43):4536-45.

Mahajan, Gurpreet. 2001. Identites and rights. Aspects of Liberal Democracy in India. New Delhi: Oxford University Press.

Mayawati, Kumari. 2001. 'Bahujan Samaj Aur Uski Rajniti, quoted in Sudha Pai' Dalit Question and Political Response—Comparative Study of Uttar Pradesh and Madhya Pradesh, *Economic and Political Weekly*, March 13, 2004, pp. 1141-1150.

Menon, Nivedita. 2000. Embodying the Self: Feminism, sexual violence and the Law in Community, gender and violence, subaltern studies XI (eds.). Partha Chatterjee and Pradeep Jaganathan, New Delhi: Ravi Dayal.

Mies, Maria. 1976. The Shahada Movement: A peasant movement in Maharashtra, Its Development and its Prospects, *Journal of Peasant Studies*, 3 (4): pp. 472-82.

Mohanty, C.T. 1991. Introduction: Cartographies of Struggle of Third world women and the politics of feminism, in Third World Women and the politics of feminism, (eds.). Chandra Talpade Mohanty and Russo Lourdes Torres, Bloomington: Indiana University Press.

Mouffe, Chantal. 1995. Feminism, citizenship, and radical democratic politics, in Social post-modernism. Beyond identity Politics, Linda Nicholson and Steven Seidman (eds.), Cambridge: Cambridge University Press.

Moya, Paula M.L. 2001. Introduction, in Reclaiming Identity: Realist Theory and the Predicament of Post-modernism, (eds.). Paula M.L. Moya and Michael R. Hames-Garcia. Hyderabad: Orient Longman.

Okin, Susan M. 1999. Is Multi-culturalism Bad for Women? Princeton: Princeton University Press.

Omvedt, G., (1993). Reinventing Revolution: New Social Movements and Socialist Traditions in India. London: ME Sharpe.

Oommen, T.K. 1990. Sources of Deprivations and Style of Protest: The Case of the Dalits. In his Protest and Change: Studies in Social Movement, New Delhi: Sage Publications.

Oommen, T.K. 2001. Civil Society: Religion, Caste and Language in India, *Sociological Bulletin*, 50(2), pp. 219-235.

Padke, Shilpa. 2003. Thirty years on. Women's Studies Reflect on the Women's Movement, *Economic and Political Weekly*, 38 (43):4567-4576.

Pai, Sudha. 2002. Dalit Assertion and the Unfinished Democratic Revolution: The BSP in Uttar Pradesh, New Delhi: Sage.

Prabhavati, M. 1995 Dalit. Women in Contemporary Indian Situation in P.G. Jogdand (ed.) Dalit Women in India: Issues and Perspectives, New Delhi: Gyan Publishing House.

Ram Nandu. 1995. Beyond Ambedkar, Essays on Dalits in India, New Delhi: Har-Anand Publications.

Rao, M.S.A. 1978. Social Movements and Social Transformation: A Study of Two Backward Classes Movements in India, New Delhi: Manohar.

Rao, A. 1988. From Atrocities to Protest Movement: An Urge for Social Development in S.K. Srivastava and A.K. Srivastava (eds.) Social Movement for Development, Allahabad: Chug Publications.

Rao, A. 1995. The Politics and Gender and Culture in International Human Rights Discourse, in Women's Rights, Human Rights J. Peters and A. Wolper (eds.), International Feminist Perspectives, New York: Routledge.

Ray, R. and A.C. Korteweg. 1999. Women's movements in the third world: Identity, Mobilisation and Autonomy, *Annual Review of Sociology*, 25: pp. 47-71.

Ray, R. 1999. Fields of Protest: Women's Movements in India. Minneapolis: University of Minneapolis Press.

Ray, R. 1998. Women's Movements and Political Fields: A Comparison of two Indian cities, *Social Problems*, 45 (1): pp. 21-36.

Reddy, Narasimha D., and Arun Patnaik. 1993. Anti-arrack agitation of women in Andhra Pradesh, *Economic and Political Weekly*, 28(21): pp. 1059-66.

Rege Sharmila. 1998. Dalit Women Talk Differently: A Critique of 'Difference' and Towards a Dalit Feminist Standpoint Position Source: *Economic and Political Weekly,* Vol. 33, No. 44 (Oct. 31 - Nov. 6, 1998), pp. WS39-WS46.

Rege, Sharmila, 2000. 'Real feminism and dalit women: Scripts of denial and accusation', Economic and Political Weekly, 35 (6): pp. 492-495.

Saberwal, Satish. 1994. Democratic and political structures, in Social change and political discourse in India: Structures of Power, Movements of Resistance, Vol. 1, T.V. Sathyamurthy (ed.). Delhi: Oxford University Press.

Sangari and Suresh Vaid, (ed.). 1989. Recasting Women. Essays in Colonial History, New Delhi: Kali for Women.

Sangari, Kumkum. 1995. Politics of Diversity. Religious Communities and Multiple Patriarchies, Published in two-parts in *Economic and Political Weekly*, 30(51): 3287-3310 and 30(52):3381-92.

Sarkar, Sumit, 1973. 'The complexities of young Bengal,' *Nineteenth Century Studies*, 4: pp. 504-34.

Sarkar, Tanika. 1991. 'The women as communal subject: Rashtra Sevika Samithi and Ram Janmabhumi Movement, *Economic and Political Weekly*, 26 (35).

Shiva, Vandana. 1988. Staying Alive: Women, Ecology and Survival in India. New Delhi: Kali for Women.

Squires, Judith. 2002. Culture, Equality and Diversity, in Multiculturalism Reconsidered, Paul Kelly (ed.), Oxford: Oxford: Polity Press.

Vijayalakshmi, V. 2004. Citizenship, Differences and Identity: Dalit Women and Political inclusion, Working paper 147, Institute for Social and Economic Change, Bangalore.

3 Contemporary Status of Dalit (Women) in India

We have seen in the preceding chapters that historically India has witnessed long struggle and sustained interventions by social reformers, that led to the emergence of India's reservation policy as a mechanism of inclusion for the excluded segments that have been subjected to social abuse, dispossession, indignity, impoverishment and discrimination for years. Moving from history to contemporary world drives us to analyse the status of Dalit including Dalit men in general and Dalit women in specific in the contemporary times.

The Dalits of India are perhaps the world's foremost example of a community whose rights are violated. In India, over 200 million dalits are also known as Untouchables or outcastes. Despite the existence of Constitutional rights and other affirmative action that is meant to address the issues, today their predicament can be described in terms of a lost humanity and a dispossessed community who live in segregated conditions. Notwithstanding the democratic values, caste hierarchy continues to dominate (feudal) system of Indian Society.

Not only the untouchability arrested the growth of personality of untouchables but also comes in the way of their 'material well-being'. It deprived them of certain civil rights. The status of untouchable suggest that they are not even considered a citizen. Citizenship is nothing but the bundle of rights. Rights which includes such as personal liberty, personal security, right to hold private property, equality before law, liberty of conscience, freedom of opinion, and speech, right of assembly, right of representation in country's government and right to hold office under the state. The untouchability of untouchables puts these rights far beyond their reach.

The widely held perception of the Dalit woman as the OTHER is the distilled impact of centuries-long alienation generated by ingrained patriarchal and Brahminical values at all levels in society, which in turn causes the high level of exclusion, invisibility and structural and domestic violence which is the experience of Dalit women. Thus even among women, she is perceived as OTHER (forms a category of her own). She is at the receiving end of a long, socially-engineered pecking order, which asserts the relative 'superiority' of one category of human being over another. She belongs to the 'lowest' category, as manifest in her condition of total social, physical, economic and political vulnerability.

Although after independence the State Government of India through its application of the provisions of equality and affirmative action in the Constitution has launched various economic and social development programmes for dalits i.e., the Scheduled Castes (SCs) and Scheduled Tribes (STs) and women, which are in line with various theories stated above, yet the goal of social integration has not been achieved, for these groups are yet to overcome the feelings of inferiority, segregation and exclusion. Majority of women have very little or nothing to inherit, educational and occupational opportunities for them are very limited, legal help costs money and above all, legal rights are meaningless as women are ignorant about them. Nevertheless, since independence, the demands of women for social justice have become more and more strident.

Unequal treatment has been the inescapable fate of the untouchables in India and that in a country like India where it is possible for discrimination and deprivation to be practiced on a vast scale and in a relentless manner, fundamental rights have no real meaning for untouchables.

Deprivation exists whenever there is a factor constraining the opportunities open to an individual, groups, community or society. Restriction of opportunities open to an individual leads to deprivation. It means that each caste or race does not get equal chance to make its preferences felt and to determine its life style. There are theories describing deprivation. According to Nozick's entitlement theory the rules governing acquisition, transfer and rectification should be such that they are not violative of anybody's rights, which place prior constraints on the action of others, including, in particular, the state.

The emphasis here is thus, on equal rights. This theory along with the Dworkins theory of the right to be treated 'equal' by the state and Rawlsian's 'theory of justice or deprivation'. In the ancient Hindu society there was no sphere of life—spiritual, moral, legal and economic which was not treated by graded inequality. The main emphasis in the Dworkin's theory is the 'right to being treated as an equal', i.e., all citizens are entitled to being treated with grave concern and respect as all others. The Rawlsian theory encompasses such things as rights, liberties, incomes, opportunities and the social basis of self-respect. According to A.K. Sen's *'Theory of functional capability'* the appropriate concern for a moral theory is one focussing on the capability and doing and a capability set is a collection of functioning which together define the freedom available to a person. Eliminating deprivation means that each caste or race has an equal chance to make its preferences felt and to determine its lifestyle. In the broadest sense, eliminating deprivation involves eliminating the present effects of past inequalities. Some of the effects are not reversible but alternative compensation such as moral regeneration of the suppressed class by providing them with *'liberty, equality and fraternity'* should form the basis of any society.

Deprivation and development are very much linked with the issues of distributive justice. Different forms of deprivation have been identified and analysed by the experts from cross section of the society. The basic tenet of inclusive development viz., social justice is eroded letting loose a process of extensive exclusion market by growing inequalities, deprivation and marginalisation. Deprivation has various discriminatory dimensions—economic, social political, etc., which led to emergence of the process of mobilisation against deprivation.

Dalit Population in India and in the State of Uttar Pradesh

According to the UNDP India Report (2007) on Human Poverty and Socially Disadvantaged Groups in India, the HDI at all India level for SCs is estimated to be 0.303, which is lower than the HDI for non-SC/ST at 0.393 for the period 1980-2000. As per 2001, the Scheduled Castes and Scheduled Tribes constituted 24.4 per cent of India's population (16.2 per cent Scheduled Castes and 8.2 per cent Scheduled Tribes). Their population (excluding the state of Jammu and Kashmir) was 166.67 million and 84.32 million respectively.

Out of which around 66 million women are Dalits, forming 48 per cent of the total Dalit population of the country. Out of this 16.3 per cent of Dalit women population in India, 81.4 per cent live in rural areas. They, along with their male counterparts, constitute a sizeable social group that continues to suffer from descent-based discrimination arising out of the caste system. The exclusion and deprivation of SCs is closely associated with the institution of caste and the practice of untouchability. The SCs were excluded from access to property rights, civil rights, and education, except as their use as labour for the castes higher than permitted. Their deprivation became more severe as they also suffered from physical and social segregation from the rest of Hindu society through the institution of untouchability. This has thus been institutionalised, and has led to multiple exclusion of the low caste untouchables, with severe consequences for their economic and social condition.

Overview of the Dalits in India and Uttar Pradesh

Table 1

Trends in Proportion of Schedule Caste Population

Census Year Population	*Total Population in Million*	*SC Population in Million*	*Proportion of SC*
1961	439.2	64.4	14.7
1971	547.9	80.0	14.6
1981	665.3	104.8	15.7
1991	838.6	138.2	16.5
2001	1028.6	166.6	16.2
2011	1210.5	201.3	16.6

(*Source:* Census of 1961-2011)

Discrimination-based on caste imposes social exclusion on persons belonging to Dalit castes. Their physical separation from the dominant castes in terms of housing patterns, strict enforcement of the prohibition of inter-dining at public places, seating arrangements in educational institutions, particularly in schools and engaging them in degrading occupation like manual scavenging and carrying of night soil (by women). Sexual control and systematic rape of Dalit women by men of the dominant castes, forced prostitution in the name of religion through Devadasi system are all violation of human dignity.

Therefore, Dalit's perpetually live in a situation of threat and fear, which is apparent when their houses and property are destroyed/burnt or when Dalit women are raped and killed, so on so forth because they are voiceless.

Positional Aspect of Dalit Women

Now, let us examine the positional aspect of dalit women in India. Dalit women in India suffer from three oppressions: Gender, as a result of patriarchy; class, from being from the poorest and most marginalised communities; and caste, from coming from the lowest caste, the 'untouchables'. Although discrimination on the basic of caste is against the Indian Constitution and prohibited by many laws, its practice is still widespread, especially in rural India. These women, are often offended, discriminated, deprived of human dignity and have been subject to inhuman treatment and ugly form of untouchability. Dalit women not only grapple with the discrimination due to caste hierarchy and untouchability but they live in poverty coupled with political, legal and religio-cultural discrimination. Access to resources such as land, water is out of reach to these women. Henceforth, Dalit women end up working as bonded agricultural labourers with low/under paid wages, in spite of their knowledge and skills in farming. The extreme perennial economic deprivation has also resulted in illiteracy, malnourishment, poor health conditions, besides this they are also overworked, oppressed and victimised by a number of factors, including patriarchal attitude within the family and community.

Now coming to the state of Uttar Pradesh, it is marked by sharp economic and social inequalities among different social groups. It is lagging behind most of the other states in terms of indicators women development. The gap is particularly high in case of indicators such as female literacy, female work participation rates (FWPR) and life expectancy. On the other hand, the fertility rate in UP is much higher than the national average. Sex ratio in the state is low and has been declining. Female literacy rates are much lower than male literacy rates and FWPRs are also extremely low. Infant and child mortality rates among girls are higher as compared to the boys. Female life expectancy is lower than male expectancy, unlike the situation in most parts of the world. The poor indicators of women's status in UP are reflective of the fact that the prevailing socio-cultural milieu in the state discriminates against women. The role of women's agency is particularly weak in UP, which has implications not only for the well-being of women but also for economic development and social progress in the society as a whole (Dreze and Gazdar 1996).

Economic Deprivation of Dalit Women

Box. 1

- Dalit Women are the most economically deprived section of Indian society.
- Dalit women labour force constitutes the backbone of Indian agriculture economy.
- The 71 per cent of them are agricultural labourers.
- The 90 per cent were cultivators (1991).
- The 32.40 per cent of the household sector and large number of them employed in unorganised labour in urban areas.
- A large number of them employed in unclean occupation.
- They are denied just and equal wages, fair-share in economic distribution, maternity benefits, the security and protection.
- Almost all the Dalit women enter the labour market before the age of 20.

Dalit Women as Victims of Caste Hierarchy and Atrocities

Vulnerably positioned at the bottom of India's caste, class and gender hierarchies, Dalit women experience endemic gender-and-caste discrimination and violence as the outcome of a severely imbalanced social, economic and political power equations. Their socio-economic vulnerability and lack of political voice, when combined with the dominant risk factors of being Dalit and female, increase their exposure to potentially violent situations while simultaneously reducing their ability to escape. Violence against Dalit women presents clear evidence of widespread exploitation and discrimination against these women subordinated in terms of power relations to men in a patriarchal society, as also against their communities based on caste. As the National Commission for Women has commented, "in the commission of offences against... scheduled caste (Dalit) women the offenders try to establish their authority and humiliate the community by subjecting their women to indecent and inhuman treatment, including sexual assault, parading naked, using filthy language, etc."

Hence, violence, which serves as a crucial social mechanism to maintain Dalit women's subordinate position in society, is the core outcome of gender-based inequalities shaped and intensified by the caste system.

Dalit Women's day-to-day struggle is one of existence, survival and justice. The everyday discrimination is dotted by mental and physical violence. Eternally, the principles of 'high and low', 'purity and pollution' has not left any scope for changing Dalit women's status. Thus, any move by Dalit women to question the system, or challenge inequality to change the life situation has resulted in retaliation with abuses such as beating, rape, naked parading, labelled as witches and harassed for murder. This further implicates in punishing the whole community by burning of houses, destruction of properties, valuables, crops etc. The crux of the Dalit Women's struggles for survival is rooted in her being at the lowest rung of the Caste hierarchy.

Twelve major forms of violence constitute the basis of this study, nine being violence in the general community—physical assault, verbal abuse, sexual harassment and assault, rape, sexual exploitation, forced prostitution, kidnapping and abduction, forced incarceration and medical negligence—and three being violence in the family—female foeticide and infanticide, child sexual abuse and domestic violence from natal and marital family members. The majority of the Dalit women have faced several forms of violence over the past five years, either in one incident, or in a series of incidents of violence, in either or both the general community and the family.

Box. 2

More frequent forms of violence that are perpetrated against the majority of Dalit women are verbal abuse (62.4 per cent of total women), physical assault (54.8 per cent), sexual harassment and assault (46.8 per cent), domestic violence (43.0 per cent) and rape (23.2

per cent), in descending order. Although the remaining forms of violence are faced by relatively fewer Dalit women (less than 10 per cent of total women per form of violence), this does not discount their gravity, precisely because of the qualitative factor of force present in these forms of violence.

Uttar Pradesh Leads in Atrocities towards Women

According to recent figures tables in Parliaments by the National Commission for Scheduled Castes and Scheduled Tribes, the number of cases of atrocities against Dalits registered in 2000, stood at 23,742 cases (including 1,034 cases of rape). Dalit women are estimated to be the first victims, in close to 75 per cent of these cases. The State of Uttar Pradesh leads in the number of cases registered under the Scheduled Castes/ Scheduled Tribes (Prevention of Atrocities) Act 1989, followed by Rajasthan, Madhya Pradesh, Andhra Pradesh, Tamil Nadu, Karnataka, Gujarat and Bihar.

Violence therefore, forms the core result of gender-based inequalities, and intensified by caste discrimination. Women are gang raped, forced into prostitution, stripped, paraded around naked, even murdered for no crime of theirs. (According to the UN Special Rapporteur on Violence Against Women—E/ CN.4/2002/83, 31st January, 2002). They are victims of worst form of degradation such as manual scavenging.

Educational Status

Though the right to primary education has been declared a fundamental right under newly-introduced/insisted Article 21A of the Indian Constitution.

Literacy Rate

The performance of literacy rate of Scheduled Castes in 2001 in states of Bihar, Jharkhand and Uttar Pradesh and that of Scheduled Tribes in states of Andhra Pradesh, Arunachal Pradesh, Bihar, Gujarat, J and K, Jharkhand, Karnataka, Madhya Pradesh, Orissa, Rajasthan, Tamil Nadu, Uttar Pradesh, West Bengal and Dadra and Nagar Haveli is below 50 per cent. Among the SCs the proportion of literates in 1991 was the highest in Kerala (79.7 per cent) and the lowest was in Bihar (19.5 per cent). The pattern was similar in 2001 with the literacy rate being 82.7 per cent in Kerala and the lowest 28.5 per cent in Bihar, thereby showing a narrowing of gaps. As far as STs are concerned, Mizoram had the highest literacy rates in 1991 (82.7 per cent) and 89.3 per cent in 2001. This was the lowest in 19.4 per cent in Rajasthan in 1991, and 28.2 per cent in Bihar in 2001.

Table 2

Female Literacy Gaps

Year	*All India Total*	*All India Female*	*SC Female*
1961	24.02	12.95	3.29
1971	29.46	18.7	26.44
1981	43.67	29.85	10.93
1991	52.21	39.29	23.76
2001	75.3	53.7	41.9
2011	80.9	64.6	56.5

(*Source:* Census of India Records of 1961-2001, Registrar General, Government of India).

There is vast disparity in literacy rates between SC women (23.76 per cent) as compared to women in general (39.29 per cent) dalit men (49.91 per cent) and Indians in general (52.21 per cent). In 2000, the literacy rate among SC and ST females (15 and above) in rural areas was 24 per cent and 23 per cent respectively as compared to 41 per cent for non-SC/ST women and national average of 29 per cent.

Illiteracy and Lack of Access to Education

Box. 3

- Lack of educational development is another important problem for Dalit Women, placing them at a disadvantages position as compared to both Dalit men as well as non-dalits.
- Dalit female literacy rate was 23.76 per cent and lowest in rural areas with only 19.46 per cent, lowest in Bihar 5.54 per cent, Rajasthan 4.73 per cent, U.P. 8.47 per cent.
- Large number of Dalit girls drop out in primary—53.96 per cent, middle and secondary levels.
- Dalit girls are denied educational opportunities because of caste and gender discrimination.

Disparities exists in urban areas also; in fact the literacy rate among SC females was the lowest, even lower than ST females. The literacy rates were 48 per cent, 54 per cent and 70 per cent respectively for SC, ST and non-SC/ST females in urban areas, the national average being 57 per cent. The relative disadvantage of the SC/ST female population in terms of educational development is thus clearly reflected in their literacy rates.

Table 3

Literacy Rate of General Population and SC Population, 1961–2001

Total			*Male*			*Female*			
	1991	*2001*	*2011*	*1991*	*2001*	*2011*	*1991*	*2001*	*2011*
General	52.2	64.80	73.0	64.1	75.30	80.9	39.3	53.70	64.6
SC	37.4	54.70	66.1	49.9	66.60	75.2	23.8	41.90	56.5

Drop out Rate

The drop out rate among the SC and ST females is also relatively high at each stage of education. As we move up in educational level, from primary/middle to high school and higher secondary school and to graduate and above, the drop out rate increases. Finally, at the graduate level and above, the share of SC and ST women (15 and above) is 0.4 per cent and 0.3 per cent respectively, as compared to 1.2 per cent for non-SC/ST women, with national average being 0.63 per cent. In urban areas, these ratios worked out to 2.7 per cent, 6.4 per cent and 10.1 per cent for SC/ST, and non-SC/ST respectively with a national average of 11.12 per cent.

Table 4

Drop Out Rates (2003-04)

Class I-V			*Class I-VIII*			*Class IX –X*			
	Total	*Boys*	*Girls*	*Total*	*Boys*	*Girls*	*Total*	*Boys*	*Girls*
General	31.47	33.74	28.57	52.32	51.85	52.92	62.69	60.98	64.92
SC	36.56	36.83	36.19	59.42	57.33	62.19	73.13	71.41	75.49

(*Source:* Selected Educational Statistics 2004–05, Ministry of Human Resource Development).

The following reasons for the high rate of illiteracy among Dalit women are: Resistance from the family to send girls to schools; fear of insecurity in villages; lack of physical facilities like accommodation, school, transport and medical facilities; girls were forced to take care of the siblings when the parents are away at work; girls were forced to do domestic chores which prevent them from attending school; working to earn for the family prevent the girls from attending school; working with parents to earn their livelihood in *beedi* factories or other unorganised sector made them illiterate; because of the sick and unemployed parents, girls were forced to work; many were forced to get married at a young age, which stop schooling; social restriction is that the girls should stop education after marriage; in some areas there are complaints from Dalit women teachers of misbehaviours, blackmail and exploitation by the male staff of other high caste people; distance of schools from home, irrelevant content of the education system; year of alienation of girls from their environment as a result of education are some of the other factors for low literacy level among SC girls. Even if the education improved the marriage prospects of the girls, the minus point is the increase in dowry. Therefore, many parents wish to withdraw the girls from schools.

Dalits women belonging to the creamy layer of the society are better with good education and socially and economically they are well off like other high castes. They are fully aware of the welfare schemes provided by the government and their percentage is very low when compared with the total dalit population. In rural areas, the first generation girls from SC need the attention of government and other organisation. Mostly the teachers of the locality provide information to them about the welfare schemes. In many Dalit associations executive positions are occupied by male members whereas very poor representation is made by women in their pasts. The women are not properly informed about the Government schemes and there is an urgent need to get a feedback about the welfare schemes where lot of money is spent for the development of Dalits. The funds are not utilised properly for their progress. Many of the schemes go unnoticed because they are not properly provided to the concerned section.

Additionally, at the level of higher education, SC girls compared men 28.5 per cent of all SC students enrolled in graduate, post-graduate and professional course (Government of India, Selected Educational Statistics 1998-1999). This gendered higher education divide ensures that only few dalit girls are equipped professionally to enter into the technology sector, restricting their opportunities for socio-eco development.

The 1991 Census revealed the great disparity between SC women illiteracy rate (76.24) and that of the general population (47.79). The SC female drop out rate at every stage of education is higher than that of either SC boys or the general female population. It is sad that over 83 per cent of SC females drop out of school at the secondary stage, the most crucial one for the next stage of higher education and for future employment.

There have been some trends showing a more rapid increase in literacy, with female and SC literacy rising at a faster rate than the overall rate in recent years. District level analysis of the literacy situation, for the Uttar Pradesh Human Development Report, shows that certain important changes seemed to have occurred in the literacy situation, which has had both positive and negative features. Between 1981 and 1991, there was a close correlation between the level of literacy of a district in 1981, and the change that it experienced during 1991.

According to 2001 Census Report, the literacy rate of UP Dalit stands at 43 per cent whereas the national average of the dalits is 54.7 per cent. The literacy rate of UP Dalits both males and females is 60.3 per cent and 30.5 per cent respectively whereas the national average of Dalits is 66.6 per cent and 41.9 per cent respectively. As such UP dalits lag behind the Dalits of many other states of India in terms of male and female literacy rates. According to Dr B.R. Ambedkar the progress of a society is measured by the progress of women, but the position of Dalit women in Uttar Pradesh is very low. It also badly reflects on the poor performance of Uttar Pradesh government on education front.

A large majority of the illiterate population comprise Dalit women, with 76.24 per cent of dalit women being illiterate. The girl drop out rate among Dalit families is increasing with girl-children being forced to work as child labourers. More and more girl children from the Dalit communities are school drop-outs and working as child labourers. Dalit women are illiterate because they have less access to education, which is an inherent part of the caste system. There are not enough secure facilities for education, taking care of small children and they join the

Table 5

Literacy Rate among Scheduled Castes and Scheduled Tribes in Uttar Pradesh

Person	*Male*	*Female*										
SC	*1961*	*1971*	*1981*	*1991*	*1961*	*1971*	*1981*	*1991*	*1961*	*1971*	*1981*	*1991*
Total	7.1	10.2	15.0	21.1	12.8	17.1	24.8	32.3	1.1	2.5	3.9	8.3
Rural	6.3	9.1	13.5	19.4	11.6	15.8	23.2	30.7	0.7	1.7	2.7	6.6
Urban	19.0	23.4	27.4	33.6	28.5	33.0	38.5	43.9	7.7	11.8	14.3	21.5

(*Source:* Population Census, India, 1961, 1971, 1981 and 1991).

adults to add to the income of the family. The resultant impact was only 43 per cent of dalit children completed primary schooling compared to 58 per cent of non-dalits and only 42 per cent completed middle schooling compared to 63 per cent of non-dalit children in the respective age groups. There are thus, clear caste gaps in educational attainment, but they vary considerably by region in the state.

When coupled with higher drop out rates among SC girls at the primary (54.0) upper primary (73.2) educational level as compared to girls in general (46.0 and 65.1 respectively) and SC boys (46.3 and 64.3 respectively), the indications are that formal education schemes are not reaching or have sufficient, sustained impact on Dalit girls. A few tables given below reflects the picture.

But still social group disparities in literacy continue to be very large in the state. Though the right to primary education has been declared a fundamental right under newly-introduced Article 21-A of the Indian Constitution but in the case of dalits the situation seems to be grim. The Census only collects information on the general population and on shows that literacy among SCs and STs has increased at a higher rate for these groups compared to the general population, but the deficit is still substantial, particularly among women belonging to these social groups.

Enrollment Ratios

Enrollment among Muslims and SCs is much lower compared to other social groups, while children belonging to high castes groups enjoy nearly universal access to education. The largest differences were between SC girls in the lowest consumption quintile, who had an enrollment rate of only 30.6 per cent and upper castes boys belonging to the high castes in the highest consumption quintile who had an enrollment rate of 95.3 per cent, more than three times as high (World Bank Report, 2000/2001).

In the UNICEF survey, trends across castes groups indicate a lower enrollment for SC/ST and OBCs as compared to upper castes. This difference is much larger in rural than in urban areas. The OBCs show the lowest enrollment in both rural and urban areas. The difference between the enrollment of girls and boys is the largest in the backward castes, including that the

Table 6

Disparity in Literacy Rate between All and Scheduled Castes Population, 1961-1991

	Person	*Male*	*Female*									
SC	*1961*	*1971*	*1981*	*1991*	*1961*	*1971*	*1981*	*1991*	*1961*	*1971*	*1981*	*1991*
Total												
India	42.9	49.9	59.0	70.2	49.4	56.7	66.4	76.2	25.4	34.2	44.0	59.3
U.P.	40.1	47.0	55.1	63.6	46.9	54.3	64.1	72.2	15.7	23.7	27.8	41.5
India	48.4	54.0	52.3	73.5	53.4	59.2	68.4	78.4	27.5	39.0	47.0	63.1
U.P.	44.1	50.2	58.6	66.8	50.2	56.4	65.9	73.9	26.9	24.3	28.7	44.0
India	44.3	54.8	63.8	73.0	54.9	63.5	72.2	79.5	26.7	40.4	50.9	63.9
U.P.	46.1	53.6	59.7	67.4	57.5	63.4	70.3	76.3	24.5	35.4	40.3	52.7

(*Source:* Computed from population Census, India, 1961, 1971, 1981 and 1991).

greatest disadvantage is faced by girls in this group. This is followed by SC/STs and upper castes. The difference across all castes groups is again larger for rural than for urban areas (UP Development Report, 2007).

Level-wise enrollment ratios estimated from the UNICEF survey shows that both gross and net enrollment ratio are higher for urban than for rural areas, Being highest in the primary level, followed by the upper primary level further analysis of these rates shows that girls in all cases have lower gross and net enrollment ratios than boys, the difference being larger for rural than for urban areas. Among castes groups, enrollment ratios are the highest for the upper castes followed by the SC/STs and OBCs. The difference between the enrollment ratios of girls and boys is also the lowest for upper castes, but is high for SC/STs and OBCs (*Ibid*).

In the rural areas proportion of drop outs for all age groups are the highest among the dalits followed by the non-dalits. In the 11-13 age group for urban population, dalits show the highest proportion of drop outs followed by non-dalits.

The major trends from the analysis of the figures on enrollment, drop outs, proportion of never enrolled and retention rates are not encouraging.

The bias against the girl is reflected in every indicator of basic education both in rural and in urban areas. This neglect is, however, greater in rural than in urban areas. Among caste groups, girls face a greater disadvantage among the dalit as compared to the non-dalits. Though the disadvantage exists in all castes groups this advantage is further accentuated in rural areas as compared to urban areas in Uttar Pradesh.

The continuing prevalence of inequality is a major infringement of the rights of women and girls and it is also an important impediment to social and economic development.

Now, the question remains as to why dalit women have poor access to all resources as compared to non-dalit women. The persisting inequality in command over resources and human capabilities could be the result of a number of factors such as continuing process of exclusion and discrimination of SCs and limited impact of the pro-poor and anti-discrimination government policies.

The foregoing analysis reveals that the rate of female literacy was quite lower than that of males in almost all social groups. The females belonging to STs/SCs had lower rate of literacy as compared to others. The rate of female literacy has been on the rapid rise over time. Nevertheless, there has been a vast illiteracy in respect of ST/SC females as compared to others. A considerable gender and social inequality in educational attainments has existed in India, especially in rural areas. It has been found that in India, especially in rural areas, a greater female illiteracy in respect of STs/SCs has prevented females from accessing qualitative employment either in agriculture or non-agriculture. The proportion of females is quite significant in casual wage employment in the case of STs/SCs as compared to others.

Consequently, a greater incidence of poverty seems to be persistent among them. The ignorance, illiteracy and the incidence of poverty among STs/SCs appear to have ghastly affected the health status of them as compared to others. It can be concluded that the health status of the weaker sections of the society mainly depends on poverty reduction and educational attainments. Further, the reduction in poverty depends on accessibility to qualitative employment. Accessibility to qualitative employment is further determined by the level of educational attainments. It is, therefore, education that plays a "linchpin" role in reducing the incidence of poverty as well as improving the health status of these socially marginalised and economically disadvantaged sections of the society. A greater emphasis, therefore, should be accorded to provide qualitative education to the weaker sections of the society for their socio-economic well-being.

Access to Water, Sanitation and Basic Amenities

According to the data on electricity-based on Houses and households' amenities data, Census of India 2001, 55.8 per cent of the households in the country have access to electricity. The extent of attainments and deprivation among SCs, STs *vis- a-vis* the 'General category' with regard to availability of electricity. The percentage access in terms of General category, SC and ST households are 61.4 per cent, 44.3 per cent and 36.5 per cent respectively. Thus, SC and ST households have lesser coverage in terms of access to electricity.

Table 7

Percentage of Houses Having Access to Electricity

Census Year	*Total*	*General*	*SCs*
1991	42.4	48.1	28.1
2001	55.8	61.4	44.3

Though during the decade 1991-2001, the access to availability of electricity among the households of General, SCs and STs population increased by 13.3, 16.2 and 13.7 per cent points respectively, still both the SCs and STs households were still deprived in comparison to General households.

Taking villages with 50 per cent or more households of the village to be ST villages and 30 per cent or more households criteria for SC villages, the following table shows the distribution of SC, ST and Other villages by percentage of households having electricity which is zero per cent, greater than zero but less than 10 per cent and more than or equal to 10 was produced using Census data.

Drinking Water

Status of drinking water supply to Scheduled Castes and Scheduled Tribes are coupled with inadequacy of available data. According to the Report of Census of India 2001, out of total 53.69 million urban households, the SCs and STs household are 7.808 million and 2.328 million respectively. The details of distribution of urban households, SCs and STs households by source of drinking water and its location contained in the 2001 census Report are given as under.

In India 45.2 per cent households among the general population are having drinking water source within premises whereas only 27.0 per cent Scheduled Castes and 15.2 per cent Scheduled Tribes households have this facility. As regards availability of drinking water sources within premises at the state level, Punjab has 89.3 per cent households among the general population, followed byLakshadweep (86.2), Chandigarh (82.8) Delhi (79.3) and Kerala (74.5). Except Goa (62.1), Maharashtra (58.5) and Gujarat (53.7) states, in rest of the states, the percentage of household shaving drinking water source within premises is below 50 per cent. In case of Scheduled Castes households, the drinking water source within premises in Punjab, Delhi, Goa, Chandigarh and Kerala are 77.8 per cent, 56.9 per cent, 53.8 per cent, 53.0 per cent and 52.5 per cent households respectively. States like, Jammu and Kashmir, Haryana, Rajasthan, Bihar, Uttar Pradesh, West Bengal, Madhya Pradesh, Andhra Pradesh and all the seven North Eastern states having drinking water source within its premises are at below 50 per cent.

There are eighteen states where general households are having drinking water source away premises higher than the national average 14.4 percentage. Of these states, Manipur leads the table in which 27.4 per cent households are having drinking water source away from their premises followed by other states. In case of Scheduled Caste Population 34.2 per cent households are having drinking water source away from their premises in Orissa followed by Madhya Pradesh (28.3 per cent), Jharkhand (27.9 per cent), Karnataka (27.7 per cent), Rajasthan (27.5 per cent), Assam (26.1 per cent), Haryana (25.9 per cent), Tripura (23.6 per cent), Uttaranchal (22.9 per cent), Meghalaya (22.8 per cent), Andhra Pradesh and Manipur (22.4 per cent), Sikkim (21.7 per cent), Kerala (21.1 per cent), Chhattisgarh (21.0 per cent), Mizoram (20.7 per cent), Jammu and Kashmir (20.5 per cent), Bihar (20.0 per cent) and West Bengal (19.9 per cent). There are thirteen states where Scheduled Caste households are having drinking water source away from their premises were below the national average of 19.5 per cent. A total of 28.2 per cent households among the Scheduled Tribes are having drinking water source away from their premises in comparison to 19.5 per cent and 14.4 per cent among the Scheduled Castes and general households respectively. The above discussions indicate that the gap between General, Scheduled Castes and Scheduled Tribes population in relation to drinking water source is high.

Sanitation

As per the 2001 Census data, 23.7 per cent of Scheduled Castes households have latrine facility. Within their premises as compared to 42.3 per cent general households. Among the Scheduled Tribes only 17 per cent households have latrine facilities. There are eighteen states where Scheduled Castes households and sixteen states where Scheduled Tribes households have latrine facility below the national average at 36.4 per cent. Of these states, Orissa (7.6 per cent), Bihar (8.1 per cent), Chhattisgarh (9.6 per cent), Jharkhand (13 per cent),

Madhya Pradesh (14.7 per cent) are the states where only less than 15 per cent households have latrine facility among Scheduled Castes households. On the other hand, Orissa (3.6 per cent), Chhattisgarh (4.4 per cent), Madhya Pradesh (5.9 per cent) Jharkhand (6.5 per cent), Rajasthan (7.1 per cent), Andhra Pradesh (12.6 per cent) and Bihar (12.7 per cent) are the states where less than 15 per cent households are have latrine facility among STs household.

As regards, households with connectivity for waste-water outlet, 50.6 per cent of general households, 42.9 per cent of SCs households and 21.8 per cent of STs households have access to this facility in India. The percentage distribution of General, SCs and STs households having connectivity for wastewater outlet is given in table below:

Housing

Housing is one of the basic requirements for human survival. For a normal citizen, owning a house provides a significant economic security and dignity in society. For a shelterless person, possession of a house brings about a profound social change in his existence, endowing him with an identity, thus integrating him with his immediate social milieu. As per the 2001 Census, 57.7 per cent of general households have permanent houses, whereas 42.8 per cent SCs households and only 24.4 per cent STs households possessed permanent houses. The condition of housing for the Scheduled Castes in Orissa (19.5 per cent), Chhattisgarh (22.2 per cent), West Bengal (23.9 per cent), Bihar (27.9 per cent), Jharkhand (29.6 per cent), Madhya Pradesh (34.8 per cent), Uttar Pradesh (41.0 per cent) and all the North-Eastern states except Mizoram are below the national average. The condition of housing for STs is predominantly Adivasi states are pitiable. Chhattisgarh has only 8.2 per cent of their Adivasi households living in permanent houses followed by Jharkhand (11.1 per cent) and Orissa (12.9 per cent).

High Incidence of Poverty

The value of HPI[1] was estimated at 33.63 per cent for all social groups taken together at all India level. The HPI for SCs was estimated to be 41.47 per cent for all India which was much higher compared to non-SC/STs (31.34 per cent) The HPI revealed significant variation across the states with values ranging from 18.62 to 59.36 per cent. The level of deprivation was greatest in Bihar (59.36 per cent) followed by Uttar Pradesh (50.03 per cent), Orissa (47.66 per cent), Rajasthan (43.78 per cent) and Madhya Pradesh (43.68), as compared to all-India level (41.47 per cent).

The poverty situation is very serious among the Scheduled Caste communities. As per information available (1993-94) 37.4 per cent was residing below poverty line in India while proportion of Scheduled Caste residing below poverty line was more pronounced (48.9 per cent). Again in the state of Uttar Pradesh 59.2 per cent persons belonging to Scheduled Castes were residing below poverty line against 45.3 per cent of general population. Thus, 27.77 per cent of the poor were SCs and STs whereas their share of India's population was only 21.57 per cent. It was also highlighted that lower the poverty line, the greater the proportion of the SCs/ STs. The poverty has caused the Scheduled Castes under perpetual indebtedness and consequently forcing them to work as bonded labour. It shows that incidence of indebted households is more pronounced in the Scheduled Castes.

Box. 4

- As most Dalit women have to depend on wage labour employment to earn their livelihood, they have a poor economic base and higher unemployment rate. This is seen in terms of their lower standard of living and higher level of poverty.
- The 51 per cent of the Dalits in rural areas and 56.48 per cent in urban areas were below the poverty line (93-94). This means more than half of the dalits did not get enough to eat and therefore, suffered from malnutrition.
- Poverty levels were quite high among the agricultural labourers.
- Lower standard of housing quality and basic amenities. About 7 per cent of the Dalit households have no electricity, 90 per cent have no sanitation facilities.
- In rural areas they have to walk long distance to collect fodder, fuel materials and water, women have to shoulder more responsibilities and the other families have to survive on their meagre labour.

Below the Poverty Line

One of the measures to analyse the state of the poor persons is the Income Gap Ratio (IGR). It essentially measures the difference between the poverty line and the average consumption of the people living below the poverty line. Though the poverty ratio between the SCs, STs, and the total population varies significantly, the income gap ratio in most of the States is not significantly different between SC, ST and All-population. This is true both of rural and the urban areas. This would seem to suggest that while the chances of SCs and STs being poor are significantly higher than that of the total population in most of the states, the condition of the poor as reflected in the consumption pattern. It may further be mentioned that this assertion needs to be examined further in detail as it could have policy implications for anti-poverty programmes. Although there has been a reduction in the incidence of poverty among all sections of society including Scheduled Castes, the reduction was comparatively lesser in the case of Scheduled Castes in urban areas. Still about 37.36 per cent of Scheduled Caste population continues to live below the poverty line, as compared to 20.36 per cent of total population (GOI, 2005).

Work Participation Rates[2]

The Work Participation Rate at All India level is the highest among the Scheduled Tribes being 49.1 per cent, followed by Scheduled Castes (40.4 per cent) and general population (30.3 per cent). The picture is somewhat similar in all the States/UTs where the Scheduled Tribes have much higher WPR followed by the Scheduled Castes. Among states like Chhattisgarh, Madhya Pradesh, Orissa, Maharashtra and Gujarat that have significant proportion of Adivasi population have reported WPR of 50 per cent or more. Among the Scheduled Castes, Andhra Pradesh has recorded the largest WPR being 50.5 followed by Himachal Pradesh (48.9), Tamil Nadu (48.1) and Karnataka (46.3).

Although the Scheduled Tribes and the Scheduled Castes appear to be doing well in the employment front, an in-depth examination of the data in terms of the availability of work throughout the year and the type of activity provides clearer picture of the deprivation. While 80 per cent of the workers among the general population are main[3] workers, the share of main workers among Scheduled Castes is 73 per cent and that among Scheduled Tribes is 69 per cent. The situation is similar

Table 8

Workers Participation Rate

Social Groups	*Persons*			*Male*			*Female*		
	1991	*2001*	*2011*	*1991*	*2001*	*2011*	*1991*	*2001*	*2011*
Scheduled Castes	39.25	40.4	40.9	51.48	50.7	52.8	25.98	29.4	28.3
All Communities Except SC and STs	35.80	39.1	39.8	51.35	51.7	53.3	18.96	25.6	25.5
Total	**37.46**	—	—	**51.55**	—	—	**22.25**	—	—

(*Source:* Census Report, 1991, 2011, Government of India, Delhi).

in the states with Jharkhand having the largest proportion of marginal workers among the Scheduled Castes (41.8 per cent) and J and K and Orissa among the Scheduled Tribes (42.6 per cent).

The employment opportunities for SC women are very rare and, they are provided very meagre income just of subsistence level. Being a part of a traditional Hindu economic system, the SCs were till now to follow the occupational pursuits only permitted the Shastric traditions. Sizeable populations among SCs still follow these occupations, which are low in hierarchy of social status. A large number of SC women are engaged in so-called unclean occupations which are considered to be inferior in nature, such as scavenging. Because of their association with these occupations, these woman face exclusion and discrimination in the social and economic sphere. In what has been called India's "hidden apartheid," entire villages in many Indian states remain completely segregated by caste.

As noted by Ambedkar, "India is admittedly a land of villages and so long as the village system provides an easy method of marking out and identifying the untouchable, the untouchable has no escape from untouchability". Every village has its ghetto, and the ghetto is where the Dalits live. "Untouchability" relegates Dalits to a lifetime of discrimination, exploitation, and violence, including severe forms of torture perpetrated by state and private actors. Because of the castes into which they are born, Dalits are forced to work in "polluting" and degrading occupations and are subject to exploitative labour arrangements such as bonded-labour, migratory labour, and forced prostitution. Dalit children are vulnerable to trafficking and the worst forms of child labour in these and other areas. Dalits are also discriminated against in hiring and in the payment of wages by private employers.

Segregation between Dalits and non-Dalits is routinely practiced in housing, schools, and access to public and private sector services. Ninety-nine per cent of Dalit students are enrolled in government schools that lack basic infrastructure, classrooms, teachers, and teaching aids. Thorat concludes that "upper-caste" social behaviour in rural India is governed by the norms and codes of the traditional caste system. Consequently, Dalits are separated from other communities, denied freedom of movement, and otherwise ostracised from shared social activities.

Table 9

Percentage Distribution of Female Workers in Primary, Secondary and Tertiary Sectors of National Economy, by Social Groups

Sector	*Industrial Category*	*Total*	*SC*	*ST*	*Others*
I. Primary		81.19	85.93	93.41	76.66
	1. Cultivators	34.57	17.53	47.00	37.06
	2. Agriculture Labourers	44.24	66.52	44.21	37.01
	3. Livestock, Forestry, Fishing and Hunting	2.05	1.50	1.70	2.32
	4. Mining and Quarrying	0.33	0.38	0.50	0.27
II. Secondary		7.98	6.77	3.00	9.59
	5. (a) Manufacturing, Processing and Repairs in Household Industry	3.50	3.08	1.30	4.17
	5. (b) Manufacturing, Processing, Repairs in other than Household Industry	3.83	2.86	1.30	4.76
	6. Constructions	0.65	0.83	0.30	0.66
III. Tertiary		10.83	7.30	3.59	13.75
	7. Trade and Commerce	2.22	1.28	0.80	2.88
	8. Transport, Storage and Communication	0.33	0.32	0.10	0.42
	9. Other Services	8.28	5.79	2.69	10.45
Total (I+II+III)		**100.00**	**100.00**	**100.00**	**100.00**

(*Source:* Census Reports, 1991, Government of India, Delhi).

The practice of economic exclusion and discrimination is also evident in the differential pricing for Dalits in the sale and purchase of items ranging from raw materials to finished goods, and in Dalits being denied the ability to purchase land for both agricultural and non-agricultural use. Migration and the anonymity of the urban environment have in some cases resulted in upward occupational mobility for Dalits, but the majority continues to perform its traditional or polluting" functions. A lack of training and education, along with the discrimination faced in seeking other forms of employment, has kept alive these traditions and their hereditary nature. A majority of the Dalit rural work force subsists on the menial wages of landless agricultural labourers, earning less than US$1 per day. Those in urban areas work mostly in the unorganised sector. India's much touted system of reservations or constitutionally reserved quotas for scheduled castes assists less than one per cent of the Dalit population. In all forms of labour, women are consistently paid less than men, compounding the dual discrimination of caste and gender detailed below.

The SC and ST women, who worked as wage labour faced discrimination in wage earning particularly in urban areas. In 2000, the SC and ST women casual wage labour received daily wage earning of Rs 37 and Rs 34 respectively as compared to Rs 56 for non-SC/ST women, while the national average was Rs 42.

Health Status among SC Women

The National Health Policy-2002 (NHP, 2002) recognises that access to and benefits from, the public health system have been very uneven between the better endowed and the more vulnerable sections of society. Against this backdrop, it is then the principal objective of NHP-2002 to evolve a policy structure, which reduces these inequities and allows the disadvantaged sectors of society a fair access to public health services by various measures including separate schemes and increasing sectoral outlays in the primary health sector.

Box. 5

- Sex ratio of females in every thousand of males has declined from 957 in 1961 to 922 in 1991.
- Women take nutrient deficient food since most of them are below poverty line (a district level study in Maharashtra).

- Around 56 per cent of Dalit Women suffer from some form of anaemia, as compared to 49.1 per cent of non-SC/ST women. Similarly, a much higher percentage of Dalit Women are under-nourished as compared to their non-SC/ST female counterparts (2nd National Family Health Survey, 1998-99).
- With significant cuts in government expenditure for public health services, on which the majority of Dalit women continue to rely, and commercialisation and privatisation of public health-care services, poor Dalit women are being forced to fend for themselves either to live with ill-health or to enter into health-related debt. This has the chain effect of affecting the health status of Dalit children and their families, besides lowering the income generating capacity of Dalit women.

Health and medical care services are not only inadequate but also unequally distributed across different parts of the country. Accessibility to health and medical care services is also not even across different sections of the society in rural areas. As the data are not available for rural areas separately, the health status of social groups can be seen in terms of few indicators at the all India level. The data presented in Table 10 below shows that the proportion of women accessing the reproductive health-care services such as family planning, antenatal checkups was lower in the case of STs/SCs as compared to others. The proportion of women suffering from nutritional deficiency, children undernourished, women and children with anaemia was quite higher in respect of STs/SCs as compared to others. The fertility rates were quite higher in the case of STs/SCs than that of others. The higher fertility rates are generally associated with more health risks and problems and hence the women belonging to STs/SCs are more likely suffer from ill-health. It has also been found that Infant Mortality Rate (IMR) and Child Mortality Rate (CMR) per thousand live births were quite significant in the case of ST/SC as compared to others. This clearly shows that the health status of STs/SCs is not satisfactory as compared to others. This can partly be attributed to a greater incidence of poverty experienced by them and the persistence of ignorance, illiteracy among them.

Table 10

Health Status among Social Groups in India, 1998-99

Health Indicators	*All*	*SC*	*Others*
Married women using a family planning method (per cent)	48.2	44.6	53.5
Any Antenatal checkups (per cent)	65.4	61.1	71.3
Women with nutritional deficiency (per cent)	35.8	42.1	30.5
Women with Anaemia (per cent)	57.8	56.0	47.6
Total fertility rate (per cent)	**2.85**	**3.15**	**2.66**

(*Source:* National Family Health Survey (NFHS) 1998-99).

Total Fertility Rate

At the National level the Total Fertility Rate (TFR) is higher among SC and STs as compared to others. In the states of Bihar, Haryana, Jammu and Kashmir, M.P. Rajasthan, Sikkim and Uttar Pradesh the TFR among SCs is more than the average TFR among SCs at national level. It is further observed that in the States of Bihar, Delhi, Gujarat, Haryana, Jammu and Kashmir, Madhya Pradesh, Sikkim, and Uttaranchal the TFR among SCs is greater than three children whereas it is more than four in Rajasthan and Uttar Pradesh.

The TFR among the Schedule Tribe population in the states shows that in the states of Assam, Bihar, Jharkhand and Sikkim it is less than the average TFR of the state as well as the TFR for others. In the states of Jammu and Kashmir and M.P. the TFR for STs is more than three and it is more than four in Rajasthan, Uttar Pradesh and Uttaranchal.

Neo-natal, Infant and Child Mortality Rate

In 1998-99, the infant mortality rate among SCs was 83 and among STs were 84.2 against others of 67.6 per 1000 live births. According to NFHS-II data, the neo-natal mortality, infant mortality, child mortality and under-five mortality is higher for SCs and STs at all India level compared with total mortality rates and mortality rates for others respectively.

The National Rural Health Mission (2005-12) seeks to provide effective healthcare to rural population throughout the country with special focus on 18 states, which have weak public health indicators and/or weak infrastructure. It has key components provisions of a female health activist in each village. But the selection criteria for these female health personnel are not pro-SCs/STs. The minimum criteria of education standards do not suit for SCs/STs especially in under-served and un-served areas.

Table 11

Basic Maternal Health Parameters among Scheduled Castes and Others

	SCs	*Total*
ANC Check up	61.1	65.4
Percentage Institutional Delivery	26.8	33.6
Percentage of women with anaemia	56.0	51.8
Percentage of children, underweight for their age	53.5	47.0

(*Source:* National Family Health Survey (NFHS) 1998-1999).

Institutional Delivery Indicator

Comparing the institutional delivery at the country level, it is observed that indicators for both SCs and STs are less than others. As it is seen in the table given above, anaemia among SC and ST women is more compared to the women of other communities. It is also seen that at national level the full vaccination among SC and ST infants is less compared to others. At national level, anaemia among SC and ST children is more than that prevalent among others. At national level, the unmet need for limiting is more for SCs compared with unmet need for limiting among others. The same is true for unmet need among SCs with regard to spacing. It is observed that at an all India level the unmet need for limiting among ST population is less compared to unmet need for limiting among others whereas the same is not true with regard to unmet need for spacing.

It was also observed that TB generally prevails among SCs and minorities. It is now well-established that TB can be deadly when occurring in a patient of HIV/AIDs, especially due to the advent of new and drug resistant forms of the disease. Much more research is needed to understand the actual extent of prevalence of HIV/AIDs in the vulnerable Dalit/Adivasi populations. The scenario for them does not look very bright, especially due to the fact that these populations have the least access to even basic health-care.

Nutritional Status can be measured by both, anthropometric measures and clinical tests. The indicator used in this paper to assess the nutritional status of women, is the Body Mass Index or BMI.[4] BMI is an effective and widely used indicator of nutritional status. In this state 36 per cent women suffer from Chronic Energy Deficiency (CED),[5] more so in rural than in urban areas. On the whole nutritional status of rural women is poorer than urban women. Non-dalit women have highest BMI of 20.6 while dalits have BMI ranging between 19-20 kg per m^2.

Anaemia is among the most widespread deficiency diseases in India, predominantly among women and children. Anaemia has a detrimental effect on women's health and may lead to enhanced risk of maternal and pre-natal mortality. According to the UP Development Report 2007, over 49 per cent of women in Uttar Pradesh had some form of anaemia. Urban women had a slightly lower prevalence of anaemia than rural women. As compared to upper castes who showed the lowest prevalence of anaemia with proportion of 45.2 per cent, the SCs women had higher prevalence of 52 per cent.

Reproductive health is of great importance in the case of women since it has a bearing on the overall life expectancy of women, especially in a country like India where material mortality is quite high. Reproductive health includes issues like the level of antenatal care preceding births, vaccination of pregnant females against tetanus, extent of post-partum checkups, etc.

As compared to SC women the upper castes women received the highest number of antenatal checkups. Antenatal care increased with increasing level of economic status of households, and also with increasing level of education of the females.

Vaccination of pregnant females against tetanus is carried out under the RCH Programme in order to prevent the incidence of tetanus in both the mother and the infant. It was seen that as 44 per cent females in rural areas had not been vaccinated against tetanus, while the figure in urban areas was much lower at 17 per cent. Three quarters of the births in urban areas had been immunised against tetanus, as compared to 46 per cent in rural areas. The percentage of vaccination among the SC women is much lower than the upper caste women.

The percentage of institutional deliveries increased from 11 in 1992-93 to 17 percentage in 1998 (NFHS, 1998-99). The percentage of births that took place in medical institutions was about five times higher in urban areas (35.4 per cent) than in rural areas. Trained personnel provide assistance to less than one-fourth of the total deliveries in the State. (IIPS 2001) Three fourths of the deliveries take place in unhygienic conditions at home. It is because of this that Uttar Pradesh is marked by a very high degree of reproductive morbidity and mortality.

Infant Mortality and Child Mortality

Infant and child mortality are critical indicators of health delivery, especially as excessive child mortality is associated with easily preventable causes—poor nutritional status of the mother, pre-natal and post-natal care, sanitation and hygiene. The state's infant and child mortality rates have shown significant improvement over the years but there are large differences between sectors, social groups and regions. The IMR across social groups shows the highest figures for SCs, followed by OBCs and STs. In the case of child mortality rate, SCs are followed by STs, OBCs, and upper castes. Thus, upper castes have lower rates of infant and child mortality than other social groups. A number of proximate factors are responsible for the high mortality among infants and children in the state. These include the poor nutritional status of expectant mothers, absence of proper antenatal care, unhygienic conditions under which children are delivered, diarrhoeas, respiratory and other diseases affecting infants and children.

Table 12

Infant Mortality Rate and Child Mortality Rate in Uttar Pradesh, 1998-99

	IMR	*CMR*
Rural	101.3	43.5
Urban	65.3	27.3
Male	94.8	28.8
Female	96.0	53.4
Social groups		
SC	110	54.1
ST	83.3	45.0
OBC	105.7	40.8
Others	82.3	32.5

Strongly ingrained gender basis in four of males ensure that India has all-time low female to male ratios. When compared by poor multinational health due to poverty and systematic violence, the ratio of SC women to men stood at 922:1000 in 1991 as conformed to 928:1000 for men SC women to men. Rural disparities are greatest 926:1000 for SCs as compared to 941: 1000 for non-SCs indicating lesser enjoyment of the rights to life and health among rural dalit women.

So far the state of Uttar Pradesh is concerned, Anaemia is the biggest killer of girls and women and is responsible for the high Maternal Mortality Rate (MMR). The state of affairs in Lucknow in no different, although slightly better than other parts of UP. According to health department sources, 50 per cent of women in the age group of 15-49 in the state are anaemic, 58 per cent of breast-feeding women have been found to be having haemoglobin level less than the prescribed 12 units. The surprising fact is that 46 per cent of the women in high income group and 45 per cent women in urban area have also been found to be anaemic due to various reasons.

Box. 6

- Sex ratio of females in every thousand of males has declined from 957 in 1961 to 922 1999.
- Women take nutrient deficient food since most of them are below poverty line (a district level study in Maharastra).
- Around 56 per cent of Dalit Women suffer from some form of anemia, as compared to 49.1 per cent of non-SC/ST women. Similarly, a much higher percentage of Dalit Women are under-nourished as compared to their non-SC/ST female counterparts (Second National Family Health Survey, 1998-99).
- With significant cuts in government expenditure for public health services, on which the majority of Dalit women continue to rely, and commercialisation and privatisation of public health-care services, poor Dalit women are being forced to fend for themselves either to live with ill-health or to enter into health-related debt. This has the chain effect of affecting the health status of Dalit children, and their families, besides lowering the income generating capacity of Dalit women.

MMR ratio (death/lakh live births) of India is 301 and of UP 517, as per the sample survey conducted by the registrar, Government of India. Nearly 77,000 material deaths are reported per year. Around 211 women die every day, of which 42 death are due to anaemia during pregnancy. UP figures among the worst performing states of the country. There are over 56 lakh births every year in the state, and around 28,000 pregnant mothers die every year, which means that out of total women dying in India during pregnancy, one-third are from UP.

Significantly, the MMR has come down in UP to 517 from 707 in 1995. Numbers of girls married before the age of 18 years has reduced from 64 per cent to 53 per cent. As per the District Level Household Survey (DLHS) of the state released earlier this year, the institution deliveries have increased from 23 per cent in 2006 to 25 per cent in 2008, because of the *Janani Suraksha Yojana* (JSY). Clearly, the situation has improved but the MMR is not dropping at a faster rate. It appears rather explicitly from this analysis that the Dalits in India and Uttar Pradesh are excluded from the basics of health facilities. This is particularly true of childhood survival, nutritional status, child health-care and maternal health-care. In spite of an improvement in survival levels, infant and childhood mortality among SCs is unacceptably high. Besides, over one-third of SC women suffer from chronic energy deficiency, as seen from the BMI.

Conclusion

Recognising the special problems of the group, the government has over the years, continuously introduced policies and programmes to build their human capacities and capabilities and the resultant impact is that there has been some improvement in the HDI, HPI and their various components, since the relative improvement in the case of dalit women has been by and large, lower as compared to non-dalit women, the disparity between them and non-dalit women has not declined substantially enough to bridge the gap and bring ratio closer to equality. As a result, the situation of dalit women with respect to all indicators of well-being such as agricultural land, education, health etc., is at much lower level as compared to non-dalit women, despite the inclusionary measures of the State.

References

1. HPI is a measure to assess the level of deprivation among a given social group with reference to Infant Mortality Rate, Poverty Ratio (Head Count Ratio), Health Status and Nutritional Status.
2. Work Participation Rate' (WPR) is defined as the percentage of total workers to total population.
3. According to Census definition a worker is categorised as 'Main Worker' if she/he has worked for six months or more, otherwise she/he is considered to be a 'Marginal Worker.'
4. BMI (Body Mass Index) is the ratio of weight (in kilograms) to the square of weight (in square meters). The grade of nutrition is determined by the value of the ratio, which indicates under-nutrition, if the value is below 18.5; normal status between 18.5 to 25 and overweight status above 25.
5. A BMI below 18.5 kg/m² indicates chronic energy deficiency (CED), caused by a highly deficient diet.

Bibliography

Agarwal, S. 1999. Genocide of women in Hinduism. Jabalpur: Sudrastan Books. Available online: http://www.dalitstan.org/books/.

Census of India, 1991, 1994. Series 1, India, Part-II A (ii) General Population Table, Delhi: Controller, Department of Publications.

Census of India 2001, 2004. Provisional Population Tables, Paper I of 2001 Delhi: Controller, Department of Publications.

Census of India 2001, 2004. Primary Census Abstract, Total Population, Tables: A-5, Delhi, Controller, Department of Publications.

Government of India. 2001. Department of Women and Child Development, New Delhi: Ministry of Human Resource Development.

Dreze, J. and H. Gazdar. 1996. 'Uttar Pradesh: The Burden of Inertia', in Jean Dreze and Amartya Sen, *Indian Development: Selected Regional Perspectives*, New Delhi. Oxford University Press.

Government of India. 2008. Inclusive Growth: Eleventh Five Year Plan—2007-2012, Vol. I, Planning Commission.

Government of India, 1978. Draft Sixth Five Year Plan, New Delhi, Planning Commission.

Government of India, 1988. Draft National Perspective Plan for Women 1988-2000, Mimeo, New Delhi: Department of Women and Child Development.

Government of India, 2000. National Family Health Survey-2, Mumbai: Indian Institute of Population Studies (IIPS).

Government of India, 2003. Annual Report 2002-03, New Delhi Ministry of Social Justice and Empowerment.

Government of India, 2004. Economic Survey 2003-04, New Delhi: Ministry of Finance, Economic Division.

Government of India, 1975. Towards Equality: Report of the Committee on the Status of Women in India, New Delhi: Department of Social Welfare, Ministry Education and Social Welfare.

Government of India, 1993. National Family Health Survey–2 (NFHS 92-93), Mumbai:Indian Institute of Population Studies (IIPS).

Government of India, 1998. Ministry of Welfare (renamed as Ministry of Social Justice and Empowerment on May 25, 1998), Government of India, Annual Report 1995-1996.

Hardinge, S., Subjectivity. 1992. Experience and Knowledge: An Epistemology for/of Rainbow Coalition Politics, *Development and Change*, Vol. 23, No. 3.

Human Rights Watch. *Violence Against "Untouchables Growing*, Says Report. Indian Government fails to Prevent Massacres, Rapes, and Exploitation. Available online at:http://hrw.org/english/docs/1999/04/14/india879.htm.

Narula. S. 1999. Broken People: Caste Violence Against India's "Untouchables." London: Human Rights Watch.

Government of India, 2004. National Crimes Records Bureau, Crimes in India Report (2004), Tables 7.4 and 7.7 News Archives.http://www ambedkar.org.

4 Process of Inclusion: Concepts and Trends

The idea of making a gift of fundamental rights to every individual is no doubt very laudable. The question is how to make them effective? The prevalent view is that once rights are enacted in a law then they are safeguarded. This again is an unwarranted assumption. As experience proves, rights are protected not by laws, but by the social and moral conscience of society.[1]

—Ambedkar in 1943

Social Inclusion: Concept

As a concept Social Inclusion, generally understood, is a strategy to combat Social Exclusion. The utility of the concept social inclusion will depend on the extent and degree to which it successfully deals with social exclusion and the extent to which it promotes social cohesion in a society that is fractured along numerous fault lines. In this conceptualisation, social inclusion can provide a coherent critique to the multiple forms of social injustices and the concomitant of institutional policies and practices.

Social Inclusion forces us to go beyond the realm of formal equality and substantive equality which is characterised by discrimination, exclusion and inequality. Social inclusion begins from the premise that it is democratic citizenship that is at risk when a society fails to develop the talents and capacities of all its members. The move to social inclusion is eroded when the rights of minorities are not respected and accommodated. For social inclusion there is no contradiction between democratic citizenship and differentiated citizenship (where people can hold dual and even multiple loyalties).

Social cohesion is clearly not the same as social inclusion. The former does not necessarily ensure the latter, for multiple forms of exclusion can exist in a cohesive society. Nonetheless, the crucial questions persist: cohesion around what vision and inclusion to what? Are we talking about assimilation? Is this a new way of managing state minority relation? As Kymlicka and Norman point out, there have been major disputes both about the legitimacy of assimilation as a way of eliminating differences, and about multiculturalism as the official recognition of differences (1999). Social inclusion recognises that identity formation is a complex phenomenon. For example, identity formation and social cohesion of immigrant groups in the urban environment is mediated by their histories in the sending countries, state in the host country and its multicultural practices, and is also mediated by the reality of discrimination and exclusion.

Social Inclusion is precisely about this democratisation of democracy. By developing a new way of approaching old problems, by positing a radically different conception of citizenship and community, by arguing for new measures of accountability, by providing the impetus for the emergences of new modes of evaluations of public policies, by arguing for increased representation and participation by marginalised groups and above all by encouraging the development of skills talents and capacities of all social inclusion will democratise democracy.

The growth of the multicultural nation therefore, is producing the conditions for the emergence of a new sense of social inclusion, what David Held calls a "cosmopolitan democracy" (Held, 1995) that recognises differences, respects differences and that argues for substantive equality and not just formal equality.

So, inclusion strives for a nation in which every one live with purpose, dignity and satisfaction. Inclusion describes what Robert Kennedy, called our desired "bond of common fate".

Indicators-based on social inclusion would not be in terms of wage and income only, but in a variety of dimension including health, education, housing, skills, advancement and opportunities. Social inclusion has considerable potential to improve our understanding of social issue and policies.

Experience of (Social) Inclusion in Different Parts of the World

In 1999, the Prime Minister of United Kingdom Tony Blair, in his speech, spelt out a vision of social inclusion that promoted advancement in the labour market, improved education outcomes, reduced health inequalities, higher qualities housing, safe neighbourhoods and importantly the reducing income inequalities.

Like UK the rest of the Europe and many other well of nations used social inclusion as an over-arching framework for addressing a myriad of social policy including income inequalities, skill levels, education, health inequalities, housing affordability etc. The precise boundary of the concept are far from determinants and differently defined by countries but at the core, social inclusion involves including every one in social institutions and relations in way that matter for well-being.

Throughout the last two decades, the international development actors have witnessed a growing concern about poverty, marginalisation and various forms of deprivation. Two concepts stand out prominently in this regard: Human Development and Social Inclusion. Both are not substitutive but complementary, addressing in-depth specific aspects of poverty understood as a multidimensional challenge. What unites the two is their focus on people which is put at the centre of the policy focus in an attempt to achieve the ultimate goal of improving their opportunities and realising their capacities.

Let us define social inclusion first. The term, while appearing frequently over the last few years, has yet to be well-defined. Although, attempts have been made to define social inclusion in ways that can be measured.

According to Freiler's notion social inclusion, is a process that encourages the development of talents, skills and capacities necessary for children and youth to participate in the social and economic mainstream of community life (2001). What makes a discourse on social inclusion more compelling than one on exclusion are the following:

- Social inclusion is the political response to exclusion. Most analyses of racism and sexism for example, focus on the removal of systemic barriers to effective participation and focus on equality of opportunity.

These analyses tend to be essentialist and consequently are unable to develop a comprehensive vision that cuts across all the areas of injustice. Social inclusion is about more than the removal of barriers. It is about the comprehensive vision that includes all.

- Social inclusion is pro-active. It is about anti-discrimination. It is not about the passive protection of rights, it is about the active intervention to promote rights and it confers responsibility on the state to adopt policies that will ensure social inclusion of all members of society (not just formal citizens, or consumers or taxpayers or clients).
- Social inclusion, by virtue of the fact that it is both process and outcome can hold governments and institutions accountable for their policies. The yardstick by which to measure good government therefore becomes the extent to which it advances the well-being of the most vulnerable and the most marginalised in society.
- Social inclusion is about advocacy and transformation. It is about the political struggle and the political will to remove barriers to full and equitable participation in society by all.
- Social inclusion is embracing. It posits a notion of democratic citizenship as opposed to formal citizenship. Democratic citizens possess rights and entitlements by virtue of their being a part of the polity not by virtue of their formal status (as immigrants, refugees, or citizens).

As it has been noted above that in recent years social inclusion has been promoted especially by the European Union (EU), which defines it as a 'process which ensures that those at risk of poverty and social exclusion gain the opportunities and resources necessary to participate fully in economic, social and cultural life and to enjoy a standard of living and well-being that is considered normal in the society in which they live'.

Hence, social inclusion is understood as both a relative concept where exclusion can only be judged by comparing the circumstances of some individuals (or groups or communities) relative to others, in a given place and at a given time; and as a normative concept which places emphasis on the individual's right of 'having a life associated with being a member of a community'.

The United Nations concept on social inclusion speaks as follows:

> "An inclusive society must be based on respect for all human rights and fundamental freedoms, cultural and religious diversity, social justice and the special needs of vulnerable and disadvantaged groups, democratic participation and the rule of law".

It is to note that the concept of social inclusion is based on subjective understanding of what 'right' or 'fair' is. This notion or understanding differs across countries, societies and individuals. Thus, there is no uniformity in the use of the term social inclusion. There are also certain issues related to it. For some, inclusion and exclusion works simultaneously. An individual or a society may be included in one desired area but may be excluded in another important area. This may be as a consequence of the inclusion or as a norm etc.

In order to achieve these rights, inclusion policies have to address institutional inefficiencies, which derive from exclusionary acts by agents based on power and social attitudes and result in multiple disadvantages-based on gender, age, ethnicity, location, economic, education, health status or disability, etc., as seen in the previous chapters. Social inclusion policies correct negative outcomes of policies, be it intentional (systematic discrimination) or unintentional ones (failure to recognise differential impact of policies on individuals or groups).

The concept of social inclusion complements that of human development in many ways. Both are people-focussed and go beyond material well-being. Human development stresses the significance of education, access to adequate social services (health and education in particular), environmental sustainability, guarantees for basic political freedom, gender equality and respect of citizens' rights.

Social Inclusion: Trends

Process of Inclusion: Indian Experience (Pedagogy and Praxis Level)

As noted in the preceding chapters, we saw how the exclusionary processes have been stumbling blocks on the road to development. Now, the question is how do we define social inclusion in Indian context and whether something has been done for the inclusion of these excluded groups at the level of pedagogy and praxis over these years? In actual how far these efforts have been instrumental in translating these attempts into a reality. Moreover, how to develop inclusive policy for different groups suffering from exclusion on the lines of caste, ethnicity, religion and gender is an issue, which is being currently discussed by the policy makers in India. All these need to be examined carefully and seriously.

Inclusive Debate

One of the basic assumptions underlying the inclusive debate is that poverty is not defined as purely material, but rather as having symbolic aspects such as lack of voice, stigma, and exclusion (Lister, 2005). The goal of inclusive debate is to act in contrast to exclusion (Lister *et al.*, 2000). Inclusive growth demands that all social groups have equal access to the services, provided by the State and equal opportunity for upward economic and social mobility. It is also necessary to ensure that there is no discrimination against any section of our society. In India, certain social groups such as the women, SCs, STs, OBCs and Minorities have historically been disadvantaged and vulnerable. Then there are certain other groups which may be discriminated against and which suffer from handicaps.

Inclusive Development in India (At the Praxis): A Historical Perspective

Conceptual perception of inclusive development has been very much in the Indian Society since ages. It can be traced back in the post-Vedic era in a couplet of post-vedic literature: "*Om sarve bhavantu sukhinah, sarve santu nir-aamayaah, sarve bhadraanni pashyanti,ma kaschid dukh bhag bhavet*" reflecting a harmonious model of co-existence in the society. It was later practised as *sarvodaya* by Gandhiji. Focus on poor man (*daridranarayan*) constructive programmes, eleven vows, trusteeship and village *swaraj* was the *summum bonum* of inclusive development, which emerged through experiments in Phoenix, Tolstoy Farm and Satyagraha Ashram during freedom struggle of apartheid in Africa and India from the British discriminatory colonial rule respectively. Vinoba Bhave emphasised on class co-ordination for inclusive development and took up this issue through *Bhoodan* and *Gramdan*. But it was not very much clear among them, that harmonious model may not work in heterogeneous class divided society. However,

Dada Dharmadhikari, an important ideologue in Gandhian folds had clearly advocated that co-ordination is almost impossible if there is existence of classes. There is need to dissolve classes for inclusive development. Scattered experiences of Gandhian practices during life time and after, have positive suggestion for inclusive development strategies in pockets but a social scientists can hardly generalise these experiments (Diwakar, 2000). The results of these experiments need to be reflected, practised and modified, time and again. But do the marginalised groups find any space among such historical formulations?

In modern terminologies Inclusive Development refers to an approach of development from inside through effective partnership of people (World Bank, 2000) in order to include more than what is done at the moment. As Amartya Sen observes: "Freedom as central feature of development emerges powerfully from the internal views. These unrestrained voices deserve attention not only of scholars and academics but also of government, international institutions, business communities, labour organisations and civil society across the world. This is a marvelous concept of development seen from inside."

Rights-based Development

The Independent India was much concern about the marginal mass. The architecture of Indian Constitution, Dr Ambedkar, on November 25, 1949, in an address to members of the Constituent Assembly, declared:

> We must make our political democracy a social democracy as well. Political democracy cannot last unless there lies at the base of it social democracy. What does social democracy mean? It means a way of life which recognises liberty, equality, and fraternity as the principles of life...
>
> On the 26th of January 1950,

We are going to enter into a life of contradictions. In politics we will have equality and in social and economic life we will have inequality. In politics, we will be recognising the principle of one man-one vote and one vote-one value. In our social and economic life, we shall by reason of our social and economic structure, continue to deny the principle of one man-one value.

There has been an effort to evolve a rights-based approach to development. The adoption of human rights framework means the need to respect the rights and entitlements of all. It emphasises the indivisibility of civil, political, economic, cultural and social rights. Thus, beginning with the 1940s there evolved strong theoretical, institutional and value premises for the pursuit of strategy of development which is inclusive in nature. But these premises are seriously threatened and a process of development with pervasive process of exclusion has emerged to the forefront since early 1980s in the form of liberalisation.

The arguments in support of remedies against discrimination that are mainly-based on historical denial of equal opportunity, due to practices of caste and untouchability-based exclusion and discrimination toward untouchables and seeking provision for equal rights, safeguards against violation of equal rights and strategies for equal access or opportunity through reservations or affirmative action.

Recent years have witnessed an upsurge of interest in strategies of inclusion ranging from affirmative action to mandatory reservations. The proliferation of democracy in the last few decades has led to the emergence of a consensus that within democratic systems one special group should not monopolise political power or governance. This has led to awareness that creating political systems that addresses the needs of various groups, especially those that are marginalised on the basis of race, religion, and ethnic background, is necessary for equity, fairness and political stability. (Hasan, 2009)

At the theoretical level, scholars and activists have questioned the dominant conceptions of liberal democracy, which is typically committed to the 'politics of ideas',[2] by rethinking the means and ends of the political process. Collective claims made by hitherto excluded groups test the limits of conventional political discourses and power structures in favour of an alternative 'politics of presence'.[3] The new politics of presence responds to a broad sense of ethnic, racial, gender and minority exclusions by questioning the separation between ideas and identity. These developments have led to a greater emphasis on inclusion and a greater focus on the political process of inclusion. Now, the question arises as to why there is need to focus on politics of inclusion. The reasons are:

(1) The increased presence of historically excluded groups is a sign of inclusiveness of public institutions, and this, in

turn, is an important marker of the fairness of democratic regimes; (2) Greater inclusion of excluded groups in decision-making institutions would provide these bodies with the presence of people, who can articulate the interests of these sections, which may otherwise be neglected by default.

Inclusive growth demands that all social groups have equal access to the services provided by the State and equal opportunity for upward economic and social mobility. It is also necessary to ensure that there is no discrimination against any section of our society. In India, certain social groups such as the SCs, STs, OBCs and Women, Minorities have historically been disadvantaged and vulnerable.

Locating at the global contours of development, India is also one of the few countries in the post-colonial world that took up the challenge of building an inclusive democracy, in a highly diverse, multi-cultural, multi-lingual and multi-religious society. The establishment of democracy and universal adult suffrage in a hierarchical society, characterised by unprecedented social inequality, deprivation and oppression was undoubtedly a revolutionary principle, a bold experiment in political affairs, perhaps the most significant in any country. Nearly sixty years after independence, India remains a major success story in respect of democracy and social inclusion. This is largely due to the primacy given to equality and social justice as the cardinal principles of contemporary political life. It was agreed that procedural democracy and formal equality were not enough to bring about substantive outcomes in terms of empowerment, justice and equality.

At an empirical level, political changes around the world have stimulated reflection on questions of exclusion of marginalised groups and ways of redressing this imbalance. Special efforts have been made to include those previously excluded in government and legislatures. In the realm of formal politics, the modes of representation are increasingly dominated by descriptive representation and participation in decision-making. Overall, it is widely believed that a more balanced representation in governance would lead to better decision-making and policy priorities that reflect people's concerns (*Ibid*).

The freedom struggle and the social reform movements prepared some ground for social equality, in the sense that they delegitimised the most rigorous forms of oppression that characterised Hindu society. The policy of providing benefits to the historically disadvantaged peoples, which was established through several provisions in the Constitution, played an important part in advancing this agenda. The term 'disadvantaged' refers collectively to all three groups officially designated as backward: the SCs, the STs and the Other Backward Classes (OBCs) (minorities are not officially included among the disadvantaged). These three groups were targetted for special advantages and protection under Article 46, and Directive Principles of State Policy.

These programmes permit departure from formal equality[4] for the purpose of eliminating social discrimination (Galanter, 1984). The constitutional understanding of equality is explicitly aimed at securing substantive equality for previously subordinated groups, and is designed to discourage merely formal understandings of equality that have often been used to oppose affirmative actions. Substantive[5] equality is not defined, but the Directive Principles give a great deal of attention to its advancement and the Fundamental Rights are themselves specified in a way that makes room for affirmative action programmes designed to advance the material situation of the disadvantaged groups. Thus, Article 15 states: 'Nothing in this article... shall prevent the State from making any special provision for the advancement of any socially and educationally backward classes of citizens or for the SCs and the STs. In short the framers of our Constitution understood the goal of equality in terms of an end to systematic hierarchy and discrimination-based on caste. The focus consequently is not on difference but rather on social disadvantage. Substantive equality is directed at eliminating institutional and systemic discrimination against disadvantaged groups, which effectively undermines their full and equal participation in society.

And as a result over the years, many policies and programmes were enacted by the State. But this act of the State had to face major arguments, debates and controversies. Most often these arguments are stated in terms of individual rights versus group rights; equality of opportunity versus equality of results; merits versus efficiency; and affirmative action versus mandatory reservations. The key issues in these debates, both for the opponents and supporters, centre on the relevance of caste, but these policies are rarely questioned on the conception of disadvantage and rarely locate the debate in the context of the social structure as it has evolved to its present stage. (Hasan, 2009).

Finally, it is useful to distinguish between reservations and affirmative action. It is important to note here that affirmative action does not necessarily mean reserving quotas in jobs for the disadvantaged sections like the lower caste or minorities, but taking these identities as a factor for preferential treatment, for example, in college and university admission and employment policies. Starting from different vantage points, both are mechanisms of preferential treatment to facilitate inclusion of disadvantaged groups. Both sets of measures address the recognition that certain patterns of disadvantage and exclusion require measures to promote equality of opportunity.

It is well-known that the government has assumed a wide ranging responsibility for the welfare of the SCs and STs. The Indian system of positive discrimination is unique, both in terms of the benefits involve and in the magnitude of the groups eligible for them. (Dushkin, 1967). Policies for the lower castes in turn fall broadly into two types:

(1) Anti-discriminatory or protective measures, and (2) Developmental and empowering measures.

Various policy initiatives have taken up to bring the deprived masses into the mainstream of development through inclusive development packages. To ensure the development programmes on empowerment of women, a national policy for the empowerment of women was also introduced in the same year (2001) to bring about changes, advancement and empowerment of women. Women access to equality, freedom and social justice was envisaged in all spheres of activities and social life. In addition to equal access and equal opportunities to women the need for changing societal attitudes and community practices is indispensible for mainstreaming a gender perspective in the development. Constitution of India lays these principles as the very basis of development policy and could be seen in retrospect as the beginning of rights-based approach to development which is inclusive in nature. The concern for human rights framework means the need to respect the rights and entitlements of all.

Social Exclusion and Policy Framework: A Historical Review

As mentioned earlier, the efforts for the social inclusion of excluded groups took place at various junctures of history, but it was only in the nineteenth century that some sort of legal framework was initiated by the British and some of the rulers of the Indian provinces which can be analysed into two parts, pre-Ambedkar efforts as well as efforts made by Ambedkar and the actual policy initiations by the State.

Pre-Ambedkar Efforts

Prior to Ambedkar apart from British, the rulers of Indian provinces, like Baroda, Travancore, Kolhapur, Cochin realised the need to introduce educational and employment rights in nineteenth—and twentieth century India for the non-Brahmins. The establishment of British rule in India introduced a western system of education, which was based on the principle of open access and universalistic criterion of admission. The Woods Despatch perhaps could be considered the first of its kind in the process of British efforts to impart education among the socially discriminated sections. In 1885, Sir Richard Temple, the governor of Bombay proposed to reserve fifty percent of free scholarships for Muslim and backward Hindu castes, because it was felt that the scholarships-based on sole criterion of merit would perpetuate the Brahmin monopoly on the education system (Jain, 1990). In Madras, a system of communal rotation was introduced to remove inequalities of representation in the services. Similarly, in Mysore order for removing inequalities in the State services were issued in 1895 that certain reservation of posts should be earmarked for all communities except Brahmins, who till then had a virtual monopoly on the entire services.[6] The Maharaja of Kolhapur, Shahuji, inspired by Mahatma Phuley, realised that the need for education among the non-Brahmins, and he founded boarding houses and also encouraged the low caste leadership to do the same for the students of their castes (Jaffrelot, 2003). It was way back in 1902 that he reserved fifty per cent of vacancies in the state administration for members of the backward communities. (Mudaliar, n.d) He became the pioneer for having provided primary education free and compulsory as early as in 1917, for the benefit of non-Brahmins including the Untouchables (*ibid*). In 1919, he categorically issued a 'Hujur Order' directing the educational institutions that 'any Untouchable student joining any state aided or helped educational institution should be treated respectfully like a gentleman, and taken into school rooms. If any man in the state education staff has any objection to his doing so, he must send in his resignation within six weeks from the receipt of this order' (Vundru, 2003). It was under these circumstances that Lord Minto responded to demands and assured the delegation of Muslim community under the leadership of Aga Khan in 1906. The demands got culminated into GOI Act, 1909 popularly known as Morley Minto Reforms. The act further enlarged the size of Legislative Councils, and introduced the system of Separate Electorates, wherby representation was bestowed upon different communities, classes, and interests *viz.*, University Senates and Chambers of Commerce and Muslim community. It was here for the first time that Muslim community on the basis of religious and social differentiation acquired Separate electorates, but no other community, not even Europeans or Sikhs were given Separate Electorates at this moment.

Now moving further, and if we situate the question of caste and discrimination question we find that the Untouchable question had not gained any substantial place till the GOI Act, 1909. But it was being recognised that they were a category apart suffering from social exclusion. It did amount to treating them equal as in the field of education without appropriate special considerations. Eleanor Zelliot has tried to explain the situation in the following words:

> The granting of an electorate for Muslims in which they alone would vote brought the idea of communal electorate for minorities to the forefront in the minds of all communities which feared their submersion in a government-run by the dominant caste-Hindu community. The granting of special electorates to the Muslim community also made numbers important. Whether the vast number of Untouchables were truly Hindu and to be counted as such, or not, became an important question for the first time (Quoted by Galanter, 1984).

Ambedkar Efforts and State Policy Initiatives

Moving ahead to Ambedkar's efforts, it can be said that it was in 1919 Ambedkar appeared for the first time for the rights of Depressed Classes. It was the formative stage of reservation policy that culminated in a proper and exhaustive policy in the Constitution of India in 1950, for which Ambedkar made systematic intellectual efforts. A systematic articulation of arguments in favour of remedies against caste discrimination was put forth by Ambedkar in his first statement, to the Southborough Committee in January, 1919 at the time of the reform in the Government of India Act, 1919. In 1928, Ambedkar submitted a statement to Simon Commission, showing his concern for providing safeguards for the protection of the Depressed Classes (BAWS, 1982). Ambedkar did not want the numerical strength of a community to be benchmark for representation but the economic and educational standing that is the lower the economic and educational standing the higher the representation and *vice-versa*. In fact, appearing for evidence before the Southborough Committee, Ambedkar outlined the kind of social system prevailing in India *vis-a-vis* DC, and why Untouchables as a distinct community needed to have separate representation in the councils, and the same was re-emphasised during 1928.

Further, while presenting the case of the Depressed Classes regarding promoting their education, Ambedkar suggested some of the measures to be adopted by the government, which included-modifying compulsory primary education, making primary education obligatory and applying the recommendations made by the Hunter Commission regarding the education of the Muslims to the Depressed Classes to make their educational progress a fact, and securing entry in the Public Service to the Depressed Classes to induce them to education (BAWS, 1982). At this juncture, Ambedkar's concern was to insist that the Depressed Classes also have the right to education provided the State. He also argued that the Untouchables, having been virtually excluded from the public services would prefer the system of appointments by selection, to the system of selection by open competition. Presenting the case, he suggested that a certain number of vacancies in Class I and Class II services to be filled by system of nomination with a pass examination for other than Brahmins.

Ambedkar's intervention in articulation of the problems of Depressed Classes during this period showed how the Depressed Classes differ as a community from the rest of the population in general, and from Hindus in particular. Although there was references of social discrimination and denial of civil rights to Depressed Classes, but the emphasis was more on political representation and less on civil rights. The questions of education and Public services were raised but the solutions were more in the context of equal rights and did not emphasise on legal safeguards against violation of rights.

During Round Table Conferences in 1930-32 he made various interventions through memorandums in the meetings of the conference which ultimately led to acceptance of reservation in the Central and State Legislatures. Taking strong stand on the issue of Untouchables, he emphatically said that though the problems of DCs were rooted in social mechanism, these need political instead of social solutions. On the question of treating Depressed Classes as a separate entity and providing them Separate Electorates, Ambedkar was confronted with the arguments of Gandhiji viz., 'will the Untouchables remain Untouchables in the times to come as the Muslims to remain Muslims and Sikhs as Sikhs...' and I would resist it (Separate Electorates for Untouchables).'[7] Differences and lack of compromise among leaders forced the British Prime Minister adjourn the second RTC *sine die* with a suggestion to put a signed requisition authorising the Prime Minister to arbitrate and give decision on the issue. Gandhiji signed but Ambedkar refused to do so asserting that the demands of the Untouchables were so reasonable having no need for arbitration (BAWS, 1982). Meanwhile, the British Prime Minister, Ramsay MacDonald, announced his decision known as Communal Award on August 4, 1932 to impart separate electorates to the Depressed Classes, which touched Gandhi, who declared 'fast' till the decision was reverted. It was on the fifth day of the fast that leaders of both sides that is Hindus and the Depressed Classes agreed on a formula that is known as the Poona Pact, signed on September 1932, by Ambedkar on behalf of the Depressed Classes and by Madan Mohan Malaviya on behalf of the caste-Hindus. Although, the RTC and its culmination in the Poona Pact had given space in Central and Provincial Legislatures, but in Ambedkar's view, it was not complete in terms of safeguards. Not satisfied with Poona Pact in 1940, Ambedkar came out openly against the Pact saying that 'Safeguards under Poona Pact are inadequate', which was reiterated in 1942, when he demanded proportional representation of SCs in the Public Services.

To sum up during 30s and 40s Ambedkar's inclusionary efforts were focussed on extension of reservation of public employment and education. In fact, it was in 1940s that the reservation policy took the definite shape it has today. While the final formation came at the time of framing of India's Constitution in 1947 that spelt out broader issues of safeguards, these statements and interventions, indeed provide insights to the evolution of reservation policy for SCs.

Constitution and Provisions for Social Inclusion

In the later years of 40s and early years of 50s, the future course of history was to be set in motion. Ambedkar tried to put inclusive policies for excluded groups during the making of the Constitution for free India by the Constituent Assembly. The Memorandum was presented by Ambedkar on behalf of the All India Scheduled Castes Federation in 1946, which was thought of as a small constitution for the protection of common citizenry, and attempted to establish social democracy and State socialism. Ambedkar suggested a dual strategy for adopting (Inclusive policy' referring to it as 'Safeguards against Economic Exploitation' and 'Safeguards Against Social Discrimination and Isolation'. And when Ambedkar got appointed the Chairman of the Drafting Committee of Assembly on December 23, 1947, he drafted and debated the provisions for safeguarding the interests of SCs in particular and other marginalised sections in general which included women too.

Ambedkar's perspective on 'inclusive policy' incorporates a dual strategy. He refers to these as 'safeguards against economic exploitation' and 'safeguards against social discrimination and isolation in his last systematic treatise on this theme (Ambedkar, 1947). Ambedkar reiterated his position that the problems of Untouchables are rooted in the historical denial of basic human rights. Therefore, he grounded the justification for remedies against caste discrimination of Untouchables in a citizenship framework. If initial effort involved creating awareness among the British regarding the position of Untouchables and demands to give citizenship rights, the second phase took him towards assertion of rights with wide description and explanations in terms of political representation in the form of Separate Electorates. In the third phase, we see the extension of representation and participation in the sphere of education and employment. The fourth phase of interventions came at the time of making the Constitution. This phase involved acceptance of the principles of non-discrimination, legal abolition of untouchability, recognition of the problem, particularly the educational and economic backwardness of the low castes and the responsibility on the state to protect the interests of the SCs and STs and women and take measures for their uplift. In the last phase of interventions, he gets back to re-assertion and rejuvenation whether it was in the sphere of political representation in the Legislatures or enlarging the spheres of State interventions.

Constitutional Safeguards

The Constitution of India adopted in 1950 is progressive not only in granting equality to women, but also in empowering the State to adopt measures of affirmative discrimination in favour of women. The Constitution further imposes a fundamental duty on every citizen to abstain from practices derogatory to the dignity of women. Yet, the Hindu Code Bill, which proposed equal inheritance for women, prohibited polygamy and liberalised divorce and custody rights, was vehemently opposed by influential Congressmen including the first President of Free India, Rajendra Prasad.

As far back as October 1938, the National Planning Committee was formed to draw an outline for independent India's planned development. One of the 29 sub-committees published a report entitled 'Women's role in planned economy', in 1947. Informed by the liberal and socialist perspectives, the report quite admirably brought into focus the dualism that existed between inside/outside, private/public, familial/economic, and informal/formal whereby 'inside, 'private', 'familial', and 'informal' were the categories belonging to women by acknowledging women's labour as a 'separate unit of production' rather than part of family work. However, many of the initial radical—liberal views on marriage reforms, divorce, adoption, and maintenance of children were retraced in the face of the explicit patriarchal resistance (Chaudhury, 1995). The contradictions arise because ironically, despite accepting gender equality as a guiding principle, the operative part of the concept was never examined in the context of the emergent nation state and its development plans and perspectives. Also, as the following discussion suggests, gender issues continued to be framed by dominant patriarchal ideologies and discourses even as insitutionalised attempts were being brought in place for expanding spaces for women in a gender equity paradigm.

As we know that the Constitution of India is a pious document which has codified almost all legal provisions relating to the development of the marginal masses. Part–III (Known as Fundamental rights contains Article 14-34), and Part-IV (in the form of Directive Principle of State Policy). These words have great significance so far social inclusion is concerned.

The Indian Constitution's spirit of liberal and democratic principles is reflected in Part IV, Directive Principles of State Policy. Some of the relevant provisions are set out in Articles 36 to 51 of the Indian Constitution, which could be seen as the principles towards inclusive development. Though these provisions are not justifiable, Constitution of India lays these principles as the very basis of development policy and could be seen in retrospect as the beginning of rights-based approach to development. But all this is in jeopardy under the restructuring initiated under the pressure of globalisation; the State is increasingly distancing itself from these constitutional obligations.

Box 1. Constitutional Inclusion to All Women

- Equality before the law. Article 14
- No discrimination by the State on the grounds only of religion, race, caste, sex, place of birth or any of these. Article 15 (1)
- Special provisions to be made by the State in favour of women and children. Article 15 (3)
- Equality of opportunity for all citizens in matters relating to employment or appointment to any office under the State. Article 16
- State Policy to be directed to securing for men and women equally, the right to an adequate means of livelihood. Article 39 (a)
- Equal Pay for equal work for both men and women. Article 39(d)
- Provisions to be made by the State for securing just and humane conditions of work and for maternity relief. (Article 42)
- To promote harmony and to renounce practices derogatory to the dignity of women. Article 51-A (e)

The Government of India has enacted legislations to ensure, and the Constitution itself provides for several safeguards for SCs. The primary consideration of the government in abolishing 'untouchability' and in enforcing several measures for protective discrimination as the nature of the disabilities that had been typically associates with untouchability.

The safeguards in the Constitution have been provided to facilitate the implementation of the directive principle contained in Article 46, which states:

Although the directive principles of state policy are not enforceable by any court of law, they are nonetheless fundamental to the governance of the country, delineating the duties and obligations of the state to apply these principles while executing and amending laws (Article 37). According to B.R. Ambedkar, the directive principles set before the state the ideals of social and economic democracy since political freedom bereft of social and economic content is meaningless.

For this express purpose, various provisions relating to SCs are contains in Parts III, IV, VI, XIV, XVI and XIX of the Constitution. These parts delineate the fundamental rights of the citizens of India, the directive principles of state policy and the appointments of ministers for the welfare of SCs. The Constitution also recognises the fundamental disparities between SCs and other marginalised groups, making a clear distinction between them under special provisions relating to certain classes. It also contains provisions for reservation for the SCs in the lower and upper houses of the people both at the union and state levels, outlines provisions for claims by the SCs to services and posts, and calls for the establishment of a permanent National Commission for the Schedules Castes and Schedules Tribes (NCSCST).

The Constitution of India guarantees equality before the law (Article14) and enjoins the states to make special provisions for the advancement of any socially and educationally backward class or for SCs (Article 15[4]). It also empowers the state to make provisions for reservation in appointments or posts in favours of any backward class of citizens (Article 16 [4]). The Constitution of India also categorically states that untouchability stands abolished and that its practice in any form is forbidden (Article 17). Further, it enjoins to promote, with special care, the educational and economic interests of the weaker sections of society-in particular of SCs-and promises to protect them from social injustices and all forms of exploitation (Article 46). Reservation of seats for SCs in democratic institutions (Article 330), and in the services (Article 335) is a measure of positive discrimination. It also empowers the state to appoint a commission to investigate the conditions of the socially and educationally backward classes (Article 340 and to specify the castes to be deemed as SCs (Article 341 [2]). In accordance with these Constitutional provisions, a number of measures have been initiated by the government to provide protection against discrimination and exclusion and to empower the SCs, both economically and politically.

The government strategy, which has evolved over time, has expanded both in terms of the spheres of intervention and the methods of implementation. This strategy has been shaped by a specific understanding of the nature of deprivations of the SCs and other marginalised social groups, and is based on the recognition of the persistence of poverty and other deprivations, which are considered as by-products of traditional restrictions, the denial of economic and social rights, and continuing discrimination and exclusion.

Therefore, to overcome the historical injustice of SCs and to bring them at par with mainstream society, it was considered necessary to empower them by assigning them some legal rights priority and ensuring them their effective participation in economic and social development as well as the political processes of the country. Several measures of general empowerment were initiated. Simultaneously, since discrimination and exclusion are continuing problems, a protective mechanism is considered as necessary. The government's current strategy conceptualises the removal of inherited deprivation and is directed towards the protection of SCs from continuing discrimination and exclusion.

Anti-discriminatory measures include the enactment of the Untouchability Offence Act, 1955, under which the practice of untouchability and discrimination in public places was treated as an offence. In 1976, the Act was reviews in order to make it more stringent and effective and was designated as Protection of Civil Rights (PCR) Act. The Act provides penalties for refusing access to SCs to places of public use.

In consideration of the fact that the normal provisions of the Indian Penal Code (IPC), and the PCR Act were thought as inadequate to provide safeguards to SCs/STs against several crimes, an additional Act, called the Scheduled Castes and the Schedules Tribes Prevention of Atrocities (POA) Act, was enacted in 1989. This Act was specifically enacted to prevent atrocities against the members of SCs/STs.

These Acts define the role of the Central government in co-ordinating measures initiates by state governments and call for the tabling of an annual report in each house of the Parliament. The rules also provide for the issuing of instructions to government servants to take serious notice of untouchability and to enforce the provisions of the Acts. Besides, the rules also mandated the establishment of administrative structures for the implementation of the provisions mentioned in them.

Consequently, various administrative structures to this effect have been put in place throughout India. Generally, in any states, the social welfare department is the nodal implementing agency for these Acts. The police and the home departments have also been made responsible for enforcing these Acts. Vigilance and monitoring committees overseeing the effective implementation of these Acts have been set up in many states. Special courts for SCs/STs have been established in many states, with some states even providing legal assistance to the victims of caste harassment and atrocities. There are provisions for the identification of untouchability-prone areas and there are incentive awards for the promotion of social integration through inter-caste marriages, with financial assistance being provided to a couple entering a marriage where either one of the spouse belongs to the SC community. Reservation in the public spheres was incorporates as a constitutional provision to ensure proportional participation of SCs in public sector employment, and to enable their entry into public educational institutions as well as various political democratic bodies and institutions. Without 'positive discrimination', this proportional participation of SCs might not have been realised due to the prevalence of exclusion and discrimination. The government's reservation policy can thus be views as one of affirmative action. Affirmative action remains the government's most powerful instrument to ensure social justice to the disadvantaged groups. It reflects the government's renewed commitment to institute a 'National Charter of Social Justice' based on the principles of social harmony, gender justice, with necessary legal measures.

The reservation policy is directed at providing:

- Safeguards for public employment/service;

- Provisions regarding entry into public educational institutions, and
- Provisions regarding reservation of seats in central and state legislations, and in various other political bodies and institutions.

Article 16(4) is to be read with Article 335, which states: 'The claims of the members of the SCs and STs shall be taken into consideration, consistently with the maintenance of efficiency of administration, in the making of appointments to services and posts in connection with the affairs of the Union or of a state'.

Thus, while forming an opinion for instituting reservation, the state shall also take cognisance of the limitation set out in Article 335, that is, whether reservation is consistent with the maintenance of efficiency of administration.

As discussed earlier, the Constitution of India, often heralded as a landmark document, was inspired by the emancipatory vision of its chief architect Dr B.R. Ambedkar—a Dalit leader who himself suffered severe discrimination and who sought to ensure equal protection and substantive equality for Dalits in independent India. As a document, the Constitution combines broad social purpose, stemming from the social content of the Independence Movement, with practical administrative detail, based on the Assembly members' experiences in government, and on the events around them. Ambedkar cautioned against adopting too "Western" a vision of what Constitutional democracy in India should look like. According to Ambedkar:

> (Such a system failed) to realise, that political democracy cannot succeed where there is no social and economic democracy. Democracy is another name for equality. Parliamentary democracy developed a passion for liberty. It failed to realise the significance of equality and did not even endeavour to strike a balance between liberty and equality, with the result that liberty swallowed equality and has left a progeny of iniquities (Rodrigues, 2002).

Indian constitutionalism attempts, however imperfectly, to balance liberty and equality of interests and in so doing foreshadows the delicate balance between formal and substantive conceptions of equality in international human rights law *(Ibid)*. Chief among these fundamental rights is the Right to Equality. Article 14 of the Constitution of India reads: "The state shall not deny to any person equality before the law or the equal protection of the laws within the territory of India." (Galanter 1984) An exception clause allows for affirmative action measures under some circumstances. "Nothing in this article... shall prevent the state from making any special provision for the advancement of the socially and educationally backward classes of citizens or for the Scheduled Castes and Scheduled Tribes."

The clause (Article-14) marks a significant departure from the American model on which India's equality provision is based and constitutionalises the validity of affirmative action in the Indian context. The Indian model is also one of substantive equality. If formal equality aims at equal opportunity, then substantive equality aims at equal results by considering the social structures in which equal results would not necessarily result from formal equality guarantees.

Protective Legislation

In addition to constitutional provisions, the government of India has pursued a two-pronged approach to narrowing the gap between the socio-economic status of the scheduled caste population and the national average: one pronged involves regulatory measures which ensure that the various provisions to protect their rights and interests are adequately implemented, enforced and monitored; the second focusses on increasing the self-sufficiency of the scheduled caste population through financial assistance for self-employment activities through development programmes to increase education and skills.

The Protection of Civil Rights Act

With an eye to eradicating pervasive discrimination practised against scheduled caste members, the Central government enacted the Protection of Civil Rights Act, 1955 ("PCR Act") to enforce the abolition of "untouchability" under Article 17 of the Constitution. The PCR Act punishes offenses that amount to the observance of "untouchability." These include, *inter alia*, prohibiting entry into places of worship, denying access to shops and other public places, denying access to any water supply, prohibiting entry into hospitals, refusing to sell goods or render services, and insulting someone on the basis of his or her caste.

Perhaps the greatest deficiency of the PCR Act was the fact that abuses against Dalits were not limited to name-calling or denial of entry into public spaces: violence was a defining characteristic of the abuse. Thirty-four years after the introduction of the PCR Act, the Scheduled Castes and Scheduled Tribes (Prevention of Atrocities) Act of 1989, was enacted purportedly to bring these other forms of abuse to an end. Recognising the relative backwardness of SCs in the society, the Constitution of India guarantees equality before the law (Article 14) and enjoins the State to make special provisions for advancement of socially and educationally backward classes (Article 15[4]). It also empowers the State to make provisions for reservation in appointment or posts in favour of SCs/STs (Article 16(4). The Constitution of India also states categorically that untouchability is abolished and its practice in any form is forbidden. Further, the State is required to promote with special care the educational and economic interests of weaker sections in particular the exploitation of SCs (Article 46). Reservation of seats in democratic institutions (Article 330), and inservices (Article 335) is another measure of positive discrimination. It also empowers the State to appoint a commission to investigate into the conditions of socially and educationally backward classes (Article 340), and to specify the castes to be deemed as SCs (Article 341).

As stated above the Scheme of the Constitution (of India) reflects a three-pronged strategy for changing the status of Scheduled Castes (and Scheduled Tribes) based on the traditional social order. This consists of:

(a) Protection: Legal/Regulatory measures for enforcing equality and removing disabilities: Providing strong punitive action against physical violence inflicted on them; Eliminating customary arrangements which deeply hurt their dignity and person; Preventing control over fruits of their labour and striking at concentration of economic assets and resources and setting up autonomous watchdog institutions to safeguard interests, rights and benefits guaranteed to them.

(b) Compensatory discrimination: Enforcement of reservation provisions in public services, representative bodies and educational institutions.

(c) Development: Measures to bridge the wide gap between the Scheduled Castes and other communities in their economic conditions and social status, covering allocation of resources and distribution of benefits. This strategy was subsequently operationalised in the State policy and the commitment to this policy has been a feature of Indian State ever since. The policy has been strengthened and revised and its ambit made wider from time to time.

These protective measures are monitored by the National Commissions for Scheduled Castes and Scheduled Tribes. The development measures for the educational, social, and economic "upliftment" of scheduled castes are administered by the Ministry of Social Justice and Empowerment.

Inclusion: Women (Dalit) Equality and Development

Gender equality has three aspects: equal opportunities, equal treatment and equal entitlements for both, men and women. It is directly linked with human development. And the gender development got reflected in the government policies with its paradigm shifts from WID[8] to WAD[9] and GAD[10] in the planning process.

Box 2. Shifts in the Approach of Five Year Plan to Women's Issues

---

- In the 1950's women were mainly looked at as recipients of welfare.
- In the 1960's women's education started to receive priority, along with measures to improve maternal and child health and nutrition services.
- There was a marked shift in the 1970's from welfare to development', recognising women as participants in the process of development.
- In the 1980's, we adopted a multi-disciplinary approach, with a special thrust on three core sectors—health, education, and employment.
- In the early 1990's, the emphasis was on training and skill development programmes to make women economically independent and self-reliant.

- In the Ninth Plan which runs from 1997 to 2002, the empowerment of women is one of its nine primary objectives. Also, the Plan attempted convergence of services available in both women-specific and women-related sectors, and
- The Tenth Five Year Plan (2000-07) has empowerment of women as a focus and also views development of children as most desirable societal investment with a rights-based approach to their development.
- The development process must be engendered to strengthen the links between economic growth and gender justice across its inter-sectional dimensions of caste, class, tribal status, poverty and other exclusions.

The First Five Year Plan sought to "promote the welfare of women" by helping them to play their legitimate role in the family and the community but emphasised that the major burden of organising activities for the benefit of the female population had to be borne by the private agencies. Five Year Plan continued to reflect the same welfare approach to women's interests though they accorded priority to education for both, men and women and launched measures to improve maternal and child health services and supplementary nutrition for children as well as expectant and nursing mothers. It was the Sixth Five Year Plan in which the focus on women's interests shifted from 'welfare' and 'development'. Planners and policy makers began to recognise women not only as partners but also as stake-holders in the development of the country. The Seventh Five Year Plan saw developmental programmes which aimed at raising the economic and social status of women and at ensuring that they get the benefits of national development. This is when 'beneficiary-oriented programmes' extending direct benefits to women in different developmental sectors began. There was a stress upon the generation of both skilled and unskilled employment through formal and non-formal education and vocational training. The Eighth Five Year Plan had a Human Development focus. It tried to ensure that the benefits of development do not bypass women, and it implemented special programmes for women to complement the general development programmes and to monitor the flow of benefits to women in education, health and employment.

The Ninth Five Year Plan was rather ambitious. It took up 'empowering women as agents of socio-economic change and development' as a major commitment. To begin with, it adopted the 'National Policy for Empowerment of Women', which among other objectives, sought to organise women into Self Help Groups to work for their own empowerment, accorded a high priority to schemes for maternal and child welfare and most importantly, made a bid at easy and equal access to education through the Special Action Plan of 1998, plans for the free education of girls up to the college level (inclusive of professional courses), and vocational training.

The Tenth Five Year Plan (2002–07) adopted a multi-pronged approach for the socio-economic development of the SCs: Social empowerment through educational development; economic empowerment through income and employment enhancing avenues; protection through effective implementation of protective legislations and eradication of occupations such as manual scavenging; and holistic development through earmarking of funds proportionate to the population. [Scheduled Caste Sub-Plan (SCSP) and Tribal Sub-Plan (TSP)].

The Scheduled Caste Sub-Plan (SCSP) is not meant to be an isolated programme/scheme. Instead its purpose was to serve as an umbrella strategy for overall development of Scheduled Castes. The strategy entails the targetted flow of funds and associated benefits from the Annual Plan of States/Union Territories, at least in proportion to the Scheduled Caste population in total population of the States/Union Territories. While the central objective of the SCP is the economic development of Scheduled Castes, it also intends to promote their educational and social development along with the fulfillment of their minimum needs and human resources development. The objective of SCP is to ensure that not only sufficient funds are allocated for the welfare of Dalits, but also that the funds are properly used and that effective and practical programmes with clear goals and targets are initiated.

For effective implementation of SCSP and TSP, the Planning Commission also issued guidelines to all State Governments/ UTs which have been revised from time to time, the last revision being on 31st December 2006 (*See* Annexure).

The central focus of the 11th Plan (2007-2012) was that Gender Equality and Gender Justice must be articulated. They were as follows:

- The development process must be engendered to strengthen the links between economic growth and gender justice.
- There must be an integrated and inter-sectoral approach. Restricting the focus to "women's issues" will yield limited results.
- Gender must be addressed across it's inter-sectional dimensions of caste, class, tribal status, poverty and other exclusions.
- The goal would be to engender every sector.

Economic Inclusivity

Gender Budgets[11]—The Concept

Historically, we have moved a long way in terms of perspectives and methodologies since the mid-1980's, when initial attempts were made to integrate gender perspectives into national budgets—from 'Women's Budgets'; to 'Gender Budgets' (reflecting the ongoing shift from a focus on women to the focus on gender and the relations between women and men) to 'Gender-sensitive Budgets' to 'Mainstreaming Gender Perspectives into Budgets', (implying that the aim is not to produce a separate gender budget but to incorporate relevant gender perspectives into overall budget processes). "Gendering the Budget (Gender Budgeting) is not meant to bargain for a larger share of the resources for women or to create a separate budget for them. The aim is to analyse the budgetary expenditures from a gender perspective.

In India, the 1974 Report of the Committee on the Status of Women in India gave a new impetus towards the search for gender perspectives on public expenditure. And, though the Eighth Five Year Plan (1992-97), for the first time, highlighted the need to ensure a definite flow of funds from the general developmental sectors to that of women ("The benefits of development from different sectors should not bypass women and special programmes on women should complement the general development programmes. The latter, in turn, should reflect greater gender sensitivity"), not much progress was made in terms of ensuring adequate flow of funds and benefits to women. It was the Ninth Five Year Plan (1997-2002), which adopted **"Women Component Plan"** as one of the major strategies of planning and budgeting and directed both the Central and State governments to ensure that 'not less than 30 per cent of the funds/benefits are earmarked in all the women's related sectors". It also directed that a special vigil be kept on the flow of the earmarked funds/benefits through an effective mechanism to ensure that the proposed strategy brings forth a holistic approach towards empowering women. The National Policy for Empowerment of Women, 2001 made concrete suggestions towards the introduction of a gender perspective in the budgeting process. Specifically, it promised:

- Developing "Gender Development Indices" (GDI), by networking with specialised agencies.
- Undertaking "Gender auditing and development of evaluation mechanisms".
- Undertaking the collection of "Gender-disaggregated data" by all primary data collecting agencies of the Central and State governments as well as research and academic institutions in the Public and Private Sectors. Already in 1998, the Department of Women and Child Development, Government of India had taken up the initiative for generating "gender-aggregated data" across the country. Based on a series of consultations, held with States and Union Territory Administrations to develop Gender Development Index (GDI) and Gender Empowerment Measures (GEM), 18 important indicators were identified for collection of gender-disaggregated data at state/district levels. But the responses were not very encouraging. The "Workshop on Engendering National Budgets in the South Asia Region", held July 2002 in New Delhi in Collaboration with the UNIFEM, was another concrete step towards a gender budgeting initiative in India. Subsequently, the National Institute of Public Finance and Policy (NIPF & P) was commissioned to study gender-related economic policy issues and the policy alternatives for building a gender sensitive national budgeting process.

The Annual Indian Economic Survey 2000-01, for the first time, contained a section on Gender Inequality in the chapter on Social Sector, based on the input provided by the Interim Report on the 'Status of Women in India and their Role in Economy', submitted by NIPF&P in January 2001. The second Report of NIPF&P, submitted in August 2001, made a 'Post Budget Assessment of the Union Budget 2001-02'; The Report categorised public expenditure in three main types: (i) Those specifically targetted to women and girls, (ii) Pro-women allocations which are the composite expenditure of schemes with women component, and (iii) Mainstream public expenditure that has gender differential impacts. Though the methodology adopted was found inadequate, needing much refinement, the salient findings of the union budget analysis brought to light some interesting trend in public fund expenditure from gender perspective and also methodological issues.

The NIPFP Reports led to the realisation of the need to analyse State Budgets with a gender perspective, since the States/UTs account for bulk of the expenditure in social sector, which impinges on the welfare, development, and empowerment of women.

The National Scheduled Castes Finance and Development Corporation (NSFDC) established in 1989, provides financial and other support to beneficiaries for taking up various income generating activities. An amount of Rs 388.80 cr was made available to the Corporation upto 31st March, 2007 as equity share contribution against the authorised share capital of Rs 1000 cr. The number of SC persons who received assistance during the Tenth Five Year Plan (up to December 2006) is 257901.

- The National Safai Karamcharis Finance and Development Corporation was established in 1997 to provide financial support to the *safai karamcharis* (scavengers) to take up various income-generating activities. During the Tenth Five Year Plan, the Corporation introduced the Micro Credit Finance Scheme and the Mahila Samridhi Yojana, benefitting 102187 persons. During 2006-07, it disbursed loans to 16545 beneficiaries (up to December 2006) for various income generating activities in 23 States and two UTs.
- The scheme of grant-in aid to the Scheduled Castes Development Corporations (SCDCs) was introduced in 1978-79 as a CSS for participating in the equity share of the State corporations in a Centre-State ratio of

49:51.The SCDCs finance employment, oriented schemes that cover: (i) agriculture and allied activities including minor irrigation; (ii) small-scale industry; (iii) transport; and (iv) trade and service sector. They also finance projects by dovetailing the loan component from NSFDC/ Banks.

- Under the Sampoorna Grameen Rozgar Yojana, provision has been made for special safeguards for weaker sections and women .22.5 per cent of the annual allocations under the first stream of SGRY has been earmarked for individual beneficiary schemes of SCs/STs. Minimum 50 per cent of the allocation to the village panchayat has been earmarked for creation of need-based village infrastructure in SC/ST habitations under the second stream of SGRY.
- Under the Swarna Jayanti Gram Swarozgar Yojana, which aims at bringing poor families above the poverty line by providing them income generating assets through a mix of credit and subsidy, 50 per cent of the Swarozgaris assisted should be from SCs/STs.
- Of the total work force engaged in handicrafts, 47.42 per cent are women, of which 37.11 per cent belong to SC/ST category (*Source*: NCAER survey, 1995-96). In this sector, about 22.5 per cent of the outlay in respect of identified Central Sector Schemes is earmarked for the benefit of the Scheduled Castes and Scheduled Tribes.
- Majority of weavers/artisans belong to the SC/ST population. These groups are normally linked to hereditary or subsistence-based occupations and that too in the unorganised sector. The Handlooms Sector employs over 65 lakh persons in weaving and allied activities. It is estimated that, of the total work force, women constitute 62.40 per cent and SC/STs category constitute 32 per cent (as per the joint census of handlooms and powerlooms 1995-96). To assist Handloom Weavers, including SC/ST and women weavers, the Government of India implements various developmental Schemes through State Governments with the objectives of (i) Employment Generation, (ii) Modernisation and upgradation of technology, (iii) Input

support, (iv) Marketing support, (v) Publicity and Exhibition, (vi) Infrastructural support, (vii) Welfare Measures, (viii) Development of Exportable Products (ix) Research and Development.

Political Inclusivity

There are two different models of political inclusion: One focusses on the inclusion of women and marginalised groups through "a politics of presence" in political institutions, e.g., gender quotas or parity (Phillips, 1995). The other model focusses on the inclusion of women and oppressed groups "from below" through a "politics of difference", e.g., voluntary association in civil society (Young, 1990).

India has gradually transformed from Women in Development to Gender and Development in the policy approaches. Affirmative action policies are developed to reach the goal of inclusive democracy and sustainable development. At global level special measures have been designed to ensure women's participation, development and empowerment. These changes in awareness, expertise, policies, laws and women's voices are efforts of many actors. At grassroots though translating these ideas is very important.

Dalits constitutes around five per cent population of the world. This large population is shackled in poverty, illiteracy, political subjugation and cultural oppression. For the Development of the Dalits in general and Dalit women in particular political participation is necessary. Developmental needs of women and Dalit marginalised are getting special attention as the 73rd Amendment gets implemented. The 73rd Amendment mirrors the developmental goal India visions for sustained grassroots democracy.

Visions of political development stress on democracy and participation as innate to its discourse. Development in this sense needs democratic decision-making of all the stake holders, informed and active civil society and inclusive political structure to reach its goal. In the Indian context, the process of democratisation with inclusive participation is envisioned through the 73rd Indian Constitution Amendment Act, 1993. The Act fosters the strengthening of grassroots' democracy by creating opportunities for inclusive participation of the marginalised groups. It provides rights to Scheduled Castes

(SCs), Scheduled Tribes (STs), and women to participate in local government. The Act aims at redressing the gender and caste inequities. Thus, it provides proportionate reservation to the SC-ST categories-based on their population and 33 per cent for women to ensure their participation in local bodies.

The resultant impact of political inclusivity of women in general and Dalit women in particular, women's participation in panchayat has been remarkably visible. This has recently resulted in Union cabinet approving a proposal of a Constitutional Amendment Bill for increasing quota (50 per cent) for women in Panchayats at all tiers (Panchayat Raj Ministry report). Ministry seminar report 2009, estimate more than 1.4 million women to occupy 2,60,768 panchayats in upcoming panchayat elections (Panchayat Raj Ministry). It also states, at present, out of the total elected representatives of panchayat numbering around 2.8 million, 36.87 per cent are women. The Panchayat Raj Ministry report indicates a significant role played by reservation in bringing, women into mainstream. According to this report, Reservation has played a significant role as four-fifths of all the representatives got elected from reserved seats. Reservation facilitated the first entry into politics for most of the elected representatives (83 per cent). Positive impact of entering politics and working as a Panchayat Raj functionary is visible as 79 per cent of women representatives reported better self-esteem; 81 per cent reported confidence-building and 74 per cent stated increase of decision-making abilities (*Ibid*). Such positive report gives a picture of better and inclusive governance that India is moving towards by applying 'Gender and Development' approach. This step foresees increased and active-participation of women in public sphere, which leads to empowerment and development.

Educational Inclusivity

With respect to the educational development of SCs, the Central government has introduced major scholarship programmes and these include... The other important schemes for the educational development of SCs are: (i) providing coaching facilities to students to prepare them for various competitive examinations being conducted by Union Public Service Comission (UPSC), State Public Service Commissions, banks, and so on; and (ii) hostel facilities to both boys and girls for pursuing education from middle level onwards.

Centrally Sponsored Schemes

A number of centrally sponsored programmes are being continued for Dalits. These are:

- Post-matric Scholarships;
- Pre-matric Scholarships for children of those engaged in unclean occupations;
- Boys and Girls Hostels;
- Book Banks;
- Upgradation of merit of SC/ST students;
- Coaching and allied schemes.
- National Overseas Scholarship and passage grants for higher studies abroad;
- Grants in aid to voluntary organisations.

In addition to these, in the central sector have also been improved, viz.

- Educational complex in low literacy pockets for development of women's literacy in Dalit areas, and
- Special educational development programmes for Scheduled Caste girls belonging to very low educational levels.

State Sponsored Schemes

- Scholarships and stipends at various levels;
- Supply of textbooks, stationary; equipment, uniform, sports material.
- Administration of Balwadis, Primary Schools, Middle Schools and Higher Secondary Schools.

Attendance Prize to students.

- Residential Schools;
- Amenities to boarders in private hostels and financial assistance for sharing rental accommodation;
- Hostels (and reservation of seats in general hostels);
- Merit Scholarships;

- Expenses of those studying in public schools;
- Reimbursement of examination fees and tuition fees at different levels of education.
- Excursions;
- Mid-day Meals (MDM);
- Loans to students for carrying on education;
- Vocational craft classes;
- Introduction of modern trades and training centers for self-employment.
- Coaching and Study centre;
- Awards to teachers;
- Houses for teachers.

In addition, the Ministries of Education, Labour and Agriculture and the University Grants Commission have also been providing various other facilities to Dalit students, namely:

- Reservation of seats in educational institutions including Medical and engineering Colleges, Technical Institutions, Sainik Schools and Navodaya Vidyalayas,
- Kendriya Vidyalayas,
- Relaxation in age and marks for the purpose of admission,
- Research scholarships and fellowship.

Carry Forward and Exchange

If a sufficient number of SC/ST candidates fit for appointments against reserved posts are unavailable, such vacancies can be de-reserved and filled by candidates from other communities. Such being the case, of promotion by selection from Group 'C' to Group 'B' to the lower rung of Group 'A', wherein the carrying forward of reservations is not permitted. While filling up reserved posts, the oldest carried-forward vacancy is to be filled first.

Vacancies reservations for the SCs/STs may be exchanged, in case no suitable candidates are available from the respective community for which the vacancy is reserved. The normal provision for them is that exchange is possible only for the reservation that has been carried forward to the third year of recruitment.

Concessions and Relaxations

Concessions and relaxations are applicable to the following:

- Reservation in services/posts in government and public sector undertaking (PSUs) to be filled up by direct recruitment or promotion.
- Relaxation of maximum age limit for direct recruitment and posts to be filled up by promotion.
- Concessions in recruitment, examination fee, etc.
- Separate interviews for SC/ST candidates for direct recruitment.
- Relaxation of qualification, experience and other criteria for appointment.
- Travelling allowance for attending written tests and interviews for recruitment.
- Extension of zone for consideration for promotions to SC/ST employees.
- Reservation in general residential accommodations.
- Provisions in the Central Civil Services (CCS) (Conduct) Rules against harassment of SC/ST employees.
- Reservation in dealerships of PSU products, and concessions in conditions related to dealership.

Procedural Safeguards

- Roster for reservation in posts,
- Annual inspection of roster,
- Annual statement on reservation,
- Monitoring and ensuring the proper implementation of concessions.

Institutional Safeguards

- Provision of liaison officers and officers and special cells to assist them to monitor and ensure the proper implementation of SCs/STs.

- Establishment of an NCSCST with purpose and functions as delineates under Article 338.
- Establishment of a committee of Parliament on the welfare of SCs/STs to examine the representations of SCs/STs in services and to make suitable recommendations for improvements.
- Establishment of NCSCST, National Scheduled Caste Finance and Development Corporation (NSCFDC), National Commission for Safai Karamcharis (NCSK), and Dr Ambedkar Foundation.

Provisions in Central and State Legislatures and Other Bodies

Under Articles 330 and 332, seats are reserved for SCs in the Lok Sabha (Lower House of Representatives), the Rajya Sabha (Upper House of Representatives) as well as in the Legislative Assemblies in all states of India. The quota of reservation in each state is based on the SC population of the respective state.

Educational Policies

The primary educational problems of the SCs are, first, the prevalence of low literacy rates among them, second, high drop out rates at the school level, and, lastly, discrimination and exclusion in some form or other, including admissions to educational institutions. The focus of the government's programme has been on improving both school-level and higher education, with various steps being incorporated at the school levels (primary, middle and secondary) as well as at the higher levels to facilitate enrollment and admission, reduce the drop out rates, improve the quality and capabilities of educational content and encourage retention at the higher levels, including professional education and research that could lead to higher degrees for SCs.

National Policy on Education (NPE), 1986

The NPE lays emphasis on the attainment of minimum levels of learning at all stages of education-primary, middle and secondary and on the overall personality development of the child. Pursuant to the NPE, the following special provisions for SCs have been incorporated in the existing schemes of the Department of Elementary Education and Literacy and the Department of Secondary Education and Higher Education:

- Relaxed norms for opening of primary schools.
- A primary school within one km walking distance from habitations of 200 people instead of 300.
- Incentives like free textbooks, uniforms, stationery and school bags to students from the SC community.
- Priority given to areas with high concentration of SCs in major programmes of the Department of Elementary Education and Literacy like the District Primary Education (NFE), and the National Programme for Nutritional Support to Primary Education (NPNSPE).
- Abolition of tuition fees in government schools in all the states, at least up to the primary level. Most states have abolished tuition fees for SC students up to the senior secondary level.
- Of the 43,000 scholarships at the secondary stage for talented children from rural areas, 13,000 scholarships are reserved for children from the SC/ST community, and 70 scholarships are reserved for SC/ST candidates under the National Talent Search Examination (NTSE).
- Strict observance of reservation of seats for SCs in Central government institutions such as the Indian Institutes of Technology (IITs), The Indian Institutes of Management (IIMs), Regional Engineering Colleges (RECs), Central universities, Kendriya Vidyalayas and Navodaya Vidyalayas. In pubic educational institutions, apart from reservation, there is also relaxation in the minimum qualifying cut-off percentages for admission. The University Grants Commission (UGC) has establishes SC/ST cells in 103 universities, including Central universities, to ensure proper implementation of the reservation policy. A standing committee has also been set up by the UGC to review the implementation of the reservation policy in various public educational institutions.
- Remedial and special coaching is provided to improve the academic skills, linguistic proficiency and levels of comprehension of SC students. The IITs have a scheme under which SC students, who fail by a small margin in the entrance examinations are provided a year's preparatory course.

- The UGC has also formulates a scheme for providing coaching to candidates from the SC/ST community to prepare them for the National Eligibility Test (NET), and to subsequently provide from among them adequately qualified candidates for recruitment as lecturers.
- SC candidates are also provided relaxation up to 10 per cent in the cut-off marks for the Junior Research Fellowship (JRF) test. All SC.
- Every year 50 JRFs are awarded in the Sciences and the Humanities to SC/ST students, who appear in NET and qualify for lectureship.
- The UGC provides a relaxation of five per cent marks– from 55 per cent to 50 per cent at the masters' level to SC/ST candidates for appointment as lecturers. For SC/ST students, the UGC has also reduced the minimum percentage of marks to appear in the NET to 50 per cent.

Alternative and Innovative Education

Along with formal schooling, alternative and innovative education is a major part of the overall strategy for covering unnerved habitations and for the mainstreaming of out-of school children, especially girls. The scheme provides for a diverse range of needs such as the following:

- A learning centre for the unserved habitation like the Education Guarantee Scheme in Madhya Pradesh.
- A special strategy for out of school children in order to mainstream them into formal streams such as the efforts of the M. Venkatrangaiyah Foundation and the *Balika Shikshan Shivirs* under the *Lok Jumbish Project*, or the creation of special mobile schools for migrant populations such as for the shepherds of Jammu and Kashmir.
- A special approach for adolescent girls to meet the diversity of their learning needs such as the *Mahila Shikshan Kendras* under the *Mahila Samakhya Project.*
- A source of remedial teaching at urban slums to meet the special educational needs of deprived children, who may enrol in school but are unable to cope-for instance, Pratham in Mumbai.

- An experimental stream where new pedagogical approaches could be tried out under innovative components, such as Rishi Vally School in Andhra Pradesh, where the idea is to non-formalise the apparatus of education.

Special Educational Schemes

The Ministry of Social Justice and Empowerment (MoSJE) implements various centrally sponsor schemes for the educational development of SCs through state governments and Union Territory (UT) administrations.

Central Sector Scheme of Upgradation of Merit of SC Students

This scheme was started in 1987-88 by Ministry of Human Resource Development (MHRD) in the Department of Education and was transferred to the Ministry of Welfare (MoW) in the middle of 1993-94.

The objective of the scheme was to upgrade the merit of SC students by providing them with opportunities for all-round development through education in residential schools. The scheme intended to remove their educational and social deficiencies, and attempted to facilitate their entry into institutions/courses where admissions were on a competitive basis. Under the scheme, 100 per cent central assistance is released to states/UTs to arrange remedial and special coaching for SC students studying in classes IX to XII.

While remedial coaching aims at removing deficiencies in subjects taught at school, special coaching is provided to prepare students for competitive examinations for entry into professional courses such as engineering and medicine. Under this scheme, coaching is provided in linguistic skills, the sciences and mathematics. Although the number of awards with respect to each state/UT is predetermined in the scheme, each state/UT is entitled to a minimum of five awards. A package grant of Rs 15,000 per students per year is provided under the scheme. The scheme also provides for additional grants for students with disabilities, such as reader's allowance, transport allowance and escort's allowance.

Centrally-sponsored Coaching and Allied Scheme

Under this scheme, funds are released for Pre-examination Training Centres (PETCs) in various parts of the country to prepare SC candidates for competitive examinations (SSCs), etc. The objective of the scheme is to improve the representation of candidates belonging to the SC community for whom posts are reserved in the state/central services.

The ongoing scheme was modified in September 2001 to 'Coaching and Allied Assistance for Weaker Sections including Schedules Castes, Other Backward Castes and Minorities' to make the scheme more cost-effective and result-oriented. Under the revised scheme, the grant-in-aid is given to a state government on a matching basis over and above its committed level of expenditure, and 100 per cent assistance is provided to UTs. In the case of directly-run centres, assistance through universities/institutions is on a 90 per cent basis. Some private institutions are also being funded on a contractual basis. The grant is released in two installments.

The salient features of the scheme are as follows:

- Assistance is provided for preparation for recruitment to all services in Group 'A' and 'B' under the central and state governments, PSUs, Banks and the private sector.
- Assistance is also provided for entrance examinations to educational institutions that run professional courses in the areas of medicine, engineering, etc.
- Coaching is emphasised for emerging areas such as information technology (IT) and other service sector activities.
- Coaching centres are entitles to financial assistance of Rs 8,000 per student per course for training in Group 'A' services, Rs 6,000 per student per course for Group 'B' services and for all other government services examinations.
- A stipend of Rs 700 per student per month for Group 'A' services and entrance examinations is provided for outstation students. In the case of local students, RS 225 and RS 125 are provided for Group 'A' and 'B' services with entrance examinations, respectively.
- The coaching institutions are requires to extend extra attention to coaching students and ensuring that at least 33 per cent of those they coach under the scheme are successful in the entrance/recruitment examinations.

Pre-matric Scholarships (PMS) for the Children of those Engaged in Unclean Professions

The scheme was introduced in 1977-78 with the objective of financially assisting the children of scavengers of dry latrines and sweepers, who had traditional link with scavenging, flaying and disabilities among the target groups were also assisted.

The scheme is implemented by state governments and UT administrations. Central assistance is provided to the state governments on a 50:50 per cent matching basis and on a 100 per cent basis to the UT administrations over and above their committed liability.

The scheme covers day scholars from class I to X with scholarship rates ranging from Rs 25 per month for classes I to V, Rs 40 per month for classes VI to VIII, to Rs 50 per month for classes IX to X. The scheme also covers hostellers from class III to X, with scholarship rates for hostellers from class III to VIII being Rs 200 per month and for those in classes IX and X Rs 250 per month. The scholarship is provided for 10 months on a year. Besides the scholarship, an annual ad hoc grant of Rs 500 is also provides to day scholars as well as hostellers.

The scheme was last modified with effect from 25 February 1994, following which there is no income ceiling prescribed. Up to two children of the same parents can get benefits from the scheme, if they are pursuing education in classes IX and X. Although no such restriction has been placed on children, who are pursuing education up to class VIII, an additional/third/ subsequent child born after 1st April, 1993 will not benefit from the scheme.

Post-matric Scholarships for the SC Students

The objective of the scheme is to provide financial assistance to students belonging to the SC/ST category to pursue post-matriculation education in recognised institutions, including correspondence course within the country.

The financial assistance under this scheme includes provision of maintenance allowance, reimbursement of compulsory non-refundable fees, thesis typing/printing charges, study tour charges, book allowance for students pursuing correspondence courses and special provisions for students with disabilities such as reader charges for blind students.

The scheme has been implemented by various state governments and UT administrations, which receive 100 per cent central assistance, over and above their committed liability. For the North-Eastern states, there is no such liability.

Book Bank for SC Students

The scheme is intended to provide SC/ST student's access to the latest text books in medicine (including Indian systems of medicine and homoeopathy), veterinary, engineering, agriculture and polytechnic courses that require expensive books. The book bank scheme also encompasses law, chartered accountancy, management and the bio-sciences.

Provisions have also been made in the scheme to include Braille books/talking books/cassettes to help visually-impaired students. Each set of books provided through this scheme is shared by two students at various stages except in the case of post-graduate course and chartered accountancy, wherein each student is provided one set.

The scheme is open to all those who receive post-matriculation scholarships. The life period of a single set of books has been fixed at three years, and the ceiling cost per set of textbooks varies from Rs 2,400 to Rs 7,500, depending on the course. The scheme also provides Rs 2,000 towards the purchase of cupboards. The scheme is implemented by the state governments and UT administrations. Central assistance is provided to the state governments on a 50:50 per cent matching basis and on a 100 per cent basis to the UT administrations.

Scheme in Girls/Boys Hostels for SC Students

The main objective of this scheme is to provide hostel facilities to SC students while they are studying in middle, high and secondary schools, colleges and universities. The scheme is implemented by the State governments and on a 50:50 per cent matching basis and a 100 per cent basis to the UT administrations for the construction of hostel buildings for up to 100 inmates, boundary walls, two-room sets for hostel wardens and one-room sets for given *chowkidars* (watch and ward staff). Non-governmental organisations (NGOs) are also given central assistance for the expansion of existing hostels on a 45 per cent central share, 45 per cent state share and 10 per cent own contribution basis.

Land is to be provided free of cost by the state/UT or beneficiary institution. A few rooms of the hostel are to be constructed in accordance with barrier-free designs and facilities like ramps being incorporated so as to enable comfortable access by disabled students, the cost of construction is worked out on the basis of the state/Central Public Works Division (CPWD) schedule of rates. The expenditure on the maintenance of these hostels is to be born by the state governments from their funds.

Centrally-controlled universities can receive financial assistance up to 90 per cent under the scheme, with the remaining 10 per cent contributed by them. Other universities can receive central assistance of up to (45 per cent) and themselves (10 per cent).

National Overseas Scholarship for SC Students

The National Overseas Scholarship is a non-plan scheme under which 17 scholarships of a total of 30 are awarded annually to SC students. The scheme, which also includes SC converts to other religions, intends to provide financial assistance to meritorious SC students, who have no means to fund themselves for higher education abroad in courses for which adequate facilities are unavailable in India.

Under this scheme, the government meets a student's entire tuition fees, provides a maintenance allowance, a contingency allowance and air passage both ways once a year. There are some subject restrictions for bachelor's, master's, doctoral and post-doctoral courses. Certain courses pertaining to science, technology, medicine, agriculture, engineering and Indian studies are excluded from the list. Specific subjects are prescribes every year in consultation with the MHRD to pursue master's and bachelor's courses. Preference is given to candidates pursuing Ph.D degrees and post-doctorates in the fields of science, technology and engineering.

The maximum duration of scholarship varies for different degrees. As for the qualifying criteria, SC candidates are requires to obtain 60 per cent in the qualifying degree along with two years research/teaching/work experience for bachelors, masters and Ph.D degrees, and five years research/teaching/work experience with Ph.D for a post-doctoral degree. A candidate's age should not exceed 35 years, and the annual income of the applicant should not exceed Rs 60,000. Only one child in a family can avail of this award.

The scheme is widely advertised every year in national and regional newspapers and in Employment News. The NCSCST, state governments and UTs are also simultaneously apprised of the advertisement. The selected candidates are given an award letter that facilitates their seeking admission abroad. Since the award is valid for three years, excluding the year of selection, it gives the students ample time to secure the necessary admission. The scholarships are forwarded to the students abroad by the Indian missions in the countries of their study.

Passage Grants for SC Candidates

This non-plan scheme provides four passage grants of a total of nine to SC students, who are already receiving a merit scholarship for post-graduate studies, research or training abroad from a foreign government/organisation or under any other scheme, wherein the coast of passage is not provided.

Candidates who apply for passage grants should possess a master's or an equivalent degree in the case of humanities or the sciences and a bachelor's degree in the case of engineering, technical and medical subjects. Their parents' income should not exceed Rs 60,000 per annum.

The scheme is advertised every year in leading newspapers, *Employment News* and regional language papers. The NCSCST, state governments and UTs are also well aware of the advertisements. Prospective candidates can apply for the scheme according to their convenience, as the scheme is a rolling programme and not restricted to a deadline.

Inclusive Policy and the State of Uttar Pradesh

The State governments are also to supposed to enact policies and devise and implement strategies and programmes for the inclusion of the Dalits on the lines of Central government. We all aware that the Government of India under National Education Policy of 1986 (as updated in 1992), and the Programme of Action 1992 reaffirm national commitment to universalisation of elementary education (means education up to class eighth). Para 5.12 of NPE resolves that free and compulsory education of satisfactory quality should be provided to all children up to 14 years of age before we enter the 21st century.

Keeping above in view, a World Bank assisted project called Basic Education Project had been undertaken in 1993, for expansion of quality basic education in the state. For the smooth running of this project, a society 'Uttar Pradesh Sabhee Ke Liye Shiksha Pariyojana Parishad (U.P. Education for all Project Board)' was established on 17th May, 1993 under Societies Registration Act of 1860. It's objectives were:

Box 3

Shiksha Mitra Yojana

- To Remove teacher shortage and improve teacher-pupil ratio in schools, the *Shiksha Mitra Yojana* (Friend of Education Scheme) is being implemented under the control of village panchayats.
- Under the scheme, educated local persons will be appointed on contractral basis at Rs 2250 per month attending to teaching related activities.
- Persons appointed on such a contractual basis will be called *"Shiksha mitras"*.
- The selection of shiksha mitra's will be done by the VECs.
- The minimum qualification for shiksha mitras will be intermediate.
- Under the scheme 50 per cent of the shiksha mitras will be women.
- Initially 10,000 shiksha mitras will be appointed under the scheme.
- Shiksha Mitra Scheme: Under the scheme, the desired teacher-pupil ratio would be achieved at relatively low cost.

The Parishad was to act as an autonomous and independent body for implementation of the Uttar Pradesh Education For All Project (Hereinafter referred to as "the Project") as outlined in the Project Document published by the Government of Uttar Pradesh and its revised version that may be prepared on the basis of review from time to time. The activities of the Parishad was to be concentrated in selected districts, but was expected to extend to the whole State of UP in respect of selected and sponsored projects. The Parishad had been established to function as a societal mission for bringing about a fundamental change in the basic education system, and through it in the overall socio-cultural situation. The following specific objectives of the Project would be pursued by the Parishad:

- Universalisation of Primary Education, viewed as a composite programme of:
  - (i) access to primary education for all children up to 14 years of age,
  - (ii) universal participation till they complete the primary stage through formal or non-formal education programmes, and
  - (iii) universal achievement at least of the minimum levels of learning.
- Provision of continuing education and skill development programmes for youth.
- Making suggestions for greater gender equality in education and female empowerment.
- Making necessary intervention to provide equal educational opportunity to children belonging to the Scheduled Castes, Scheduled Tribes and the poorest sections of society.
- Laying special emphasis on all educational activities on culture and communication, science and environment and inculcation of a sense of social justice.

The district primary education programme-II was started in 1997 in 22 districts of the state which ended in 2003. Moreover, DPEP-III was started in 32 districts of the state in 2000 and has ended on 31st March, 2006.

- *Janshala project* was implemented in district Lucknow during 2000-2003.
- *Sarva Shiksha Abhiyan* was started in the state in 16 districts in 2001-2002 and now covers all 70 districts of the state.

Prior to 1972, the primary and upper primary schools in Uttar Pradesh were run, maintained and controlled by District Boards and municipalities including municipal corporations, etc., constituted under various acts related to management of local bodies, i.e.,

- UP Kshettra Samiti and Zila Parishad Adhiniyam, 1961.
- UP Municipalities Act, 1916.
- UP Nagar Mahapalika Adhiniyam, 1959.

Considering urgent need to improve literacy in the state, it was felt that education needed planned interventions from the state Government. In this background, the Government of Uttar Pradesh passed the Uttar Pradesh Basic Education Act, 1972 (UP Act No. 34 of 1972).

The main objective of this act is to organise, co-ordinate and control imparting of basic education in schools other than high schools or intermediate colleges. By this Act, an Autonomous Body named 'Uttar Pradesh Board of Basic Education' was constituted under chairmanship of the Director, Basic Education. All schools which were managed and controlled by local bodies have since then been transferred to the Board. The Board of Basic Education controls appointment, transfer and posting of basic school teachers, determines school timings and gives recognition to private schools imparting basic education in the state.

Uttar Pradesh Board of Basic Education Act, 1972 has been amended in year 2000, incorporating principle of devolution of powers to the village community and management of education has been decentralised for empowering grassroots participatory agencies. Other acts relating to basic education were also amended and most crucial one has been United Provinces Panchayati Raj Act, 1947 where in there is a committee for each village or group of villages called *Gram Shiksha Samiti* whose constitution is as follows:

- Gram Pradhan—Chairman.
- Three Guardians (one woman) of students of basic schools-members.
- Head Master of Basic School or senior most head master-member secretary, (if there is more than one school in Gram Sabha).

Box 4

The Gram Shiksha Samitis

Constitution

- The Pradhan of the gram panchayat is the chairperson.
- Three guardians of the student of Basic school at least one of whom is a woman.
- The head teacher of a basic school situated in the gram panchayat.

Roles

- Establish, administer, control and manage basic schools in the panchayat area.
- Prepare basic schemes for the development, expansion and improvement of such basic schools.
- Promote and develop education, non-formal education and adult education in the Panchayat area.
- Make suggestion to the Zilla Panchayat for the improvement of basic schools.
- Make recommendations for minor punishment in such, manner as may be prescribed for a teacher or other employees of a basic school situated within the limits of the panchyat area.
- Other functions pertaining to the basic education as may be entrusted to it by the State government.

Source: Uttar Pradesh Basic Education Act (Amendment), 2000.

It was believed that *Gram Shiksha Samiti* would establish, control and plan basic schools in its panchayat areas. It would prepare plans for development and improvement of the schools. Major functions also include giving advice regarding building and other improvement plans to Zila Panchayat.

Still there is a long way to go, as challenges remain with wider dimensions to be addressed despite having various policy interventions by the government and advocacy by the experts and activists. A long march to attain social justice for the deprived sections of the society and to bring them into mainstream of development is awaited.

Pedagogical Inclusion

Here, it becomes necessary to say that the way we construct curricula, pedagogies and position, the narratives, that is, how we learn, are at least as important as what we learn. In this process of construction of knowledge-based instead of democratising, it has been found colonised by certain sections of the society on the lines of caste and gender, which needs to be deconstructed and reconstructed.

Feminist Perspective

Women had no history because the expropriation of history is an important mechanism for reproducing in the ideological sphere, social inequality. The expropriation of history from the women is a means of reinforcing male dominance. Topics that were intimately interwoven with women's lives, household and agricultural technology, religious rituals and sentiments, fertility and family size, furnishings, jewellery and clothing, inheritance and property rights, and marriage and divorce, were largely overlooked.

The historical evidences cited earlier confirmed that women have been left out of history, or when included, relegated to the periphery. This revelation startled the feminist historians at large and they realised the need to rethink historiography and rewrite history, which would not only enrich the knowledge about women in the past societies but would also reformulate traditional concepts and categories. The concern of the women historians with gender further altered the shape of history. It was in the late 20th century that gender became a category of historical analysis. Earlier, it was absent from the major bodies of social theory.

The reconstruction of women's history is made difficult because of the nature of available historical sources.[12] As most of the historical sources were written and collected by men, and libraries and archives organised their materials within the traditional categories of male-oriented history, there were few entries under 'women', and women were generally subsumed under the "male" category.[13] Recent Feminist scholarship illustrates the possibilities, which arise from looking at older sources afresh, from a different perspective and with a new set of questions in mind.

Contributions to enrich our knowledge have come from many quarters: Scholars both men and women, action groups, legal practitioners, creative writers, social workers, people committed to the emancipation of women. It is out of this theorising began to emerge. In an attempt to reconstruct women's history on the lines of caste and class one has to go back to historical formulations framed from time to time.

The Report of the Committee on the Status of Women in India (1974) known as Towards Equality was a major landmark in evaluating the position of women. It argued for the inclusion of all women, from minority communities, marginalised groups, and the lower socio-economic strata in the nation's progress and its history. This report not only influenced historians about history of women, it set the research agenda for the future. From the mid-1970s to the mid-1980s, historians focussed on locating and preserving women's records, making women visible, and documenting the lives of non-elite women. Consequent upon, this period saw scholars utilising the new historiography to reread and recast existing sources and examine newly-discovered and preserved records. Initiatives to write a more inclusive history that is honest about differences and conflicts over these differences have started gaining ground. In the late 1980's feminist scholars began talking about the need for a specialised archive for women that would collect materials and at the same time become 'an agent of conscientisation' (Sparrow, 1997-98).

As we discussed earlier that this work is undertaken for the study of women in general and dalit women in particular, which leads to consideration of the interlocking of multiple structures of oppression—caste, class, gender, which shape the multiplicity of these women's subjectivities. The patriarchal Brahmanical upper middle class perspective sees these women as lowest of the low; a paternalistic perspective sees them entirely passive victims annihilated under the combined weight of oppressive structures, to be uplifted only by benevolent outsider. But we need to point out that dalit women are in some respects freer and more self-sufficient than upper caste women. At the same time, it is necessary to remind ourselves that a ritually high status is what ensures that one is perceived to be an 'Indian woman' and confers upon 'upper' caste women the right/moral duty to feel (consciously or sub-consciously) superior to or contemptuous of dalits in general dalit women in particular.

The newer challenges to the task of writing women's history come from the subaltern school and from historians interested in resistance in everyday life. In their attempts to explain hegemonic processes, subaltern historians have uncovered and articulated the stories of suppressed peoples. Although they have paid some attention to women, the uncovering of women's subalternity has not been their forte. However, Feminist historians, both male and female, have brought to light these lacunae of traditional history. They claim that the ignorance of women's contribution to the society in the past made it easier to deny their contribution in the present too. Thus, the scholars of women's history took up the dual task of "restoring women to history" and 'restoring history to women'. There are three ways in which feminist historians have altered our perceptions of the past.

They have redefined methods and categories. They have focussed on sex along with race and class as a category of analysis which helped them in rejecting stereotypes attributed to women's nature.They have further transformed our understanding of social changes: how domestic and public spheres diverged and as a consequence, women lost control over production, property and their own personhood. Gerda Lerner (1979)[14] cites the two approaches towards writing women's history by traditional historians; 'Compensatory history' and 'contributory history'[15] both reflected male bias.

Lerner opines that till very recently women's history which has been written as a compensatory history, is a history of few notable women, ignores the majority, and their experiences. It also ignores the fact that different classes of women have different historical experiences and to comprehend the full complexity of society at a given stage of its development, it is essential to take into account such differences.

The next approach of conceptualising women's history has been "contribution history". It describes women's contribution to, their status in, and their oppression by male-defined society. However, this contribution is judged first of all with respect to its effect on the movement or event and secondly by standards appropriate to men. (Lerner, 1979)[16] Even the conceptual frameworks adopted by historian have been male-centric in nature.

Pedagogical Inclusion of Women

After Towards Equality report, scholars utilising the new historiography and examine newly discovered and preserved records. The results were impressive, for example "Women Writing in India", edited by Susie Tharu and K. Lalitha, is a translated and edited collection of women's writing from 600 BCE (Tharu and Lalitha, 1990-93). Other historians have edited recovered writing for publication. Here mention would be on the memoirs of Shudha Mazumdar, Manmohin Zutshi Sahgal and Haimabati Sen (Forbes 1989, 1994, 2000). Tanika Sarkar's translation and analysis of Rashsundari Devi's memoir (Sarkar, 1999), and Rimli Bhattacharya's translation of Binodini Devi's Memoir (Bhattacharya1998). These works both retrieve women's writings and encourage reflection on issues of agency, victimhood and cultural difference. Initiatives to write a more inclusive history that is honest about differences and conflicts over these differences have started gaining ground.

As mentioned in the previous chapter that how as an agent of conscientisation feminists under the leadership of C.S. Lakshmi started Spparow (Sound and Picture Archives for Research on Women), in the process of creating space for women in the knowledge base.

Established institutional structures and traditions of practice are extremely powerful in framing how we understand ourselves as people, our place in our communities, our cultures and identities. Insights into the processes of exclusion related to gender and sexual identities have much to offer an understanding of the exclusion of marginalised groups and the ways that these interact with gender. However, these processes are necessarily contextually constructed as people in different contexts do not have access to the same range of possibilities (Gubrium and Holstein, 2000). This implies the importance of recognising multiple gender configurations.

While SC and ST women share common problems of gender exclusion with their high caste counterparts, they also suffer from problems specifically related to their caste and ethnic backgrounds. Keeping this in mind, it becomes necessary to incorporate 'Dalit perspective' while dealing with the Dalit women.

Dalit Perspective

History writing in India was consciously served to nationalist recovery of India's self, as in post-colonial societies. History in post-colonial societies assumes a crucial role in not only retrieval of the past but also in constructing identities. Historical enterprise in India encapsulates this crisis in the selective appropriation of the past. Vijaisri, 2004. The outcastes constitute a community conscious of its discrimination and exclusion in historical narratives. The current historiographical trends, as regards outcaste history, are ambiguous, elusive in nature. Frequently, the acts of outcastes are categorised as 'parochial' elements. For instance, censorious references to them appear in 'nationalist historiography, a narrative of 'struggle' for freedom. This narrative does not recognise non-elite and non-brahmin contribution towards national movement. Likewise, Cambridge historiography, while it contests the ideological basis of the national narrative, does not initiate a dialogue with the social periphery and projects the 'lower' castes as mere passive followers of elite leaders. Marxist historians, working within the rigid class perspective, show reluctance to address issues related to caste. Finally, the subaltern school of thought that emerged in 1980's postulated an alternative framework but their research suffer from the same limitation that they failed to raise fundamental issues related to outcaste historical experience.

Alternative history develops out of existing knowledge sources to identify historical/existing points of view that have been ignored, overlooked, or unseeable. It usually denotes a history told from an alternative viewpoint, rather than from the view (actual or ascribed, obvious or inferred) of imperialists, conquerors or explorers. A search for 'inclusivity at the level identity formation, consciousness building, awareness generation have started taking deeper roots among the intellectual community. They can be enumerated as following points:

- Question the existing brahminical sources and break the brahminical mindset.
- Strengthen knowledge base of Dalit writings, which often invokes social memory as the source of their knowledge system. This also helps in maintaining the historical continuity.

- Dalit literature has emerged as a creative intervention of dalit intelligentsia. It also serves as means for Dalit writers to reclaim narrative authority over the construction of the 'Dalit Self'.
- An attempt of marginalised group to renegotiate narrative authority of autobiography, which has been originally defined and continually policed according to the interests of the dominant sections.

Dalits have not become a part of Indian historiography, though such a study is of immense relevance and significance with regard to the inherent radical democratic identity of their movement and their role of being productive community. Available scholarship on Dalit's history suffers from lack of historical and written documentation. Yet once again, this is not to rule out the immense significance of a few analytical and comprehensive studies on Dalit history. As a result, attempts towards historically locating 'untouchables' are impeded by an acute shortage of direct evidence about the realities of Dalit social life. Real initiatives to reconstruct Dalit history generally draws from traditional historical sources, like archival material, reports of censuses, commissions, committees, and gazetteers. Biographical and autobiographical writings of Dalit organic intellectuals do exist in literary form like poems, novels, dramas, contemporary press reports, and caste association activities, etc., available in vernacular language etc.

In the recent years there have been attempts to develop Dalit discourse on the issue of human rights. The Dalits have been protesting against the system for humanity and not for charity. This perspective is more viable and gets reflected in their culture and productive activities. Human rights perspective of the Dalit bahujans is a way to know about their own self which was denied by the brahminical forces (Jogdand, 1999). 'Right to be human' is an important dimension of this perspective[17] (Guru, 1997). One recent and welcome development being evident in many fora is the growing depth and breadth of dalit scholars and the possibility of a new Dalit studies intellectual movement similar to subaltern studies. Ultimately, this Dalit studies in future seems to be more vibrant with Dalit scholars exercising leadership and agency.

Since the early years of Indian society, the brahminical mode of composing defining and interpreting history, culture and stories became the basis of formation of narratives in the form of puranic stories, vrat kathas, folk lores loaded with brahminical values, ritual stories and songs. Through this, the Brahmans created a brahminical mind-set and a normative frame of reference by which accorded an inferior position.[18] To counter such oppressive historical constructions, the subaltern groups have continuously engaged in communicating their own stories, which they had composed in various forms. They have also constructed a plethora of symbols which are used as tools for empowerment in response to the urge to acquire self-respect. The creation and compilation of contesting histories and narratives are ongoing process that is transmitted to the Dalit at the grassroots level in the form of stories, riddles and genealogies.

Apart from these, Dalit literature as a creative intervention of Dalit intelligentsia played a significant role in constructing Dalit history. The historical consciousness is very much internalised in the structure of their literary narratives. The importance of Dalit writings lies in authentic representation of the community by questioning the existing brahminical and progressive writings. The protest against the caste and class dominance is central to the Dalit writings. Mostly, Dalit literary writings are autobiographical reflections of the community. Dalit writings are conscious effort of bridging the oral and written cultures. Dalit writings often invoke social memory as the source of their knowledge system. This also helps in maintaining the historical continuity.

Dalit intellectuals and academicians believe that Dalits of many castes played significant roles as leaders and commanders in the revolt. The mainstream academicians on the other hand opine that the Dalits as a community have always been docile, inactive and subjugated.

The term 'Dalit literature' can be traced to the first Dalit literary conference in 1958, which passed a resolution defining the term. But nothing tangible was seen. In the 70s thinking Dalit critics began to theorise on Dalit literature and its role. A number of young writers, full of a new awareness, had started writing for periodicals like *Asmitadarsha.* The poets Daya Pawar, Waman Nimbalkar, Trryambak Sapkale, Arjun Dangle, Namdeo Dhasal,Umakant Randhir and JV Pawar, and short story writers Tarachandra Khandekar, Yogiraj Waghmare, Avinash Dolas,

Yogendra Meshram and Bhimrao Shirvale are a few, who developed during this period. The Dalit writer began to realise more and more than there was no point in merely writing provocative poetry against injustice. The Dalit writers had also become familiar with the Black movement and literature with in the USA. The result was that the youths Nandeo, Dhasal, Arjun Dangle, and JV Pawar took the initiative and established the political movement called the Dalit Panthers in Bombay, in 1972. The leaders of the Dalit panthers were all writers. Thus a wave of writing describing experience in provocative language swept Marathi literature. This was probably the first time in India that creative writers became politically active and formed an organisation.

Dalit literature is not simply literature. Although today, most Dalit writers have forgotten its origins, Dalit literature is associated with a movement to bring about change. It is a consciousness of these beginnings. The Dalit autobiography is a literary form marked by a great quantity of writing, however, its quality is equal to its quantity. The journey from Shankarrao, Kharat's *Tara Antaral*, to the young writer Sharan Kumar Limbale's 'The Bastard' is the whole saga of Dalit social history.

Dalit Feminist Standpoint

Over the last decades women's studies in India had raised important questions about invisibility, distortion and marginalisation of gender as a category of analysis in mainstream disciplines and their practices of canonisation (standardisation, acceptance as the genuine standard work). Despite feminist critiques of the mainstream social sciences, the classical frameworks of caste have left their imprint on women's studies too (Rege, 2006). Dalit feminist critiques of the 1990's posed challenges to feminists' canons, curricular protocol and alliances with brahmanical power and privileges (*Ibid*). Except for a few notable exceptions, women's studies scholars did not seriously engage with Dalit feminist critiques and reflections on the transcoding of caste (beyond/across) code in feminist discourse and practices have been rare (*Ibid*).

The women's movement and women's studies have brought forth shifts in our ways of thinking but this does not mean that all prior assumptions have been discarded or even clearly stated. The relative lack of engagement with the non-brahmanical renderings of caste and gender in mainstream social sciences have been reproduced in women's studies. As we have been studying that the method of narrating and deconstructing experiences has been used by feminists, in the same way Indian Dalit bahujan thinkers like Mahatma Phule, Ambedkar and Periyar Ramaswamy Naicker have also used this method.

The linkages between the Brahmans' control over knowledge and the canonical understanding of caste cannot be ignored. Chakravarty, has succinctly summarised this politics of knowledge of caste:

> It is not surprising that sociological writing—whose practitioners have mostly been men—often intellectualises and thereby masks rather than explains the structure of the caste system. It gives an overemphasis on the ideology of the caste system, namely, on its ritual aspect, to the exclusion of material conditions and questions of power. This is a consequence of focussing on the brahminical view drawn from brahminical texts. It completely evades the views of dalit writers, who provided a counter view on the caste system by focusing on the experiential dimensions of caste-based oppression (Chakravarty 2003).

The introduction of Dalit testimonies as historical narratives of experience is a way of introducing the counter views on caste system (Rege, 2006). As Guru (2003) puts it succinctly, testimonies have the ability to convert what is considered pathological into subversive chemicals'. These writings perform a double function; they inflict an inferiority complex in the minds of adversaries by resurrecting Dalit triumphalism and bring out guilt in the minds of 'upper castes' by recording social wrongs done by ancestors (Guru, 2003).

The life narratives by Dalit women namely Shantabai Dhanaji Dani, Mukta Sarvagod, Shantabai Krishnaji Kamble, Baby Kondiba Kamble, Kumud Pawade, Urmila Pawar, Janabai Kachru Girhe, Vimal Dadasaheb More present Dalit women's interpretation of society and in engaging with these texts, the set of interrelated questions outlined by Kamble (1998) in his work on Dalit interpretations of society can provide significant insights. How do Dalit women contest and redefine upper caste definitions of their social status and that of their community? How do they view the institutions and practices prevalent in Indian society? Do they see the caste system as an irrevocable reality? What kinds of struggle do they suggest for the annihilation of caste? What are the ways in which Dalit women resent, note their dissent against and compromise with brahmanical domination? (Kamble, 1998).

In the earlier chapter we discussed that Dalit women have participated actively in the Dalit movement, which brought consciousness of questioning and paved the way for intellectual ferment. Consequent upon many autobiographies by Dalit women have been published. Shantabai Kamble's *Maya Jalmachi Chittarkatha* and Kumud Pawde's *Antasphot* are representative of these. Shantabai Kamble's is a struggle for identity and growth against a rural background while that of Prof Pawde is set in an urban educated ethos.

In these autobiographies, relating to different periods of time and set in different levels of society, we see varying facets of the Dalit movement, the struggle for survival, the emotional universe of a Dalit's life, the man-woman relationship, an existence crushed under the wheels of village life, the experiencing of humiliation and atrocities, at times, abject submission, at other times, rebellion.

Gopal Guru opines that 'history, for instance, cannot be real, unless a person has lived experience of an historical event; any written history about that event is inauthentic'. To quote him: 'You cannot have a Dalit experience unless you are a Dalit yourself or at least experience what it means to be a Dalit subject with no choice to be otherwise'.

In this regard he is not interested if the writing of the non-Dalits is complimentary or derogatory about Dalits. It is just that non-Dalits have no moral right to theorise about Dalits[19] (Sarukkai, 2007).

The efforts to create an alternative space by subverting the mainstream culture through their own cultural resources like their myths, legends, folktales and folk heroes, etc., are being constructed through these efforts. Dalit women's contribution their personal narrative has been instrumental in portraying their lived experiences full of sorrow and agony as voice of an agency (Other).

Challenges

The above realisation naturally necessitates going beyond the fixed conventional academic and theoretical frameworks.

For a focussed policy orientations, governance must participatory and representative of various castes and on the lines of gender. Besides generating of disaggregated data is also required.

References

1. B.R. Ambedkar, speech delivered on Jan. 18, 1943, in Dr. Babasaheb Ambedkar: Writings and Speeches, Vol. 1, 222 (1979).
2. The politics of ideas suggests "a broadly secular understanding of politics as a matter of judgement and debate, and expects political loyalties to develop around policies rather than people".
3. Politics of presence privileges the question of "who" rather than "what" and demands equal representation of women, ethnic minorities, and other groups that see themselves as excluded.
4. Formal equality is a principle of equal treatment: individuals who are alike should be treated alike, according to their actual characteristics rather than stereotypical assumptions made about them. It is a principle that can be applied either to a single individual, whose right to be treated on his or her own merits can be viewed as a right of individual autonomy, or to a group, whose members seek the same treatment as members of other, similarly situated groups. What makes an issue one of *formal* equality is that the claim is limited to treatment *in relation* to another, similarly situated individual or group and does not extend beyond the same-treatment claims to any demand for some particular, *substantive* treatment.
5. Substantive equality' is a conception of equality that is concerned with the ensuring ability of persons to compete on an equal basis, having regard to various obstacles (including discrimination) that may impede this equality of opportunity. An even more far-reaching conception of 'equality' is concerned with equality of *outcome*. In particular, claims of 'substantive equality' seek to highlight significant social obstacles (particularly discrimination-based on social characteristics) to equal access to such goods as education, employment, goods and services. For instance, an unequal distribution of childcare responsibilities between women and men may make it more difficult for women with children to undertake jobs with long working hours without additional support or accommodation. Accordingly, merely eliminating sex discrimination on the *hiring* stage may not be enough to ensure that female workers have the same employment opportunities as male workers. It suggests that it may be necessary to take further steps to

accommodate or assist female workers with children so that they may compete on equal terms with their male counterparts.

6. Mysore Government Circular No. 218-98, dated 19/21 January 1895, quoted in BR Ambedkar: Perspectives on Social Exclusion and Inclusive Policies by Sukhdeo Thorat and Narender Kumar, OUP, New Delhi, 2008.
7. Proceeding of sub-committee, Vol. II, sub-committee No. II Minorities, India Round Table Conference 1930-31, pp. 77-78.
8. Women in Development discourse deconstructs the economic growth paradigm and focusses on women specific statistics and indicators, policies and schemes, plan allocation and programmes on health, education and employment.
9. Women and development model integrates women in the development work as active change agents. Affirmative action by the state and pro-active approach by the civil society through NGOs and women's groups are advocated by this model for empowerment of women against the forces of patriarchal class society. NGOs-voluntary organisations implementing this approach have become powerful force during 1990s.
10. Gender and development model is based on an understanding of gender relations that empowers the weak (he or she). Gender is socially constructed and gender relations are power relations based on caste, class, ethnicity, race and religion. Here power is an important analytical category. This approach seeks to analyse the causes of gender inequality within the context of relations between women and men and social structure, and to change stereotyped division of labour as well as institutions and systems that bring about gender disparity. The GAD approach emphasises empowerment of women, who are economically and socially disadvantaged while paying due consideration to the role of men in eliminating gender inequality http://www.mofa.go.jp/policy/oda/category/wid/gad.html.
11. Gender budgeting is a methodology, with its own tools, designed to facilitate the application of gender analysis in the formulation of Government budgets and the allocation of budgetary resources. The objective is to enhance fiscal policy-making and measures by providing a mechanism for ascertaining their impacts on women vs men, girls *vs* boys. To ignore the gendered impact of policies and budgeting constitutes 'gender blindness'.
12. Now many more sources are being explored daily which are offering newer and fresh insights about women's lives and

how gender shapes and is shaped by wider social and political contexts.

13. See, Gerda Lerner, *The Majority Finds its Past*, London, Oxford University Press, 1979, p. 173.

14. Gerda Lerner, *The Majority Finds its Past*, New York, Oxford University Press, 1979. pp. 145-46.

15. The terms 'Compensatory History' and Contribution History Used', in Marie J. Buhle, Ann. C. Gordan and Nancy Schrom, *Women in American Society: An Historical Contribution*, Radical America, Vol. 5, No. 4-July-August, 1971 pp. 3-66.

16. Gerda Lerner, *The Majority Finds its Past*, New York, Oxford University Press, 1979, p. 146.

17. In 1998 the National campaign on Dalit Human Rights has given a charter of Dalit Human Rights which runs as Follows: We assert that 'Dalit Rights are Human Rights', we demand that full protection of dalits in the Panchayati Raj Institutions of the country, we demand reservations to Dalits in all private bodies, we demand white paper be placed in Parliament on the atrocities on Dalits etc. (*See* for details a Document on 'National Campaign non-Dalit Human Rights', 10th December-14 April, 1999.

18. Intellectual subordination of Dalit issues by the non-Dalit groups should be examined with this cultural change. Gopal Guru is very much concerned about the 'theoretical exploitation' of Dalits. It is frustrating for Guru when he finds non-Dalits taking over the Dalit experience in order to theorise about it. He says that 'It is just that non-Dalits have no moral rights to theorise about Dalits' (Guru, 2007).

Bibliograhy

Chakravarty, Uma. 1993. Conceptualising Brahmanical Patriarchy in Early India: Gender, Caste, Class and State, *Economic and Political Weekly*, April 3, pp. 579-85.

Chaudhuri, M. 1995. Citizens Workers and Emblems of Culture: An Analysis of the First Plan Document on Women', *Contribution to Indian Sociology*, New Series, Vol. 29, Nos. 1-2, pp. 211-35.

Galanter Marc, 1984. Competing Equalities: Law and the Backward Classes in India, New Delhi: Oxford University Press.

Government of India. 2001. Report of National Commission for the Scheduled Castes and Scheduled Tribes, VIth Report, 1999-2000 and 2000-2001, New Delhi.

Government of India. 1998. Ministry of Welfare (renamed as Ministry of Social Justice and Empowerment on May 25, 1998), Government of India, Annual Report 1995-1996.

Guru, Gopal. 2003. Review of 'Joothan: A Dalit's Life by OM Prakash Valmiki (Translated into English by Arun Prabha, Mukkherjee)', *Seminar*, No. 530, October, pp. 70-71.

Guru, Gopal. 1997. Human Rights and the Dalits—An Enquiry into the Human Rights Discourse in India, *Indian Journal of Human Right*, University of Hyderabad, Jan-June, pp. 107-117.

Hasan Zoya, 2009. Politics of Inclusion: Caste Minorities and Affirmative Action, New Delhi: Oxford University Press.

Jaffrelot Christophe. 2003. Indian's Silent Revolution: The Rise of Low Castes in Indian Politics, New Delhi: Permanent Black.

Jain, Kalpana,1990. 'A Myth the Muslim Created'. *Indian Express*, 5th October 1990.

Kamble, Ramesh. 1998. Dalit Interpretations of Society, *Seminar*, No. 471, November 1998, pp. 19-24.

Lister, R. Beresford, P., Green, D.A. and Woodard, K. Bradshaw, J. and Sainsbury, R. (eds.). 2000. Where are 'the poor' in the future of poverty research?. *Researching Poverty,* pp. 284-304. Ashgate, Aldershot.

Marc, Galanter.1984 Competing Equalities: Law and the Backward Classes in India, California: University of California.

Government of India. Report on Prevention of Atrocities against Scheduled Castes: Policy and Performance, National Human Rights Commission, India, p. 175.

Conclusion

Social Exclusion has become a buzzword in recent academic and political discourse all over the world. As a concept social exclusion, thus essentially refers to the processes through which groups are wholly or partially, excluded on the basis of group identity from full participation in economy and society in which they live. It involves two crucial dimensions, namely the 'societal relations' (causing exclusion) and their 'outcome' (causing deprivation). For understanding the nature of exclusion, therefore, the insight into societal interrelations and institutions of exclusions is as important as the outcome in terms of deprivation for excluded groups. It is also necessary to recognise that in 'group exclusion' people are excluded because of their group identity and because of individual attribute. In case of exclusion of group, however, individuals with certain social and cultural identity such as social origin like caste, ethnicity, religion gender, or colour, are excluded from having access to sources of income, employment, education civil rights and other social needs. Thus, 'group exclusion' is based on social and cultural identity of persons, irrespective of the attributes of individuals within social/cultural group.

It has to be recognised that Indian society is characterised by multiple forms of exclusion which revolves around the societal institutions that exclude, discriminate, isolate and deprive some groups on the basis of group's identity like caste, ethnicity, religion, gender and others in various spheres of our society, polity and economy. This has important policy implications. While in the case of 'individual exclusion' the focus will have to be on enhancing the individual capabilities in the form of pro-poor policy, while in the case of 'group exclusion' the focus of the policy will be targetted on the group as a whole covering all individuals in the social/cultural group.

However, the exclusion based on caste is one example and patriarchy is another, which is systemic or constitutive exclusion. And the primary concern in India is that about 200 million people are discriminated on the basis of caste, which historically has regulated the social cultural and economic life of people in India and as a result the structural location of Dalits in Indian society becomes unique. There have been instances of social exclusion and discrimination, extreme vulnerability to violence, sexual abuse against dalit women, trafficking, discrimination in schools and institutions of higher education, lack of access to disaster relief and mitigation measures, exclusion from markets, water sources and public services and public places, and reprisals when Dalits demand equality and justice. This is a systemic discrimination which permeates structures of governance, media and the criminal justice administration to intervene in their own level to bring justice for dalit in general and dalit women in particular. Now referring to dalit women, specifically it can be said that because of their unique location in the social matrix owing to hierarchical and power dominance and caste ridden society, exclusion and exploitation of dalit women takes place, which separates them from general/upper caste women.

In the name of religion the project of Brahminisation has alienated the women in general and dalit women in particular from their original religious forms and spirituality. However, this alienation found expression in the form of consciousness raising efforts which could be traced back to history when we find spells of dalit assertion or movement emerging during the medieval and colonial as well as contemporary period for liberating the dalits from discrimination and exploitation which the academic discourse has always negated. The recorded history has always set aside various forms of assertions, agitations, and negations, etc., shown individually or collectively by the dalits in different regions during the subsequent periods. However the efforts of intellectuals like Phule, Ambedkar and Periyar for creating an egalitarian society through their consciousness raising efforts gradually got translated into organised dalit assertion and movement. Ambedkar wanted self-representation of the dalits, because he was also convinced that only the dalits could voice these interests. He aptly pointed out that they are distinctively their own interests and none can truly voice them. Untouchability, constitutes a definite set of interests which the untouchables alone can speak for. Ambedkar's teachings have distanced them away from Hindu traditions and customs and as a result majority of dalits have rejected the Hindu religion.

No doubt, the dalit movements have left some definite marks on the position of the dalits and proved to be instrumental at least indirectly in bringing some changes in 'others' attitudes, behaviours. In fact the dalit movements which could be termed as protest movements opposed to the injustices caused on dalits by certain social collectivities, dominant group's communities and so on. But ironically these dalit movements appeared patriarchal and failed to take up the issue of dalit women. And it is quite true that dalit women are dalits among dalits. Unfortunately, the issues of dalit women neither figured in the agenda of dalit movement, their caste fraternity nor by the mainstream movements their gender fraternity.

Similar to dalit movement the women's movement has been as much attacked by dalit women for being *savarna* as the dalit movement has been attacked for being patriarchal, and feminists of minority communities have challenged the women's movement for being Hindu by default, in its claim to being secular. Ultimately, it gave birth to Dalit Feminist Standpoint (DFS) which started vouching for them. Dalit feminist standpoint argues that the liberation of women is not a uniform or undifferentiated domain. Notions of liberty vary from community to community. A Dalit woman is a separate category and they have different problems as compared to other women in the society.

In other words, feminist politics has been coming to the difficult recognition that "women" do not simply exist as a category that is available for feminist mobilisation—the question then remains, *who is the subject of feminist politics*? If "women" must be located within the grid of other identities that circulate, then what a "feminist" position would be? For what we are talking about here is more than simply the truism that "women have many identities". So, we must go much further than saying that "women" mobilise as upper-caste/dalit and so on. Rather, we need to come to the more complex recognition that under different circumstances, and given different kinds of political mobilisation, "people" identify and come together as "dalits", "muslims", "working class", or much less often, as "women". This is the difficult political fact to face—that women coming together as upper-caste/dalit may not necessarily be coming together as upper-caste/dalit *women.* We are forced to see the creation of "women-as-subject" as the end or goal of feminist politics, not the starting point.

However, this social consciousness and assertion of the Dalits including Dalit women in specific and women in general, got nourished by a number of legislative measures enacted in the form of protective and positive discrimination after independence for their inclusion. Although these measures as well as schemes have not produced desired results in concrete terms, these have certainly increased their consciousness, assertiveness and agitational capacity through out the years.

Most of its ideals, adopted after Independence, lay only in principle and needs to be fully and properly translated into practice for which more vigorous and sustained movements are to be organised at various levels. Otherwise transformation with a real democratic polity and an egalitarian socio-economic system, may remain an illusive agenda, further aggravating social tensions with the dominated and suppressed.

Some social changes seem to have taken place so far, can be categorised at structural, cultural and social levels. At the structural level, these socio-economic status, political participation and limited access to power, rise in their socio-political consciousness, and their assertion for social justice and equality as compared to that in the past has been found. This can also be inferred from their assertion for dignified and respectful social identity. However, notwithstanding differences in the nature of Dalit movements and meaning of identity, there has been a common quest in all these (Dalit) movements—the quest for equality, dignity and for eradication of untouchability'.

In order to have a right and to act to claim a right, the first step is the appreciation of the 'right to have a right'. This is critical for women in general and dalit women in particular because they have poorer access to the means to actualise their entitlements, and also because they are often not seen and do not see themselves as worthy of having rights. The devaluation and disparagement by others leads to self-devaluation and self-denigration, which deprives individuals of agency. Women's subordinate position in the hierarchical social relations of gender results in self-definitions that mitigate against rights-claiming over and beyond what ascribed relations entitle them to have.

In the Indian context, given the multiple forms of exclusion associated with group identities like caste, ethnicity, gender, and religion in various spheres of economy, polity, society and culture. It is important to formulate an inclusive policy to overcome deprivation associated with multiple forms of discrimination. To develop inclusive policies for multiple forms of exclusion associated with caste, ethnicity, religion, gender, and other forms of exclusion is an issue, which is currently being discussed by the Indian government and policy makers. It is to be recognised that the nature of inclusive policies will be necessarily governed by exclusionary character of Indian society, it would further depend on the forms and spheres of discrimination and their specific consequences on discriminated groups.

As regards Hindu society, the principle of 'graded inequality' implies that not all caste the caste hierarchies suffer equally from the hierarchical entitlement of rights. While the castes located at the bottom of the caste hierarchy namely the former Untouchables suffer the most, the OBCs follow closely. The OBCs in all probability do not suffer from the notion of Untouchability, but they have historically faced social exclusion in education, employment and in certain other social spheres.

Facts and figure mentioned in the previous chapters, clearly demands focussed intervention at country level for the Dalits (the Scheduled Castes and the Scheduled Tribes) communities on gender lines. This require large scale mobilisation of the Dalit groups around their rights and entitlements, so that they could actively participate in their own developmental attainment process.

It is time for the academicians, researchers, policy makers, the civil society to begin the explorations, the way caste pervades our lives creating hierarchy and power and how insensitive we are about the seriousness of the issue. The complexity of the structures and its relationship to hierarchy and power-based on caste and gender has different implications for those, who being privileged and dominant and for OTHER—the suppressed, dominated and excluded lot.

The Way Forward...

Social Policy can neither be formulated nor advanced, if some groups of the population are excluded from full participation in the society. Re-examining social policy on exclusion through a gendered lens is a necessity considering the pluralistic configuration of the society. A modern social policy must integrate inclusion across the range of needed (social, political and economic) interventions to effectively address exclusions.

Need for Statistical Visibility

Improving the ability to gather data disaggregated by caste, gender, ethnic background, religion, disability and other features related with exclusion is a basic step for governments in promoting inclusion. Such information is necessary for better programme design and more effective targetting and programme evaluation. In India, it is necessary that National Statistical Data System which includes population census and specialised household surveys such as National Sample Survey, National Family Planning and Health Survey and others should include specific questions related to excluded groups covering their situation and also the nature and forms of discrimination in multiple spheres.

Social inclusion should be one of the key themes in all the developmental measures that should drive and shape the current government. In doing so, it should be recognised that there are some groups that are harder to reach and last to benefit from policies that aims at targetting social exclusion, such as women, *janjatis* and Dalits. It should thus be noted that only macro-level policies will not be sufficient to address the issue of Dalit women inclusion in totality, but micro-level intervention is required as well to reach out to these sub-groups who can easily be overlooked. A systemic reform needs to be accompanied by interventions designed to reach these sub-groups, provide incentives, come up with more flexible approaches, and tackle their unique problems of exclusion so that every person is able to participate fully in public services.

The government should heed the demand of Dalit women for an inclusive democracy by interweaving inclusion into the mainstream programme and recognising Dalit women's issue as a cross-cutting issue. To translate these, the government should ensure direct representation of Dalit women at various levels of governance, although there has provision of reservations for dalits, tribes and women under the 73rd Amendment Act, revise the regime of Central government funding to ensure that local government and authorities get the money they need to promote inclusion, and consider the voluntary, community organisations and local groups that are actively involved in promoting inclusion as government's natural allies in a strategy for social inclusion. The women's quota in Panchayati Raj Institution (PRI) reminds us of a central truth: power is not something people give away. It has to be negotiated, and sometimes wrested away from the powerful. Enshrining political change within the law has forced both the pace and direction of such change. Democratic politics is, in reality, the interplay of vested interests and the PRIs' great achievement has been to mandate a vested and mutual interest, between women and the political process.The lesson of PRIs is clear, 'If the wisdom of grassroots organisations and especially the courage and clarity of women is to become policy, it will not be through the art of intellectual persuasion but by the arrangements made within the political system for their voice to have power. Bringing women into power is therefore, not only a matter of equity and fairness, but a matter of correcting an unjust and unrepresentative system'. Many believe that the removal of poverty and the achievement of full employment and social integration cannot be effectively addressed without the democratisation of the representative process. Political restructuring is the key to economic growth with justice.

Moving ahead, it can be stated that the significant role transnational networks can play in combating exclusion can not be overlooked. International agencies can help raise awareness on the issue of (Dalit women) exclusion and enrich debate nationally and internationally, they can exert pressure on the government, finance important projects and provide technical assistance and expertise to tackle the causes and consequences of exclusion. Above and beyond, the collective commitment of various stakeholders within the country, such as different associations, enterprises, financial bodies and trade unions, employers and public authorities in various fields, cannot be overlooked. This calls for the government to launch a national strategy for social inclusion, which emphasises on all the sectors playing their part, including the private sector, the voluntary and community sectors, local government and wider public sector. Furthermore, the most efficient way of putting balanced solutions into place can only be achieved by Dalit women themselves being firm and strong in dealing with the exclusion issue and achieving desirable inclusion. Studies, forums and the outcome of interactions with elected women (dalit) across India reveal that in spite of embedded patriarchy, in spite of the rigid nature of the systems within hard core politics and patronage, in spite of roadblocks put before the women—by their families, by civil servants, by parliamentarians, by legislators, by academics and by the NGOs—elected women politicians are not only speaking out, but speaking out about power.

The government should be successful in delivering the policies to deal with social exclusion (of Dalits) in its entirety (including Dalit women), by abiding and inheriting the true spirits of the *Convention on the Elimination of all forms of Discrimination Against Women (CEDAW 1979), International Convention on the Elimination of all forms of Racial Discrimination (ICERD 1965), International Covenant on Civil and Political Rights (ICCPR 1966),* and *International Covenant on Economic, Social and Cultural Rights (ICESCR 1966),* including all other relevant conventions and declarations which condemn discrimination and exclusion in all its forms and which calls for the modification of social and cultural ways in order to eliminate prejudice, customs and all other practices based on the idea of inferiority or superiority.

Even though there is no single universally accepted strategy or methodology for addressing Dalit exclusion, it is possible to identify a number of strategic approaches which give positive results. Integration, partnership, participation and spatial approachs are the cornerstone on which most programmes aimed at combating exclusion of Dalit women, are based. The principle of *Integration* aims at multi-dimensional action programme (on various dimensions of exclusion such as inadequate income, poor health, low levels of schooling, precarious jobs, absence of rights etc.), instead of having compartmentalised policies for each of them. *Partnership* calls for mobilising a coalition of interests and the commitment of a range of partners (including the actors at the economic, social and political levels) without whose collaboration it is difficult to achieve any substantive progress. *Participation* implies involving people in all the sectors (covering economic, social, political and cultural dimensions) because of inter-linkages between them. The important aspect of participation is the active involvement of people in all its levels, including information, organisation, consultation and decision-making stages. Lastly, the S*patial approach* calls for the need to create local units for the identification of the characteristic structures, mechanisms and processes of exclusion so as to carry out spatially significant analysis and intervention.

We need to push the question much further. Have we taken seriously the ways in which the core operating principle of bourgeois democracy—universal suffrage—is reshaped by the principle of reservations for groups in representative institutions? And have we confronted how the very understanding of "democracy" can take different forms over space and time? For western liberal democracies, as Anne Phillips points out, the institutionalisation of group representation seems to conflict with the historical movement of democracy away from group representation and group privilege and towards the ideal where every individual vote counts equally as one. The question of group identity in those societies has therefore been at the centre of heated debate, the most well-known form of which has been the individualist/communitarian debate. Will Kymlicka points out that the acceptance of group identity and group rights is usually on the understanding that they are "a temporary measure on the way to a society where the need for special representation no longer exists". Ideally society should seek to remove the oppression thereby eliminating the need for these rights.

In India, where both the demand for reservations as well as the opposition to it, is posed in a way that challenges the universal abstract citizen; the demand itself introduces the difference of "women" into the category of "citizen" while the opposition to it poses further differences (caste/community) against that of "women" (the "quotas within quotas" position). In India, as we have already seen, the opposition to the demand of reservations for women comes from a position that would push *further* the critique of the abstract unmarked citizen.

"Speaking for women" has been demonstrated to arise from very different kinds of concerns. It is impossible to sustain an argument defending reservations for "women" on the basis of an assumed shared experience while at the same time rejecting any notion of a shared experience that is "Dalit".

Phillips of course, does not make "shared experience" a criterion for quotas—as we saw, she considers "presence" a sufficient condition to justify them. What she shares with the positions discussed above though, is the assumption that the presence of "women" can be clearly demarcated from that of "race", "caste" or "religious" identity—the belief that while these are politically produced categories, "women" pre-exist politics.

If identities emerge in and through political mobilisation, then we need to guard against the possibility that some identities may freeze into new formations of power, thus blocking the emergence of new identities and new alignments. Cautioning against the possibility of collective rights "overtaxing" the theory of rights "tailored to individual persons", Habermas fears that group rights could represent "a kind of preservation of species by administrative means":

> "For to guarantee survival would necessarily rob the members of the very freedom to say yes or no if they are to appropriate and preserve their cultural heritage." Here Hebermas thought we have been neglecting individual freedom in the name of group rights.

Although Habermas uses this critique to limit the recognition of group rights, a debate we have already seen to be framed very differently in post-colonial societies, nevertheless this point must be taken seriously. We would however, need to take it in the opposite direction to the one taken by Habermas. That is, rather than reasserting the need as Habermas does, for "political integration of citizens" we would need to push the possibilities of continuing "pluralisation". Here, we can analyse the distinction made by William Connolly—"*pluralism* is often presented as an achievement to be protected, while the eruption of new drives to *pluralisation* is often represented as perils to this achievement." If democracy remains unresponsive to the emergence of new configurations of identity, then once-emancipatory identities can entrench themselves into formations blocking further democratisation.

The distinctive historical trajectories of the Indian democracies—a post-colonial democracy that came into being two hundred years later—have created different sets of concerns about citizenship and representation to achieve the goal of unity (in the form of integration) in diversity. This very initiation gives some hope among the excluded lot like Dalit and women. But mere institutional codification can not bring any real transformation among Dalit women. Because, they are struggling against all the odds, that is exclusion within exclusion. Real transformation or genuine inclusion can be possible, if they are introduced and their active participation can be recognised at policy level and pedagogy level/in curriculum of educational system. The academician by showing serious interest and providing an alternative space in the knowledge system along with the civil society can play a vibrant role in bringing awareness among the group at large and the Dalit women in particular. The Dalit women themselves can form organisation and assert their rights which they never claimed before to make them more active citizens. In this context, the questions that arise for feminist politics (particularly in the context of Dalit Women) from such a recognition (demand for Inclusion) of the significance of differential "locations", both temporal and geographical for Dalit women must be dealt with a holistic approach. The relevance of knowing how the social structures and institutions reproduce such forms of discrimination is only proportional to the urgency of resisting such discriminations.

To sum up, it can be said that there is a need for new approach and theoretical perspective for the study of all Indian social reality of crucial issues concerning exclusion of Dalit women. It is time now to call the academy into question, and to engage with systems and processes that produce such colonised knowledge. And by providing alternative paradigms of knowledge, theory and understanding, through decolonising the epistemological and pedagogical base and asserting their legitimacy within the academy can be a way forward.

Above all the polity, society and economy will have to be more inclusive and participatory, only then democracy as a means of governance would become meaningful for one and all. If a society practices discrimination, then the impetus for change should come both from the State and Civil society.

Annexures

ANNEXURE 1

Constitutional Provisions

- The Constitution emphasises 'safe-guards' for Scheduled Castes under the 'Special Provisions Relating to Certain Classes' in Part XVI of the Indian Constitution. The Constitution also provides for protection and promotion of their social, economic, educational, cultural and political interests to bridge the disparities and to bring them at par with other sections of the society. In addition, many articles in Parts III (Fundamental Rights), IV (Directive Principles of State Policy), IX, IX A and in the fifth schedule of the Constitution are a measure of the Constitutional concern and commitment.
- The constitutional provisions include general measures found inequality before law (Article 14); Prohibition of discrimination (Article 15), Protection of life and personal liberty (Article 21).
- The social safeguards extended specifically to address untouchability and caste-based work and discrimination are found in—Abolition of untouchability (Article 17), Prohibition of trafficking in human beings and forced labour (Article 23), Prohibition of employment of children in hazardous jobs, etc., (Artical 24), Freedom to practice religion (Article 25).
- The economic safeguards are provided under—the provisions of Articles 23 and 24 stated above as well as under promotion of educational and economic interests of SCs under (Article 46 in Part IV, Directive Principles of State Policy).
- Educational and cultural safeguards are specified in—provision for reservation (Article 15 (4) and that admission into educational institutions will not be denied (Article 29 [2]).
- Employment provisions are made under—equality of opportunities under (Article16), and claim to services and posts (Article 335).

- Political representation was based on a compromise between Mahatma Gandhi and Ambedkar—Reservation of seats in Parliament and State Legislatures under Articles 330, 332, 334.
- Monitoring of safeguards provided under Constitution and all other provisions and policies is also provided for by—Setting up commission under (Article 338).

Other Legislations

- In addition some of the legislations of general nature have greater relevance to Dalit communities.
- The Untouchability Offences Act, later reformulated as the Protection of Civil Rights Act (1955) and Rules 1977.
- The Scheduled Caste/Scheduled Tribe (Prevention of Atrocities) Act, 1989, and rules1995, Bonded Labour (system) Abolition Act, 1976.
- Employment of Manual Scavengers and Construction of Dry Latrines (Prohibition) Act, 1993.
- Devadasi System Abolition Act in the States of Andhra Pradesh, Maharashtra and Karnataka.
- Child Labour (Prohibition and Regulation) Act, 1986.
- Minimum Wages Act, 1948.
- Equal Remuneration Act, 1976.
- Land Reforms Act in different states.
- **Special Component Plan (SCP).**
- **Budgetary Allocation for SCs: Special Component Plan.**
- **Massive Injustice and Loss of Opportunities for Dalits.**

  Analogous to the "The Scheduled Castes and Scheduled Tribes (Prevention of Atrocities) Act, 1989", the Government of India does have a potentially powerful mechanism for the economic empowerment of Dalits. The mechanism is the Special Component Plan (SCP) for Dalits. SCP, in the words of the Indian Planning Commission is "a policy instrument designed to ensure the fulfillment of constitutional guarantees and entitlements enjoined for the Scheduled Caste communities."
- **The Concept of Budgetary Allocation**

  The SCP, initiated during the Indian Government's 6th Five Year Plan (1980-85), envisaged a radical redefinition of planning and budgeting for Dalits. It was based on the realisation by the Government of India that decades of planning and hundreds of millions of rupees spent in the name of "Welfare of SCs and STs" had not brought any substantial changes in the Socio-economic lives of Dalits. Hence, the SCP was brought in as a radically reworked strategy of Dalit welfare and empowerment.

- "The Sixth Five Year Plan marked a shift in the approach to the development of the SCs. The SCP, launched for the SCs, was expected to facilitate easy convergence and pooling of resources from all the other development sectors in proportion to the population of SCs and monitoring of various development programmes for the benefit of SCs."
- The programme was made obligatory for all the State Governments and all their departments as well as all Central Government Ministries. And in 1986, a scheme of Special Central Assistance of 100 per cent grant to the States for the implementation of SCP was also initiated.
- The main elements of the philosophy of the SCP, as regularly stressed by the Ministry of Social Justice and Empowerment of the Government of India, are Proportionality, Convergence, Universal Application and Auto-decision making.
- **Proportionality**

  According to SCP, funds allocated for the welfare of Dalits out of the total annual plan outlay, should be at least proportional to their population percentage at the national and states level. This means that as Dalits constitute 16.5 per cent of the Indian population, at least 16.5 per cent of the outlay of the Central Budget should be allocated as SCP funds. Similarly, in a State like Tamil Nadu, where Dalits constitute 19 per cent of the State population, at least 19 per cent of the plan outlay of the State Budget should be allocated as SCP funds.
- **Convergence**

  In contrast to the earlier practice of numerous schemes by different departments and ministries, rarely leading to any significant impact, SCP envisages an approach whereby holistic programmes, in accordance with specific historic needs and priorities of Dalits, would be evolved and sufficient funds allocated for the programmes. The targets fixed under SCP are to be desegregated into district-wise and sector-wise targets. At the district level, the district collectors are responsible for co-ordinating the implementation of the schemes under SCP.
- **Universal Application**

  As per SCP, no State Government Department and no Central Ministry or Department can claim exemption regarding the implementation of SCP. SCP also makes it clear that no mere notional allocations of funds, based on the unacceptable logic of indivisibility of projects, are allowed. Every department/ ministry must initiate concrete steps to evolve proper programmes under SCP, as per specific Government Orders (G.Os). Separate budget heads have to be shown in the Budget Link Book, clearly mentioning the receipts-expenditures details of SCP, ensuring prevention of any diversion, under-utilisation or mis-utilisation of funds earmarked for Dalits.

- "An important operational principle of SCP is that in all sectors of plan programmes, outlays for development SCs should be incorporated and no distinction can be drawn between the so-called "indivisible and divisible" sectors, as the outlays are allowable in relation to the needs of scheduled castes".

- **Auto-Decision-Making**

- SCP visualises also that Dalits themselves (and those that legitimately represent them) should have the final say in terms of the implementation of SCP. SCP demands that at both Central and State levels, the department concerned with Scheduled Castes Welfare, such as the Scheduled Castes Development Corporations should act as the nodal agency for the formulation, implementation and monitoring of SCP.

- **Proportionality**

  According to SCP, funds allocated for the welfare of Dalits out of the total annual plan outlay, should be at least proportional to their population percentage at the national and States level. This means that as Dalits constitute 16.5 per cent of the Indian population, at least 16.5 per cent of the outlay of the Central Budget should be allocated as SCP funds. Similarly, in a State like Tamil Nadu, where Dalits constitute 19 per cent of the State population, at least 19 per cent of the plan outlay of the State Budget should be allocated as SCP funds.

- **Convergence**

  In contrast to the earlier practice of numerous schemes by different departments and ministries, rarely leading to any significant impact, SCP envisages an approach whereby holistic programmes, in accordance with specific historic needs and priorities of Dalits, would be evolved and sufficient funds allocated for the programmes. The targets fixed under SCP are to be desegregated into district-wise and sector-wise targets. At the district level, the district collectors are responsible for co-ordinating the implementation of the schemes under SCP.

- **Universal Application**

  As per SCP, no State Government Department and no Central Ministry or Department can claim exemption regarding the implementation of SCP. SCP also makes it clear that no mere notional allocations of funds, based on the unacceptable logic of indivisibility of projects, are allowed. Every department/ ministry must initiate concrete steps to evolve proper programmes under SCP, as per specific Government Orders (G.Os). Separate budget heads have to be shown in the Budget Link Book, clearly mentioning the receipts-expenditures details of SCP, ensuring prevention of any diversion, under-utilisation or mis-utilisation of funds earmarked for Dalits.

- "An important operational principle of SCP is that in all sectors of plan programmes, outlays for development SCs should be incorporated and no distinction can be drawn between the so-called "indivisible and divisible" sectors, as the outlays are allowable in relation to the needs of scheduled castes".

- **Auto-Decision-Making**

- SCP visualises also that Dalits themselves (and those that legitimately represent them) should have the final say in terms of the implementation of SCP. SCP demands that at both Central and State levels, the department concerned with Scheduled Castes Welfare, such as the Scheduled Castes Development Corporations should act as the nodal agency for the formulation, implementation and monitoring of SCP.

ANNEXURE 2

Major Scholarship Schemes under the Ministry of Social Justice and Empowerment

- **Post-matric Scholarships (PMS)** implemented since 1944–45 to promote higher education among SCs by extending scholarships to pursue studies beyond matriculation. In the Tenth Plan, an amount of Rs 1822.25 cr was utilised to reach the coverage of 29.59 lakh students in 2006–07.

- **Pre-matric Scholarships** are being awarded since 1977–78 with an objective to encourage children of scavengers and those engaged in menial works, to pursue education. The 4.72 lakh children were awarded pre-matric scholarships for which Rs 56.41 cr was utilised in the Tenth Plan.

- **Upgradation of Merit for SC Students Scheme** in operation since 1987–88 to extend remedial and special coaching offered to students to remove their deficiencies in school subjects (class IX to XII) into professional and technical courses. An expenditure of Rs 14.68 cr was incurred to benefit 10625 students.

- **Rajiv Gandhi National Fellowships** launched in the Tenth Plan in 2005–06 as a special incentive to extend scholarships to SC students to pursue higher studies and research degrees such as M.Phil. and Ph.D. An amount of Rs 50.20 cr was earmarked for this scheme in the Tenth Plan to benefit 2666 SC students.

Special Provisions/Incentives for Education of SCs/STs in India

The following special provisions for SCs and STs have been incorporated in the existing schemes of the Departments of Elementary Education and Literacy and Secondary and Higher Education:

- *Sarva Shiksha Abhiyan* (SSA) aims to provide useful and quality elementary education to all children in the 6-14 age group by 2010 in the country.
- Relaxed norms for opening of primary schools: A primary school within 1 km walking distance from habitations of 200 population instead of habitations of 300 populations.
- Priority is given to the areas of concentration of Scheduled Castes and Scheduled Tribes under the programmes of District Primary Education Programme (DPEP), Lok Jumbish (LJ), Shiksha Karmi (SK), Non-Formal Education (NFE) and National Programme for Nutritional Support to Primary Education.
- Under the Scheme of Strengthening of Boarding and Hostel facilities for girl students of Secondary and Higher Secondary Schools preference is given to girl hostels located in educationally backward districts, particularly those predominantly inhabited by SC, ST and educationally backward communities.
- The scheme of Kasturba Gandhi Swatantrata Vidyalaya is to improve literacy among the women belonging to SCs, STs, OBCs and Minorities.
- The *Mahila Samakhya* (MS) programme enables women, especially from socially and economically disadvantaged and marginalised groups to address and deal with problems of isolation, lack of self-confidence and oppressive social customs.
- The higher educational institutions administered by the Central Government reserve 15 per cent seats for Scheduled Castes and 7.5 per cent for Scheduled Tribes in case of admissions as well as in appointments (teaching and non-teaching posts). Seats are also reserved in hostels attached to the Central universities/colleges.

- Abolition of tuition fee in all States in Government Schools at least up to upper primary level. Most of the states have abolished tuition fee for SC/ST students up to senior secondary level.
- Providing various incentives like free textbooks, uniforms, stationary, school bags for SC/STs, etc.
- There is 15 per cent reservation of seats for SCs and 7.5 per cent for STs in Central Government Technical educational institutions including IITs, IIMs, Regional Engineering Colleges, etc. Apart from reservation, there is also relaxation in the minimum qualifying marks for admissions for SCs and STs. There is fee exemption book bank facility and scholarships in IITs.
- Relaxation in the minimum qualifying cut off stages for admission in Universities, Colleges and Technical Institutions, apart from reservation. From an analysis by the Task Group on Development of Scheduled Castes and Scheduled Tribes on selected items in the National Common Minimum Programme (2004-2005).
- University Grants Commission provides relaxation of five per cent from 55 per cent to 50 per cent at the Master's level for appointment as Lecturer from SC/ST.
- UGC has established SC/ST Cells in 113 Universities including Central Universities to ensure proper implementation of the reservation policy.
- Kendriya Vidyalayas provide 15 per cent reservation for SCs and 7.5 per cent for STs. Norms are relaxed in admissions, if necessary and tuition fee is exempted.
- Navodaya Vidyalayas provide reservation of seats in admissions for SC and ST students in proportion to their population in the district subject to the national minimum, i.e., 15 per cent and 7.5 per cent for SCs and STs respectively.
- Out of 43,000 scholarships at the secondary stage for talented children from rural areas 13,000 scholarships are awarded to SC/ST students. Out of 1000 scholarships, two scholarships are exclusively reserved for SC/ST students under the National Talent Search Scheme.
- Development of Indian Languages by CIIL, Mysore through research, manpower, production of materials in modern Indian Languages including tribal languages.
- The 244 districts have been identified as special focus districts on cross-matching basis from among those, consisting of areas

of Minority Concentration blocks/tehsils, ITDP blocks, Schedule V and Scheduled VI areas and districts with SC female literacy less than 10 per cent for focussed attention by Centre as well as by States/Union Territories in implementation of Programmes/Schemes.

- Allocation 15 per cent and 7.5 per cent funds on notional basis from the budget of the Department of Elementary Education and Literacy and Secondary and Higher Education under the Special Component Plan (SCP) and Tribal Sub-Plan (TSP) for Scheduled Castes and Scheduled Tribes respectively.

ANNEXURE 3

Main Guidelines for SCSP and TSP

- Earmarking of funds for SCSP and TSP from the total State Plan outlay should at least be proportionate to the SC and ST population of the State/UT.
- Making the Social Welfare/Tribal Welfare Department—which are concerned with the well-being and development of SCs and STs—the nodal department for formulation and implementation of SCSP and TSP.
- Placing the funds earmarked for SCSP and TSP at the disposal of the Principal Secretary/Secretary, Social Welfare/Tribal Welfare, who will work as Planning Secretary and have exclusive authority for the reallocation of funds to other line departments of SC and ST development schemes.
- Placing the funds earmarked for SCSP and TSP under separate budget head/sub-head for each development department.
- Backing the SCSP and TSP earmarked funds by 100 per cent budget provision, sanctions and timely release of funds to the line departments and implementing agencies.
- Including only those schemes under SCSP and TSP that ensure direct benefits to individuals or families belonging to SCs or STs.
- Preparing a detailed SCSP and TSP document with physical and financial targets against each Scheme with the objective of bridging the gap between the rest of the population and the SCs and STs within 10 years.
- Ensuring that the other line departments co-operate in the proper implementation of the SCSP and TSP schemes allocated to them and put up the schemes to the nodal departments for sanction and release of funds.
- To circumvent the problem of non-divisible nature of funds

for certain sectors like major irrigation, power, roads, and so on, SCSP and TSP funds may be accounted only to the extent of about five per cent or the actual area being covered or benefitted by the SCs and STs by the projects and not the population percentage. The percentage of SC and ST beneficiaries and the area being covered/benefitted is always less than the population percentage of the SC and ST population in the State/UT.

- Preventing the diversion and lapse of funds allocated to SCSP and TSP in the Annual Plans. The SCSP and TSP should not be allowed to be changed at Revised Estimate (RE) stage by the Planning Commission.
- Carrying forward the lapsed/unutilised SCSP and TSP amount to the next Annual Plan of the State/UT as an additional fund for SCSP and TSP.
- All the CSS and SCA Schemes of the Centre necessarily should have a SCSP and TSP component in them as per the proportion of SCs and STs in the States/UTs.

ANNEXURE 4

Education

Uttar Pradesh has made significant contributions in the field of Education and Social Welfare. The State has made major investments over the past few years at all levels of education and has achieved significant success. UP has recognised and supported the continuing critical-role of private-sector in the expansion of education in the State.

Schools in the state are either managed by the government or by private trusts. Hindi is used as a medium of instruction in most of the schools except the schools which are affiliated to the Central Board of Secondary Education (CBSE) or Council for Indian Schools Certificate Examinations (ICSE) boards. A primary school is present at a distance of 1.5 km and upper primary school at three km. A secondary school is present at every eight km. in rural areas and there is a secondary school for girls in every block. Efforts are being made to establish at least one degree college in every block.

The policy of free and compulsory education has been introduced in the state to achieve universalisation of education at primary and secondary level. There are several statutory bodies which decide the fee structure in educational institutions. For non-professional courses, fee is determined by the concerned university. For professional courses, fee is regulated by a committee constituted by All India Council for Technical Education (AICTE).

Uttar Pradesh has four Central universities, 20 state universities, eight deemed universities, one institute of national importance and several polytechnics, engineering colleges and industrial training institutes. Prestigious institutes like Indian Institute of Technology (IIT)—Kanpur and Indian Institute of Management (IIM)—Lucknow are known worldwide for their quality education and research in respective fields. This provides the State with a firm basis for providing opportunities for higher education to its youth.

ANNEXURE 5

Educational Institutions

Category	*Total Number*	*Total Enroll-ment*	*Number of Teachers*	*Teacher-Student Ratio*
Pre-primary School	50	215	—	—
Primary School	94476	15	312669	42
Elementary School	20675	10	103943	30
Secondary School	3149	1	31343	39
Senior Secondary School	5190	1	109030	41
Pre-degree/Junior College	—	—	109030	41
Board of Intermediate/ Secondary Education	676 (Arts/Sc./ Com.)	773013 (BA/BSc. B.Com)	—	—
Degree College	34	17775 (B.E./B.Sc./ B.Arch.)	—	—
Engineering College	—	—	—	—
Professional College	—	—	—	—
Medical College	—	6910 M.B.B.S.	—	—
All University	—	144856 (MA/M.Sc/ M.Com.) 8073 (Ph.D/ D.Lit/D.Sc.)	—	—
All University	—	144856 (MA/M.Sc/ M.Com.) 8073 (Ph.D/D.Lit/ D.Sc.)	—	—
Central University	—	—	—	—
State University	—	—	—	—

Deemed University	5	—	—	—
Institution of National Importance	1	—	—	—
Research Institution	10	—	—	—
Teacher Training College	121	17775 (B.Ed./ B.T.)	—	—
Teacher Training School	64	4421	—	—
Polytechnic Institutes	95	25293	—	—
Technical/Industrial/Arts and Craft School	122	50221	—	—

ANNEXURE 6

UP for all Project Board

UP Education for all Project Board

The Government of India under National Education Policy of 1986 (as updated in 1992), and the Programme of Action 1992, reaffirm national commitment to universalisation of elementary education (means education upto class eighth). Para 5.12 of NPE resolves that free and compulsory education of satisfactory quality should be provided to all children upto 14 years of age before we enter the 21st century.

Keeping above in view, a World Bank assisted project called Basic Education Project had been undertaken in 1993, for expansion of quality basic education in the state. For smooth running of this project, a society "Uttar Pradesh Sabhee Ke Liye Shiksha Pariyojana Parishad (UP Education for all Project Board) has been established on 17th May, 1993 under Societies Registration Act of 1860. It's objectives are:

The Parishad shall act as an autonomous and independent body for implementation of the Uttar Pradesh Education for all Project (Hereinafter referred to as "the Project") as outlined in the Project Document published by the Government of Uttar Pradesh and its revised version that may be prepared on the basis of review from time to time. The activities of the Parishad will be concentrated in selected districts, but may extend to the whole State of UP in respect of selected and sponsored projects. The Parishad has been established to function as a societal mission for bringing about a fundamental change in the basic education system, and through it in the overall socio-cultural situation. The following specific objectives of the Project would be pursued by the Parishad:

Universalisation of Primary Education, viewed as a composite programme of (i) access to primary education for all children up to 14 years of age; (ii) universal participation till they complete the primary stage through formal or non-formal education programmes; and (iii) universal achievement at least of the minimum levels of learning.

Provision of continuing education and skill development programmes for youth.

Making suggestions for greater gender equality in education and female empowerment.

Making necessary intervention to provide equal educational opportunity to children belonging to the Scheduled Castes, Scheduled Tribes and the poorest sections of society.

Laying special emphasis on all educational activities on culture and communication; science and environment and inculcation of a sense of social justice.

The district primary education programme-II was started in 1997 in 22 districts of the state which ended in 2003. Moreover, DPEP-III was started in 32 districts of the state in 2000, and has ended on 31 March, 2006.

Janshala project was implemented in district Lucknow during 2000-03.

Sarva Shiksha Abhiyan was started in the state in 16 districts in 2001-02 and now covers all 70 districts of the state.

Background

Prior to 1972, the primary and upper primary schools in Uttar Pradesh were run, maintained and controlled by District Boards and municipalities including municipal corporations, etc., constituted under various acts related to management of local bodies, i.e.,

UP Kshettra Samiti and Zila Parishad Adhiniyam, 1961.
UP Municipalities Act, 1916.
UP Nagar Mahapalika Adhiniyam, 1959.

Considering urgent need to improve literacy in the state, it was felt that education needed planned interventions from the State government. In this background, the Government of Uttar Pradesh passed the Uttar Pradesh Basic Education Act, 1972 (UP Act No. 34 of 1972).

The main objective of this act is to organise, co-ordinate and control imparting of basic education in schools other than high schools or intermediate colleges. By this Act, an Autonomous Body named "Uttar Pradesh Board of Basic Education" was constituted under chairmanship of the Director, Basic Education. All schools which were managed and controlled by local bodies have since then been transferred to the Board. The Board of Basic Education controls appointment, transfer and posting of basic school teachers, determines school timings and gives recognition to private schools imparting basic education in the state.

Uttar Pradesh Board of Basic Education Act, 1972 has been amended in year 2000, incorporating principle of devolution of powers to the village community and management of education has been decentralised for empowing grassroot participatory agencies. Other acts relating to basic education were also amended and most crucial one has been United Provinces Panchayati Raj Act,1947 wherein there is a committee for each village or group of villages called Gram Shiksha Samiti whose constitution is as follows:

- Gram Pradhan—Chairman.
- Three Guardians (one woman) of students of Basic schools—Members.
- Head Master of Basic School or senior most head master—member secretary (if there are more than one school in Gram Sabha).
- Gram Shiksha Samiti would establish, control and plan basic schools in its panchayat areas. It would prepare plans for development and improvement of the schools. Major functions also include giving advice regarding building and other improvement plans to Zila Panchayat.

ANNEXURE 7

Educational Indicators

No. of Primary Schools (Govt. + Private Recognised)	135112
No. of Upper Primary Schools (Govt. + Private Recognised)	41595
No. of Regular Teachers in Parisadiya Primary Schools	202076
No. of Shiksha Mitras in Parisadiya Primary Schools	
No. of Regular Teachers in Parisadiya Upper Primary Schools	70200
Teacher Pupil Ratio at Primary Level	1 : 45
Teacher Pupil Ratio at Upper Primary Level	1 : 39
EMIS - 2005-06 Student Classroom Ratio	1 : 64
Repetition Rate (per cent)	1.59
Transition Rate for Class V to VI (per cent)	73
Percentage of Girls in Primary Enrollment	48
Percentage of Girls in Upper Primary Enrollment	46

Percentage of SC in Primary Enrollment	28
Percentage of SC in Upper Primary Enrollment	28
Percentage of Female Teacher Ratio	30

ANNEXURE 8

Schemes

Girls who comprise almost one half of the eligible child population, fall into category of children requiring special attention as their participation in primary education has been unsatisfactory. In this context, it must be realised that the participation level trends are not up to mark in the case of special social groups such as scheduled castes, tribes and minorities, other backward castes etc. The Primary schools have clearly indicated that girls' enrollment and retention have been low as compared to boys and this has widened gender gap. Therefore, to combat such situations, different interventions are being adopted for expansion of education for girls.

Strategies

(A) Maa-Beti Mela and Women Parliament

Objectives

Creating awareness about importance of girls education, for this purpose relevant material is being widely disseminated.

- Orienting mothers about importance and significance of education for girls.
- Putting in place a functional relationship between the teachers and parents.
- Drawing attention of teachers towards problems of girls.
- Holding discussions on gender concerns and trying to change peoples' attitudes towards their daughters and sons. Efforts are, thus, made to sensitise them and make them realise how their negative disposition prevents daughters from coming out of their shells.
- Holding discussions on present education system and appealing to those present to participate in making it more effective and responsive to expressed needs.

(B) Model Cluster Development Approach (MCDA)

Specific strategies for girls are being adopted in certain areas of the project districts. One such strategy is the MCDA, which focusses on to improved participation of girls in Primary Education.

Criteria for Selection of the Clusters

- Low female literacy rate.
- Poor enrollment and retention of girls.
- Dominance of minority or Scheduled Castes/Other Backward Castes population.
- Clusters having 10-12 villages.
- Presence of active Village Education Committees.
- Presence of some active women's groups or motivated individuals.

Education Guarantee Scheme/

Alternative Schooling

Even after opening new schools in unserved habitations by way of formal schools, many children who are dropouts, never enrolled, working children, children living in isolated villages and hamlets and girls needing flexibility in school timings to adjust to domestic demands of sibling care and household chores, need to be provided access to some form of schooling facilities. For such children, Alternative Schooling (AS) facilities have been provided in the project districts. Moving away from a rigid centre-based approach, alternative schooling facilities that are more contextual, location specific and flexible have been evolved.

Alternative Schooling Strategy: The strategy for AS is to provide alternative learning facilities to children with express purpose of mainstreaming as many children as possible into formal system. The implementation of strategy is done with active involvement of the Village Education Committee (VEC), and the community. The VEC and the community have freedom to determine time duration, venue and holiday pattern for the AS centre as per learner convenience aiming at transacting on an average four hours of learning. The AS centres are completely managed by the Village Education Committee. Priority is given to small and remote habitations with 15-30 children which do not have a school facility within one km radius. Other strategies have focussed on main streaming out of school children to regular schools or providing alternative schooling facility that is more flexible and accessible to disadvantaged children.

Civil Works

During the project period, in DPEP-III the construction of block resources centres, building for new and building less/reconstruction of primary schools, additional classrooms were taking existing schools were repined, drinking water and toilet facilities were provided.

While in SSA the upper primary school buildings were also taken up.

The most significant aspect of uncivil work programme is involvement of this community and inclusion of innovation designs and child-friendly elements in civil works.The district was given freedom to choose one of the five designs on local condition and requirement of this district:

ANNEXURE 9

Shiksha Mitra

Shiksha Mitra Scheme as Para Teachers for UP Basic Shiksha Parishadiya Primary Schools

Need

- Universalisation of elementary education.
- Non-availability of minimum two teachers for each parishadiya primary schools.
- Deployment problem in rural interior schools.
- Teacher Pupil Ratio is very high in rural areas. To maintain teacher pupil ratio as per norms in remote areas.
- To involve VEC support in primary education.

Objectives of the Scheme

- To provide minimum two teachers in each parishadiya primary school.
- To minimise the teacher pupil ratio up to the norms.
- To make provision for local youths to serve their community.
- To ensure active participation of Village Education Committee in primary education.
- To make provision for local educated ladies to serve in schools and promote Community confidence in girls education.
- To increase retention of children.
- To ensure enrollment of out of school children by focussing Shiksha Mitras on largest classes I and II in schools.

To obtain, aim of five teachers per school, in 3:2 ratio of regular teachers and Shiksha Mitras.

Assumption of Shiksha Mitra Scheme:

It is a Government of Uttar Pradesh scheme and applicable to all Parishadiya Primary Schools since 1st July, 2000.

1. Willing and qualified teachers are not available for primary schools in remote village of backward areas.
2. Arrangement for primary education through young persons having education up to intermediate belonging to the same village and willing to serve the community.
3. Local person through rigorous training can serve and teach up to class Second easily.

Vision

Focus Points

- Child and teacher relationship.
- Learning Content.
- School Environment.
- Teaching learning process : Culture of the class room.
- Long-term perspective.
- Learning from 'Basic Education Project' UP.
- Common understanding on pedagogical issues.
- Involvement of various institutions : SCERT, SPO, SIE, DIETs, SRG integrated in UPDPEP.
- Take freshness of spirit from outside.
- Resource network.
- Pedagogical Improvement plan: Multigrade situation has significant bearing on teaching learning process. Therefore, multigrade teaching has been a major concern in pedagogical plan of UPDPEP.

Overall Processes

- State Resource Group (SRG).
- Orientation and capacity building.
- Visioning workshops-state level, district level.
- Conceptual workshops I and II.
- Exposure visits and school placement.
- Review and revision of curriculum (Class I - V and VI - VIII), Text books (class I - V and VI - VIII).
- Teacher Training.
- Pupil evaluation: Continuous and comprehensive evaluation system (CCE).
- Development, Trial, Review and Finalisation.

Implementation

- Preparation and capacity-building for implementation.
- Identifying people and capacity-building in place.
- Follow-up and feedback mechanism.
- Better Educational Support for Teachers (BEST). Academic supervision and support System.
- Use of distance education.
- Innovation.

Block Resource Centre/

Naya Panchayat Resource Centre

The Block Resource Centre (BRC) at block level and Naya Panchayat Resource Centre (NPRC) at cluster level provide regular academic support, conduct teachers training, follow-up workshops, meetings and opportunities for peer learning as well as sharing of good practices.

Introduction (Need and Expansion)

Constitution of India under Article 14 (A), resolves to provide free and compulsory education for all children of the age group of 6-14 years of age. To realise national commitment of providing free and compulsory education, the universalisation of elementary education (UEE) was conceptualised.

The UP State government, in consonance with national commitment, has been doing sincere efforts to achieve and accelerate the UEE in the form of providing non-formal and formal/alternative education to children, setting up primary parishadiya schools within a radius of 1.5 km for a habitation of 300 in conformity with GOUP norm and upper primary schools within a radius of three km and opening of alternative school centres, shiksha ghar and Aganwadi centres. Alongwith this, schools have been provided with drinking and toilet facilities and construction of additional classrooms has been done where it was needed.

No doubt, all these efforts helped in increasing the enrollment of children and reducing the dropout rate of children but it led to the question of maintaining the quality of education and improving the learning achievement of children.

Though there was Assistant Basic Shiksha Adhikari already who was responsible for providing academic supervision and support and maintaining the quality of education, but a sudden spurt in the number of schools and increment in enrollment, led to academic situation out of his control which resulted in educational crises. Consequently, to rectify the anomalous situation, Kothari Commission conceptualised school as a cluster and came up with the idea of 'school cluster' and suggested to have a 'committee' in each school that would work towards improving the quality of education and learning achievement of education.

Under UP Basic Education Project, DIETs have been entrusted with the responsibility of improving the quality of education and speeding up the educational activities at district level. The Block Resource Centre at block level and Nyaya Panchayat Resource Centre at NPRC level have also been set up with the sole aim of providing academic support and guidance to teachers and schools and to significant role in the management of wide variety of quality improvement interventions at school level. Under the Project, NPRCs are nothing but school clusters as envisaged by Kothari Commission.

In spite of fact—that there was already a team of BSA, Dy. BSA, ABSA and SDI for school monitoring and supervision but various survey findings had revealed a regression in the achievement level of students of Class five as their achievement level was found to be equivalent with that of achievement level of students of class three a need of establishing an educational institution. Therefore, DIETs, established at district level have been entrusted with the responsibilities for providing teacher support activities and educational and extra curricular activities and conduct school monitoring and supervision.

ANNEXURE 10

State Plan of Distance Education

The State Project Office organised a scheme to explore and identify possibilities of distance education to support and strengthen ongoing teacher training programme. The exercise focussed on needs of teacher training, primary school curriculum and the role of other academic support institutions like DIETs, BRCs, CRCs. Teleconferencing, video programmes, self-instructional material, dovetailed with the ongoing teacher training schedule were identified as modes for strengthening and enriching training programme through distance education. A State Work Plan was evolved having the following activities:

- Capacity Building of Institutions and individuals for the use of Distance Education Technology.
- Orientation of core group.
- Supply of equipments facilitating use for D.E. material such as TV, VCR, STD, FAX, Generator, Two-in-one, etc., to DIETs.
- Providing 'down link' or 'talk back' facility to each DIET for teleconferencing.

Annexure 11

Free Text Books Distribution

Site Designed and Developed by Education For All

In UPDPEP II, UPDPEP III, Janshala (Lucknow) and Sarva Shiksha Abhiyan Programme, there is a provision of free text book distribution to all girls and Schedule Caste and Schedule Tribe boys studying in parishadiya primary, upper primary and government schools.

Free Textbook Distribution System

The Directorate of Basic Education which houses the State Text book office is responsible for ensuring the timely printing and distribution of the Free text-books and timely availability of text books in the market.

- Specifications of the Job are finalised by the Government of Uttar Pradesh and communicated to the Director, Basic Education and the State Text Book Officer (State text book office).
- Technical and financial bids are invited for inner text and cover page separately through National Tendering process.
- A tender committee with the Director, Basic Education, as the Chairperson is constituted with State Textbook officer as the Member Secretary. After the publishers and printers are shortlisted by the committee on the basis of their technical bids, their financial bids are assessed and the final selection is made.
- The lowest price quoted by the successful bidder becomes the cost prize for all other successful bidders, who agree to work on that lowest price. The price fixed includes the cost of paper, printing, transportation up to the district headquarters in case of textbooks for free distribution, binding, purchase of the textbook cover. Transportion cost is borne by the wholeseller and retailer for books that are sold in the market. The Printers/ Publishers give 7.5 per cent discount on the price of the book for free distribution and 1.5 per cent as royalty to Government through State Text-Book Office for the number of books for which agreement is made.
- In order to check the number of copies of textbooks to be printed and right amount of royalty to be paid, printing of the covers is entrusted to private security presses accredited by the Reserve Bank of India.
- Each of selected printers is allocated a unique code. This code has to appear near the spine of every textbook printed by the

Printers. This serves the dual purpose of monitoring the quality of the printing job by every printer and also reduces the possibility of unauthorised copies of the textbooks from reaching the market.

- Printers/publishers are given the manuscript on CD-Roms and the corresponding hard copies of the textbooks. In this way, the processing time at the printers end is eliminated and they are in a position to prepare the positives and negatives of the print material, plate making, etc., to start printing work immediately. For books which are not given on CD-Roms, the printers/publishers are required to make a model copy and get it approved by the subject specialists positioned in State Text book office and the Tender committee.

- After the printing job is over and the end product is verified for conformity with quality standards laid down for the job, every publishers/printer has to submit at least five finished copies of the textbook printed by them to Assistant Director (Basic) of that Region and EBSA of that district.

Janshala: Joint GOI-UN System education Programme is being implemented in Lucknow District from April 2000 with a view to providing programme support of the Government of India (GoI) regarding ongoing efforts towards goal of making primary education more accessible and effective for all primary school going children. Joint GoI-UN system Education Programme is, known as Janshala programme, a collaborative effort of the five lead United Nations Agencies viz., UNICEF, UNDP, UNESCO, ILO and UNFPA along with the Government of India.

In order to achieve above goal, Janshala programme aims at bringing into the mainstream of primary education all those children, particularly girls of 6-14 years age, who have been deprived of this opportunity so far. The focus is on children of the scheduled castes, minority communities, working children, children belonging to poorer sections of society and of parents living in slum areas and disabled children. The right of children namely right to survival, right to protection, right to development and right to participation are being kept in view simultaneously through different activities aiming at making schools child-friendly. In connection with objectives of Janshala Programme, six principal elements of the Joint GoI-UN system support for community-based primary education have been enunciated as under:

- Strengthening community-based mechanism for school management and support.

- Transforming government school into empowered community schools.

- Improving teaching methodology.
- Developing a teacher empowerment package.
- Facilitating information exchange on best class-room practices, policy and community participation.
- Applying an integrated social development approach.
- The programme is being implemented in eight blocks and all the 110 urban wards of Lucknow District.

Project Outlay

- Total project outlay is Rs 14.08 cr in which share of UN agencies is Rs 11.96 cr and rest of Rs 2.12 cr, share of Uttar Pradesh, Government.

Approach and Strategies

- Strengthening community-based mechanisms for school management support.
- Develop government schools as empowered community schools.
- Improving teaching methodology for multi-grade classrooms through pre and in-service teacher development programmes.
- Developing teacher empowerment package for teachers of empowered community schcols.
- Facilitating information exchange on best classroom practices, policy and community participation.
- Applying an integrated social development approach, which converges educational and development activities and resource inputs by all agencies and ministries.

Annexure 12

Education Guarantee Scheme/Alternative Role of Community Schooling/Bridge Courses

In National Education Policy 1986, special emphasis has been given on:

- Giving pre-eminence to people's involvement, including association of non-governmental agencies and voluntary efforts. Inducting more women in the planning and management of education.
- Establishing the principles of accountability in relation to given objectives and norms.

Village Education Committees, Mother/Parents-Teacher Associations and Women Motivator Groups. (Illustrations 1 to 3). These are the grassroots level bodies which play a pivotal role in enlisting community participation for education and bringing the community and schools closer to establish an interactive and effective school management system. These bodies are expected to assume leadership to inspire and influence community thinking and guide their decisions in favour of their children, particularly girls. These organisations are also envisaged to motivate the spirit of community ownership of schools and the education system to the extent of mobilising community resources for school improvement. There are about 55,000 village education committees, 6768 Mother/Parents Teachers Associations and 3621 Women Motivator Groups, which have been sensitised and activated under the Education Projects.

Thrust Areas

The Strategy of the state is to encourage partnership with the community and voluntary agencies. Thus, a synergetic government-community partnership would be built to achieve the objective of Universalisation of Elementary Education. Specifically, the following would be encouraged:

- To make more collaborative efforts with the community and voluntary agencies.
- To improve functioning of government schools in partnership with willing community partners, within the broad parameters of the state policy.
- To focus attention within the community, especially on women for raising awareness relating to girl's education. Efforts to be made to ensure peer pressure on guardians for girl's education.
- To encourage greater participation of women in structures like the Village Education Committees, Parent Teacher Associations, Women Motivator Groups.

These details clearly lead to an environment where state and community both are equal partners in the spread and quality of elementary education. The influence of local community is critical to grassroots capacity-building for universalisation of elementary education. In Uttar Pradesh, three types of community-based organisations are in function.

ANNEXURE 13

- **Major Scholarship Schemes under the Ministry of Social Justice and Empowerment**
- **Post-matric Scholarships (PMS)** implemented since 1944–45 to promote higher education among SCs by extending scholarships to pursue studies beyond matriculation. In the Tenth Plan, an amount of Rs 1822.25 cr was utilised to reach the coverage of 29.59 lakh students in 2006–07.

- **Pre-matric Scholarships** are being awarded since 1977–78 with an objective to encourage children of scavengers and those engaged in menial works, to pursue education. 4.72 lakh children were awarded pre-matric scholarships for which Rs 56.41 cr was utilised in the Tenth Plan.
- **Upgradation of Merit for SC Students Scheme** in operation since 1987–88 to extend remedial and special coaching offered to students to remove their deficiencies in school subjects (class IX to XII) into professional and technical courses. An expenditure of Rs 14.68 cr was incurred to benefit 10625 students.
- **Rajiv Gandhi National Fellowships** launched in the Tenth Plan in 2005–06 as a special incentive to extend scholarships to SC students to pursue higher studies and research degrees such as M.Phil. and Ph.D. An amount of Rs 50.20 cr was earmarked for this scheme in the Tenth Plan to benefit 2666 SC students with margin money out of their own funds and subsidy out of the SCA.

ANNEXURE 14

Protective Measures for people belonging to SCs are the Protection of Civil Rights Act, 1955 and the Scheduled Castes and Scheduled Tribes (Prevention of Atrocities) Act, 1989. However, despite these Constitutional provisions, atrocities and crimes on members of SCs, especially the women, continue to occur in all parts of the country in varying degrees. As per the National Crime Records Bureau Report 2005, the crimes against SCs in the last few years were mainly atrocities followed by hurt and rape.

- Implementation of the Scheduled Caste Sub-Plan (SCSP) and Tribal Sub-Plan (TSP)

In view of the persistent and wide spread socio-economic backwardness of SCs and STs, a distinct need was felt for innovative policy intervention to enable these groups to share the benefits of growth in a more equitable manner. The government prepared a separate plan:

- Development Plan called Tribal Sub-Plan for STs in 1976. It was followed by the Special Component Plan for the SCs in 1978 (recently renamed the Scheduled Caste Sub-Plan [SCSP]).
- The SCSP and TSP aim at facilitating convergence and pooling of resources from all the other development sectors in proportion to the population of SCs and STs respectively for their overall development.
- At present, 27 States/UTs are implementing SCSP through different mechanisms. The State Governments generally divide

their resources into 'divisible' and 'non-divisible' components and earmark funds for SCs only from the divisible pool. As a result, the actual funds flowing directly to SCSP from the total State Plan becomes much less than the proportion of SC population to the total population of the State.

- The State Government of Maharashtra has pioneered a special mechanism to ensure effective operationalisation of SCSP and TSP. Other States could explore replication of this mechanism.
- The Prime Minister has reiterated the need for effective implementation of SCSP and TSP during the 51st and 52nd NDC meetings held on 27th June, 2005 and 9th December 2006. He emphasised that the SCSP and TSP strategies should become an integral part of the Annual Plans as well as the Five Year Plan so that full inclusion of SCs and STs in socio-economic development is achieved within a period of 10 years.
- All Central Ministries/Departments are also expected to formulate SCSP and ensure that the flow of funds to SCSP in their plans is at least in proportion with the SC population of the country.
- At present, 17 Central Ministries/Departments have done so. These are the Ministries of Labour, Coal, Commerce and Industries, textiles, non-conventional Energy Sources, Women and Child Development, Steel and Rural Development, and the Departments of Agriculture and Cooperation, Small-Scale Industries and Agro and Rural Industries.
- Biotechnology, Science and Technology, Health, Family Welfare, Elementary Education and Literacy and Secondary and Higher Education. Many Ministries/Departments maintain that they are unable to provide funds for SCSP because their funds are devoted expenditure on large projects and are not divisible.
- The implementation of SCSP and TSP leaves much to be desired. This applies equally to the Central as well as State governments. Though there may be several reasons for this lacklustre implementation, lack of statutory or clear-cut administrative sanction is an important one.
- To look into the issues related to TSP and SCSP, a Central Standing Tripartite Committee (CSTC) which includes representatives of the Planning Commission, National Commission for SCs and STs, the Ministries of Social Justice and Empowerment and States/UTs Ministries/Departments, was set-up in May 1999. The CSTC was reconstituted in early 2006 to review the formulation, implementation and monitoring of SCSP and TSP and advice the Planning

Commission and Prime Minister on measures which would serve the interests of the SCs and STs more effectively.

- For effective implementation of SCSP and TSP, the Planning Commission also issued guidelines to all State Governments/ UTs which have been revised from time to time, the last revision being on 31st December, 2006. The main guidelines are given in.

Main Guidelines for SCSP and TSP

- Earmarking of funds for SCSP and TSP from the total State Plan outlay should at least be proportionate to the SC and ST population of the State/UT.
- Making the Social welfare /Tribal Welfare Department—which are concerned with the well-being and development of SCs and STs—the nodal department for formulation and implementation of SCSP and TSP.
- Placing the funds earmarked for SCSP and TSP at the disposal of the Principal Secretary/Secretary, Social welfare/Tribal welfare who will work as Planning Secretary and have exclusive authority for the reallocation of funds to other line departments of SC and ST development schemes.
- Placing the funds earmarked for SCSP and TSP under separate budget head/sub-head for each development department.
- Backing the SCSP and TSP earmarked funds by 100 per cent budget provision, sanctions and timely release of funds to the line departments and implementing agencies.
- Including only those schemes under SCSP and TSP that ensure direct benefits to individuals or families belonging to SCs or STs.
- Preparing a detailed SCSP and TSP document with physical and financial targets against each Scheme with the objective of bridging the gap between the rest of the population and the SCs and STs within 10 years.
- Ensuring that the other line departments cooperate in the proper implementation of the SCSP and TSP schemes allocated to them and put up the schemes to the nodal departments for sanction and release of funds.
- To circumvent the problem of non-divisible nature of funds for certain sectors like major irrigation, power, roads, and so on, SCSP and TSP funds may be accounted only to the extent of about 5 per cent or the actual area being covered or benefitted by the SCs and STs by the projects and not the

population percentage. The percentage of SC and ST beneficiaries and the area being covered/benefitted is always less than the population percentage of the SC and ST population in the State/UT.

- Preventing the diversion and lapse of funds allocated to SCSP and TSP in the Annual Plans. SCSP and TSP should not be allowed to be changed at Revised Estimate (RE) stage by the Planning Commission.
- Carrying forward the lapsed/unutilised SCSP and TSP amount to the next Annual Plan of the State/UT as an additional fund for SCSP and TSP.
- All the CSS and SCA Schemes of the Centre necessarily should have a SCSP and TSP component in them as per the proportion of SCs and STs in the States/UTs.

ANNEXURE 15
STRATEGIES

(A) Maa-Beti Mela and Women Parliament

Objectives

- Creating awareness about importance of girls education, for this purpose relevant material is being widely disseminated.
- Orienting mothers about importance and significance of education for girls.
- Putting in place a functional relationship between the teachers and parents.
- Drawing attention of teachers towards problems of girls.
- Holding discussions on gender concerns and trying to change peoples' attitudes towards their daughters and sons. Efforts are, thus, made to sensitise them and make them realise how their negative disposition prevents daughters form coming out of their shells.
- Holding discussions on present education system and appealing to those present to participate in making it more effective and responsive to expressed needs.

(B) Model Cluster Development Approach (MCDA)

Specific strategies for girls are being adopted in certain areas of the project districts. One such strategy is the MCDA, which focusses on to improved participation of girls in Primary Education.

Criteria for Selection of the Clusters

- Low female literacy rate.

- Poor enrollment and retention of girls.
- Dominance of minority or Scheduled Castes/Other Backward Castes population.
- Clusters having 10-12 villages.
- Presence of active Village Education Committees.
- Presence of some active women's groups or motivated individuals.

Education Guarantee Scheme/

Alternative Schooling

Even after opening new schools in unserved habitations by way of formal schools, many children who are drop outs, never enrolled, working children, children living in isolated villages and hamlets and girls needing flexibility in school timings to adjust to domestic demands of sibling care and household chores, need to be provided access to some form of schooling facilities. For such children, Alternative Schooling (AS) facilities have been provided in the project districts. Moving away from a rigid centre-based approach, alternative schooling facilities that are more contextual, location specific and flexible have been evolved.

Alternative Schooling Strategy: The strategy for AS is to provide alternative learning facilities to children with express purpose of mainstreaming as many children as possible into formal system. The implementation of strategy is done with active involvement of the Village Education Committee (VEC), and the community. The VEC and the community have freedom to determine time duration, venue and holiday pattern for the AS centre as per learner convenience aiming at transacting on an average four hours of learning. The AS centres are completely managed by the Village Education Committee.

Priority is given to small and remote habitations with 15-30 children which do not have a school facility within one km radius. Other strategies have focussed on mainstreaming out of school children to regular schools or providing alternative schooling facility that is more flexible and accessible to disadvantaged children.

Bibliography

Agarwal, S. 1999. Genocide of Women in Hinduism. Jabalpur: Sudrasan Books.

Agnes, Flavia .1994. Women's movement within a secular framework, *Economic and Political Weekly,* 29 (19):1123-27.

Akerkar, Supriya. 1995. Theory and practice of women's movement in India: A discourse analysis. *Economic and Political Weekly,* 30 (17): WS2-23.

Alyosius, G. 1997. Nationalism without a Nation in India. New Delhi: Oxford University Press.

Ambedkar, B.R. 1979. Caste in India: Their Mechanism, Genesis and Development (first published in (1917) in Dr Babashaeb Ambedkar: Writings and Speeches, Vol. 1, Bombay: Government of Maharashtra.

Anveshi Law Committee. 1997. Is gender justice only a legal issue? Political stakes in UCC debate. *Economic and Political Weekly,* 32 (9-10): pp. 453-58.

Arputhamurthy, Savitri. 1990. *Women Work and Discrimination,* New Delhi: Ashish Publishing House.

Arya, Sudha, (2000). Women Gender Equality and the State. New Delhi: Deep and Deep Publications.

Askonas, Peter and Angus Stewart (2000). Social Inclusion: Possibilities and Tensions. New York: St. Martin's Press.

Babu, Shyam D., Chandra Bhan Prasad (2009). Six Dalit Paradoxes, *Economic and Political Weekly,* June 6 , Vol. XLIV, No. 23, pp. 22-25.

Bandyopadhyay, Jayanta. 1999. Chipko Movement: Of floated myths and flouted realities. *Economic and Political Weekly,* 34 (15): pp. 880-82.

Banerjee, Sumantha. 1989. Marginalisation of women's popular culture in Nineteenth Century Bengal, in Kumkum Sangari and Suresh Vaid, (ed.), Recasting women. Essays in Colonial History, New Delhi: Kali for Women.

Barnard, Jessie. 1981. Socio-economic Status of Women in *The Female World*, New York: Free Press.

Barrett, M. 1980. Women's Oppression Today, Problems in Marxist Feminist Analysis, London: Verso.

Basu, Amrita, 1992. Two faces of protest: Contrasting modes of women's activism in India. Berkeley: University of California Press.

Basu, Amrita. 1995. Introduction in A. Basu (Ed). The Challenges of Local Feminisms: Women's Movements in Global Perspectives. Boulder, CO: Westview.

Basu, Amrita. 2001. The dialectics of Hindu Nationalism. In the success of India's democracy (ed.), Atul Kohli, Cambridge: Cambridge University Press.

Baxi,Upendra. 1994. Emancipation as Justice: Babasaheb Ambedkar's Legacy and Vision in Ambedkar and Social Justice, Vol. I, Edited and Published by Ministry of Information and Broadcasting, Delhi: Government of India.

Beall J., Hassim S., Todes A. 1989. 'A bit on the side?' Gender struggles in the politics of transformation in South Africa,' *Feminist Review*, 33: pp. 30-56.

Beall, J. and L.H. Piron. 2003. *DFID Social Exclusion Review*. London: LSE/ODI.

Bhalla, Ajit and Frederic Lapeyre. 1997. Social Exclusion: Towards and analytical and operational framework. *Development and Social Change*, 28: pp. 413-433.

Bhambri, C.P., 1991. State and Communalism in India, 1947-87. New Delhi: Vikas Publishing House.

Biradar, R.R. 2005. *Dynamics of Employment and Unemployment among Social Groups in India: Emerging Issues*, a paper presented at the National Seminar being organised by, Mangalore University, Mangalore during 4-5 September 2005 (mimeo).

Bourdieu, Pierre. 1977. Outline of a Theory of Practice. Cambridge: Cambridge University Press.

Bourdieu, Pierre. 1973. Cultural Reproduction and Social Reproduction. In R. Brown (ed). Knowledge, Tavistock, London: Education and Cultural Change.

Brydon, Lynne and Chant, Sylvia. 1989. Women in the Third world Gender issues in Rural and Urban Areas, England: Elgar Publishing Ltd.

Butler Judith. 1990. Gender Trouble: Feminism and the Subversion of Identity, London: Routledge.

Cecile Jackson. 1999. Social exclusion and gender: Does one size fit all? *The European Journal of Development Research,* Vol. 11, Issue 1 June 1999, pp. 125-146.

Census of India 1991. 1994. Series 1, India, Part II-A (ii) General Population Table, Delhi: Controller, Department of Publications.

Census of India 2001. 2004. Provisional Population Tables, Paper I of 2001 Delhi: Controller, Department of Publications.

Census of India 2001. 2004. Primary Census Abstract, Total Population, Tables: A-5, Delhi, Controller, Department of Publications.

Chakravarti, Uma. 1998. Rewriting History: The Life and Times of Pandita Ramabai. New Delhi: Kali for Women.

Chakravarty, Uma. 2003. Gendering Caste: Through A Feminist Lens, Calcutta: Stree.

Chakravarty, Uma. 1993. Conceptualising Brahmanical Patriarchy in Early India: Gender, Caste, Class and State, *Economic and Political Weekly,* Vol. 27, No.14 *April 3, pp. 579-85.*

Chambers, Clare. 2002. 'All must have prizes: The Liberal Case for Interference in Cultural Practices', in Paul Kelley (ed.), Multiculturalism Reconsidered, Cambridge: Polity Press.

Chandhoke, Neera. 1995. State and Civil Society: Exploration in Political Theory, New Delhi: Sage Publications.

Charles Gore and Jose B. Figueiredo. 2005 Social Exclusion and anti-Poverty Policy in Rorden Wilkinson (ed). The Global Governance Reader, Geneva: International Institute of Labour Studies.

Chatterjee, P. 1989. The Nation and its Fragments: Colonial and Post-colonial Histories, Bombay: Oxford University Press.

Chatterjee, Partha. 1989. The nationalist resolution on the women's question, in recasting women. Essays in colonial history (eds) Kumkum Sangari and Suresh Vaid, New Delhi: Kali for women.

Chatterjee, Partha. 1997. 'Beyond the Nation? Or within?' *Economic and Political Weekly* Vol. 32, No.1 January 4-11, 1997: pp. 4-11.

Chauhan, Poonam.1996. Women in Preparatory in Lengthening Shadows: Status of Women in India, New Delhi: Manak Publications.

Cynthia, Stephen. 2009. Feminism and in India by 16th November, 2009 Source:http://www.countercurrents.org/stephen161109.htm. It is a snapshot of the page as it appeared on 7th Jan, 2010, 19:26:10 GMT.

Danaher Geoff, Tony Schirato and Jean Webb. 2002. Understanding Foucault, New Delhi: Sage Publiication.

Dattar Chayya. 1999. Non-brahmin renderings of feminism in Maharashtra: Is it a more emancipatory force? *Economic and Political Weekly*, Vol. 34, No. 41 October 09, *1999.*

De Haan, Arjan. 1998. Social Exclusion: An alternative concept for the study of deprivation? *IDS Bulletin*, Vol. 29, Issue 1, January 1998, pp. 10-19.

Desh Pande, G.P. (edited with annotations and introduction). 2002. Selected Writings of Jotirao Phule, New Delhi: Leftword.

Diwakar, D.M. and G.P. Mishra (ed.). 2006 Deprivation and Inclusive Development, New Delhi: Manak Publications.

Dreze, J. and A. Hari Gazdar. 1997. 'Uttar Pradesh: The Burden of Inertia' in Indian Development—Selected Regional Perspectives (ed.) by Jean Dreze and Amartya Sen, New Delhi: Oxford University Press.

Dube, Leela. 1996. Caste and Women in Caste: Its 20th Century Avatar (ed) Srinivas M.N., New Delhi: Viking for Penguin Books of India Pvt. Ltd.

Dunne M., S. Humphreys and F. Leach. 2006. Gender violence in schools in developing countries, *Cender and Education*, Vol.18, No. 1, pp. 75-98.

Forbes, Geraldine. 2005. Women in Colonial India; Essays on Politics, Medicine, and Historiography, New Delhi: Chronicle Books.

Forbes, Geraldine. 1996. Women in Modern India. Cambridge: Cambridge University Press.

Gabriele Dietrich. 1992. Dalit Movements and Women's Movements, in Reflection on the Women's Movement in India, New Delhi: Horizon India Books.

Galanter Marc. 1984. Competing Equalities: Law and the Backward Classes in India. New Delhi: Oxford University Press.

Gandhi, Nandhita and Nandita Shah. 1992. The issues at stake. Theory and practice in contemporary women's movement in India, New Delhi: Kali for Women.

Geoff Danaher, Tony Shirato and Jean Webb. 2002. Understanding Foucault, New Delhi: Sage Publication.

Gerda Lerner.1979. The Majority Finds its Past, New York, Oxford University Press.

Giddens, A. 1991. Modernity and Self-Identity, Self and Society in the Late Modern Age. Cambrige: Polity Press/Blackwell.

Giele and Smock. 1977. Women's Roles and Status in Eight Countries, New York: John, Wiley and Sons.

Gopal Guru. 1995. Dalit Women Task Differently' *Economic and Political Weekly*, Vol. 30, Nos. 41/4214-21 October, 1995, pp. 2548-50.

Gopal Guru, 2000. Dalits, Reflections on the Search for Inclusion in Peter R. de Souza (ed.) Contemporary India: Transitions. New Delhi: Sage Publications.

Government of India. 1993. National Family Health Survey-2 (NFHS 92-93), Mumbai: Indian Institute of Population Studies (IIPS).

Government of India. 2000. National Family Health Survey-2, Mumbai; Indian Institute of Population Studies (IIPS).

Government of India. 2003 Annual Report 2002-03, New Delhi: Ministry of Social Justice and Empowerment.

Government of India. 1975 Towards Equality: Report of the Committee on the Status of Women in India, Department of Social Welfare, New Delhi. Ministry of Education and Social Welfare.

Government of India. 1978. Draft Sixth Five Year Plan, New Delhi, Planning Commission.

Government of India. 1988. Draft National Perspective Plan for Women 1988-2000, Mimeo, New Delhi, Department of Women and Child Development.

Government of India. 2004 Economic Survey 2003-04, Ministry of Finance, New Delhi: Economic Division.

Government of India (2001). Department of Women and Child Development. New Delhi Ministry of Human Resource Development.

Government of India. 1998. Ministry of Welfare (renamed as Ministry of Social Justice and Empowerment on May 25, 1998. Annual Report 1995-1996.

Guha, R. 1989. The unquiet woods. New Delhi: Oxford. Hasan, Zoya., 1994. 'Introduction. Contextualising Gender and Identity in Contemporary India', in (ed.) Z. Hasan, Forging Identities. Gender, communities and the State, New Delhi: Kali for Women.

Guru, Gopal. 2003. Review of Joothan: A Dalit's Life by Om Prakash Valmiki (Translated into English by Arun Prabha, Mukherjee), *Seminar*, No. 530, October, 70-71.

Guru, Gopal 2002. How Egalitarian are Social Sciences in India, *Economic and Political Weekly,* Vol. XXXVII, No. 51, December 14, pp. 5003-08.

Guru, Gopal. 1997. Human Rights and the Dalits—An Enquiry into the Human Rights Discourse in India, *Indian Journal of Human Right*, University of Hyderabad, Jan-June, pp. 107-117.

Guru, Gopal. 2001, The language of Dalit- Bahujan Political Discourse' in Shah G. (ed.) Dalit Identity and Politics, New Delhi: Sage Publications.

Haksar, Nandita. 1986. Demystification of Law for Women. New Delhi: Lancer Press.

Hall, S. 1996. Introduction: Who needs 'identity'? In S. Hall and P. du Gay. (Eds.) Questions of cultural identity. London: Sage Publications.

Hasan Zoya. 2009. Politics of Inclusion: Caste Minorities and Affirmative Action, New Delhi: Oxford University Press.

Hillary, 2003 India's *"Untouchables" Face Violence, Discrimination*. National Geographic News, June 2, 2003. Available online at: http: //news.nationalgeographic.com/news/2003/06/ 0602_030602_untouchables_2.html.

Hobsson, Barbara, Jane Levis Birte Siim. 2002. Contested Concepts in Gender and Social Politics, US/UK Edward Elgar Publishing.

Human Rights Watch.1999.*Violence Against Untouchables Growing*, Says Report. Indian Government Fails to Prevent Massacres, Rapes, and Exploitation. Available online at:http://hrw.org/english/docs/ 1999/04/14/india879.htm.

Ilaiah, K. 1996. Why I Am Not A Hindu: A Shudra Critique of Hindutva Philosophy, *Culture and Political Economy*, Calcutta: Samya.

Illaih, Kancha, 1994. BSP and Caste As Ideology, *Economic and Political Weekly, XXIX, No.12,* March,19, pp. 668-69.

Jackson, C. 1991. "Social Exclusion and Gender : Does One Size Fit All?" in *The European Journal of Development Research 11(1),* pp. 125-146.

Jalal, A. 1991.'The convenience of subservience: Women and the state of Pakistan', in Women, Islam and the State (ed.) D. Kandiyoti, Philadelphia, PA. : Temple University Press.

Jogdand P.G. 2007. Problems of Hindu Women in Thorat, Sukhdeo and Aryama, Ambedkar in Retrospect: Essays on Economics, Politics and Society, Jaipur, India: Rawat Publications.

John, Mary, 2000. Alternate Modernities? Reservations and women's movements in 20th century India' *Economic and Political Weekly*, Vol. 35 No. 43/44: Oct. 21 - Nov. 3, 2000WS22-WS29.

Kabeer, N. 2000. Social Exclusion, Poverty and Discrimination: Towards An Analytical Framework *IDS Bulletin* Vol. 31, No. 4: 83-97.

Kabeer, N. 2002. Citizenship, Affiliation and Exclusion: Perspectives from the South', *IDS Bulletin*, Vol. 23, No. 2, pp. 12-23.

Kamble, Ramesh. 1998. Dalit Interpretations of Society, *Seminar*, No. 471, November, 19-24.

Kannabiran, Kalpana and Vasanth Kannabiran. 2002. De-eroticising Assault: Essays on Modesty, Honour and Power, Strect, Calcutta.

Kapur, R. and B. Cossman. 1996. Subversive Sites: Feminist engagements with the law in India, New Delhi: Sage.

Kapur, R. 2002. The tragedy of victimisation rhetoric: Resurrecting the 'native' subject in international/post-colonial feminist legal politics. Harvard Human Rights Journal, 15(2), 1-38. Retrieved March 1, 2004 from www.law.harvard.edu/students/org/hrj/iss15/index.html.

Kapur, Ratna, and Brenda Cossmam. 1993. 'Communalising gender/engendering community. Women, legal Discourse and Saffron Agenda', *Economic and Political Weekly*, Vol. 28, No. 17:WS35-WS44.

Katzenstein Mary, Smithu Kothari, and Uday Mehta. 2001. 'Social Movement Politics in India: Institutions, interests and identities', in Atul Kohli (ed.) The success of India's Democracy, Cambridge: Cambridge University Press.

Keer Dhananjay. 1964. Mahatma Jotirao Phooley, Father of Indian Social Revolution, Bombay: Popular Prakashan.

Kishwar, M. 1986. 'Pro-women or anti-Muslim? The Shah Bano Controversy', Manushi, Vol. 32: 4-13.

Kosambi, Meera. 2007. Crossing Thresholds: Feminist Essays in Social History. Ranikhet: Permanent Black.

Krishnaraj, M. 2003. 'Challenges before Women's Movement in a Changing Context', *Economic and Political Weekly*, Vol. 38, No. 43, October 25, 2003 pp. 4536-4545.

Kumar, A.K. Shiva .1996. UNDP's Gender Related Development Index: A Computation for Indian States, *Economic and Political Weekly*, Vol. 31, No. 14, April 6,1996, pp. 887-895.

Kumar, Naresh. 1993. Regional Dimensions of the Status of Women in India, *Social Change*, March 1993, Vol. 23, No.I, pp. 20-29.

Lazreg, M. 2005. Decolonising Feminism. In O. Oyewumi (ed.) African Gender Studies: A Reader. New York: Palgrave McMillan.

Leach, F. and S. Humphreys. 2007. Gender Violence in Schools, Taking the 'girls-as-victims' discourse forward. *Gender and Development*, Vol. 15, No.1, pp. 51-64.

Lerner, G. 1979. The Majority Finds its Past, London: Oxford University Press.

Limaye, Champa. 1999. Women: Power and Progress, New Delhi: B.R. Publishing Corporation.

Mahajan, Gurpreet. 2001. Identites and Rights. Aspects of Liberal Democracy in India. New Delhi: Oxford University Press.

Malini, M. 1993. Caste and Patriarchy: Ambedkar's Insight into the status of Women, in K.S. Chalam (ed.). Relevance of Ambedkarism in India, Jaipur: Rawat Publications.

Mamdani, M. 1996. Citizen and Subject, Contemporary Africa and the Legacy of Late Colonialism, Princeton: Princeton University Press.

Manorma, R. 2003. 'Dalit Women: Issues and Perspectives', Paper presented at the International Dalit Conference, Vancouver, Canada, 16 May.

Marie J. Buhle, Ann. C. Gordan and Nancy Schrom. 1971. *Women in American Society: An Historical Contribution*, Radical America, Vol. 5, No. 4 July-August, pp. 3-66.

Marshall, T.H. 1950. Citizenship and Social Class and Other Essays, Cambridge: Cambridge University Press.

Mathew, Thomas. 1991 Ambedkar: Reform or Revolution, Segment Books, New Delhi.

McNay, Lois. 1992. Focault and Feminism: Power, Gender and the Self, North Eastern University Press.

Menon, N Recovering Subversion: Feminist Politics Beyond the Law, Permanent Black, Delhi.

Menon, Nivedita. 2000. Embodying the self: Feminism, sexual violence and the Law, in Community, gender and violence, subaltern studies XI (eds). Partha Chatterjee and Pradeep Jaganathan, New Delhi: Ravi Dayal.

Mies, Maria. 1976. The Shahada Movement: A peasant movement In Maharashtra, Its development and its Prospects, *Journal of Peasant Studies*, Vol. 3, No. 4: pp. 472-82.

Mohanty M. 2004. Class, Caste, Gender, New Delhi: Sage Publications.

Mohanty, C.T. 1991. Introduction: Cartographies of Struggle: Third World women and the politics of feminism. In C.T. Mohanty, A. Russo, and L. Torres (Eds.) Third World Women and the Politics of Feminism. Indiana: Indiana University Press.

Mohanty, C.T. 1991. Under Western eyes: Feminist Scholarship and Colonial Discourses. In C.T. Mohanty, A. Russo, and L. Torres (Eds.) Third World women and the politics of feminism. Indiana: Indiana University Press.

Molyneux, M. and S. Razavi. 2002. 'Introduction' in M. Molyneux and S. Razavi, ed. *Gender Justice, Development, and Rights*, London: Oxford University Press.

Morgan, Robin. 1970. Sisterhood is Powerful: An Anthology of Writings from the Women's Liberation Movement, New York: Random House.

Mukherjee, Prabhati. 1999. Hindu Women: Normative Models, Calcutta: Orient Longman.

Mukhopadhyay, M. 1998. Legally Dispossessed: Gender, Identity and the Process of Law, Calcutta: Stree.

Mukhopadhyay, M. and S. Meer. 2004. Creating Voice and Carving Space: Redefining governance from a gender perspective, Amsterdam: KIT Publishers.

Government of India 2003. National Crimes Records Bureau, Crimes in India Report (2004), Tables 7.4 and 7.7.

Nur Yalman. 1962. On the Purity of Women in the Castes of Ceylon and Malabar, *Journal of the Royal Anthropological Institute of Great Britain and Ireland*, pp. 25-28.

O'Hanlon, Rosalind. 1985. Caste, Conflict and Ideology: Mahatma Jotirao Phule and Low Caste Protest in Nineteenth Century Western India, Cambridge: Cambridge University press in association with Orient Longman Ltd.

Okin, Susan M. 1999. Is multi-culturalism bad for women? Princeton: Princeton University Press.

Omvedt, G. 1993. Reinventing Revolution: New Social Movements and Socialist Traditions in India. London: ME Sharpe.

Omvedt, Gail. 1976. Cultural Revolt in a Colonial Society: The Non-Brahmin Movement in Western India, 1873 to 1930, Pune: Scientific Socialist Education Trust.

Oommen, T.K. 2001. 'Civil Society: Religion, Caste and Language in India', *Sociological Bulletin*, Vol. 50, No. 2 pp. 219-235.

O' Reilly, Dermot. 2005. Social Inclusion: A philosophical anthropology. *Politics*, Vol. 25, No. 2: pp. 80-88.

Padke, Shilpa, 2003. 'Thirty years on. Women's studies reflects on the women's movement', *Economic and Political Weekly*, Vol. 38, No. 43, pp. 4567-4576.

Pai, Sudha, 2002. Dalit Assertion And The Unfinished Democratic Revolution: The Bahujan Samaj Party in Uttar Pradesh, New Delhi: Sage Publication.

Patton, Laurie L. 2002. Jewels of Authority: Women and Textual Tradition in Hindu India, New Delhi: Oxford University Press.

Government of India. 2002. Planning Commission National Human Development Report, Planning Commission, Government of India, March, 2001.

Rao, A. 1995. 'The Politics and Gender and Culture in International Human Rights Discourse', in Women's rights, human rights J. Peters and A. Wolper (eds.), *International Feminist Perspectives*, New York: Routledge.

Rao, Anupama, (ed.). (2001). Gender and Caste, New Delhi: Kali for Women.

Rao, Y.C. 2007. Writing Dalit History and Other Essays, New Delhi: Kanishka Publishers and Distributors.

Ray, R. and A.C. Korteweg. 1999. Women's Movements in the third world: Identity, Mobilisation and Autonomy, *Annual Review of Sociology*, Vol. 25, pp. 47-71.

Ray, R., (1998). Women's movements and political fields: A comparison of two Indian cities, *Social Problems*, Vol. 45, No. 1, pp. 21-36.

Ray, R.1999. Fields of Protest: women's movements in India. Minneapolis: University of Minneapolis Press.

Reddy, Narasimha D., and Arun Patnaik. 1993. 'Anti-arrack agitation of Women in Andhra Pradesh', *Economic and Political Weekly*, Vol. 28, No. 21, May 22, 199, pp. 1059-66.

Reddy, P.R. and Sumangala. 1998. Women in Development Perspectives from Selected States of India, New Delhi: B.R. Publishing Corporation.

Rege, S. 1998. Dalit Women Talk Differently: A Critique of 'Difference' and Towards a Dalit Feminist Standpoint Position Source: *Economic and Political Weekly,* Vol. 33, No. 44, Oct. 31. Nov. 6, 1998, pp. WS39-WS46.

Rege, Sharmila. 2006. Writing Caste/Writing Gender: Reading Dalit Women's Testimonios, Zubaan, An Imprint of, New Delhi: Kali for Women.

Rege, Sharmila. 2000. 'Real Feminism and Dalit Women: Scripts of Denial and Accusation', *Economic and Political Weekly*, Vol. 35, No. 6, pp. 492-495.

Rosalind O' Hanlon. 1985. Caste Conflict and Ideology: Joytirao Phule and Lower Caste Protest in Ninteenth Century Maharashtra, Cambridge: Cambridge University Press.

Rowbotham, S. 1981. The Trouble with Patriarchy, in Feminist Anthropology Collective (ed.). No Turning Back. Writings from the Women's Liberation Movement, 1975-80, London: Women Press.

Saberwal, Satish. 1994. Democratic and Political Structures, in Social Change and Political discourse in India: Structures of Power, Movements of Resistance, Vol. 1 T.V. Sathyamurthy (ed.) Delhi: Oxford University Press.

Sangari and Suresh Vaid, (ed.). 1989. Recasting women. Essays in colonial history, New Delhi: Kali for Women.

Sangari, Kumkum. 1995. Politics of Diversity. Religious communities and Multiple Patriarchies, published in two parts in *Economic and Political Weekly*, Vol. 30, No. 51: 3287-3310 and Vol. 30, No. 52: pp. 3381-92.

Sarkar, Tanika. 1991. The women as communal Subject: Rashtra Sevika Samithi and 'Ram Janmabhumi Movement, *Economic and Political Weekly*, Vol. 26, No. 35.

Sarukkai, Sundar. 2007. Dalit Experience and Theory, *Economic and Political Weekly* October 6, Vol. XLII, No. 40, pp. 4043-4048.

Saunders, K. 2002. Introduction: Towards a Deconstructive Post-development Criticism. In K. Saunders (Ed.) Feminist Post-development thought: Rethinking Modernity, Post-colonialism and Representation. London: Zed Books.

Sen, A. 2000. Social Exclusion: Concept, Application and Scrutiny in Social *Development Paper No. 1*, Asian Development Bank.

Sen, Amartya. 2000. Social exclusion: Concept, Application, and Scrutiny. Manila: Asian.

Shah Ghanshyam. 2001 (ed.) Dalit Identity and Politics, New Delhi: Sage Publications.

Shiva, Vandana.1988. Staying Alive: Women, Ecology and Survival in India. New Delhi: Kali for Women.

Shyam babu, D. and Prasad, C.B. 2009, Six Dalit Paradoxes, *Economic and Political Weekly*, Vol. XLIV, No. 23 June 6, 209.

Silver, H. 1994. "Social Exclusion and Social Solidarity: Three Paradigms" in *International Labour Review,* Vol. 133 Nos. 5-6) pp. 531-578.

Squires, Judith. 2002. "Culture, equality and diversity," in Multiculturalism Reconsidered, Paul Kelly (ed.), Oxford: Polity Press.

Squires, Judith, 2002. "Culture, equality and diversity," in Multiculturalism Reconsidered, Paul Kelly (ed.), Oxford: Polity Press.

Stewart, Frances. 2003. Social Exclusion and Conflict: Analysis and Policy Implications. In, Sundaram, K. and S.D. Tendulkar (2003), "Poverty among Social and Economic Groups in India in 1990s", *Economic and Political Weekly,* Vol. 38, No. 50.

Thiruchandran, Selvy. 1997. Ideology, Caste, Class and Gender, New Delhi: Vikas Publishing House Pvt. Ltd.

Thorat S. 2007. Human *Poverty and Socially Disadvantaged Groups in India,* Discussion Paper Series: 18, Human Development Resource Centre, New Delhi: (HDRC)/UNDP.

Thorat S. 2009. Dalits in India: Search for Common Destiny, New Delhi: Sage Publications.

Thorat Sukhadeo and Narender Kumar 2008 B.R. Ambedkar: Perspectives on Social Exclusion and Inclusive Policies, New Delhi: Oxford University Press.

Thorat, Sukhadeo. 2004. *Persistence of Poverty: Why do Scheduled Castes and Scheduled Tribes Stay Chronically Poor?* Working Paper for Centre for Chronic Poverty, London. UNDP (1996), *Human Development Report 1996,* New York. Oxford University Press.

Thorat, V. 2001. Dalit Women Have Been Left Behind By The Dalit Movement And the Women's Movement, *Communalism Combat,* Vol. 69, No. 12.

Tsing, A. 1993. In the Realm of the Diamond Queen. Princeton, NJ: Princeton University.

UNDP. 1995. *Human Development Report,* Published for the United Nation's Development Programme, 1995, New Delhi: Oxford University Press.

V. Geetha. 1998. Periyar, Women and an Ethic of Citizenship, *Economic and Political Weekly.*

Vijayalakshmi, V. 2004. 'Citizenship, differences and identity: Dalit women and political inclusion', Working paper 147, Bangalore *Institute for Social and Economic Change.*

World Bank. 2000, Overview of Rural Decentralisation in India, Vol. I, September 27, 2000. http;/media.worldbank.org.

World Commission on Dams (WCD) (200), Dams and Development: A New Framework of Decision Making, Report of the World Commission on Dams, Earth Scan, London, November.

Young, Iris, Marion. 2000 Inclusion and Democracy. Oxford: Oxford University Press.

Zelliot, Eleanor.1992. From Untouchable to Dalit: Essays on the Ambedkar Movement, Delhi: Manohar.

Zelliot, Eleanor. 2001. Dalit Traditions and Dalit Consciousness in N.G. Jayal and S Pai (eds). Democratic Governance in India, New Delhi: Sage Publications.

Ziyauddin K.M. and Eswarappa Kasi. 2009. Dimensions of Social Exclusion: Ethnographic Explorations UK Cambridge: Scholars Publishing.

Index

M

N